POLITICAL THINKERS
edited by Geraint Parry
University of Manchester

I

HEGEL

HEGEL

Raymond Plant

Lecturer in Philosophy in
the University of Manchester

London
George Allen & Unwin Ltd
Ruskin House Museum Street

Printed in Great Britain
in 10 point Plantin type
by Unwin Brothers Limited
Old Woking, Surrey

Ye are as aliens in a foreign land.
St. Peter

Le déracinement est loin la plus dangereuse maladie des sociétés humaines.
Simone Weil

Ich ist in der Welt zu Hause, wenn es sie kennt, noch mehr, wenn es sie begriffen hat.
Hegel

To live in Main Street is, if one lives in the right spirit, to inhabit the holy city.
Findlay

PREFACE

This book arose out of a certain dissatisfaction with existing commentaries on Hegel's work. Generally speaking, such commentaries fall into two types. There is the general study of his central metaphysical doctrines and of his logical writings; but studies of this sort, such as Findlay's *Hegel: A Re-examination*, tend not to be concerned with a close analysis of how these general metaphysical views work themselves out in his writings on particular modes of human experience, for example, the artistic, the political and the religious. At the other extreme there are works, particularly on his political thinking, which tend to minimize or discount the metaphysical dimension to his theorizing. A work in this latter *genre* would be Pelcynski's essays introducing *Hegel's Political Writings*. The present book attempts to steer a *via media* between both of these trends. It will seek to deal in some detail with his central metaphysical doctrines, arguing that an understanding of these doctrines is, *pace* Pelcynski, a necessary condition of making his writings on political philosophy intelligible.

It was originally my intention to preface this approach with a short account of Hegel's development, but as time passed I realized that such an approach was inadequate. It seemed to me to be more and more clear in the light of my understanding of his development that this period is really *the key* to the understanding of his mature philosophical work and that in addition, taken this way, one could not easily distinguish a metaphysical centre of his work, a philosophical core, which was then worked out in detail in his discussion of various modes of experience, the political among them. On the contrary, it seems to me that the whole of Hegel's work has a social and a political dimension, that his whole philosophy, and not merely his explicit political and social theorizing, was a response to certain problems in social and political experience. In order to make this thesis plausible, however, it has been necessary for me to deal in some detail with his early unpublished writings in which these social and political problems are diagnosed, and which constitute the *problematic* of his later, mature philosophical achievement. In arguing this thesis about the social and political commitment of Hegel's whole work I do not intend to be taken as providing some kind of support for Karl Popper's interpretation of Hegel in the second volume of *The Open Society and Its Enemies*. Conceived in ignorance of Hegel's philosophical achievements, Popper's discussion of Hegel is a conjecture which has had in the past, and also receives in the present work, a firm refutation. The refutation supplied in this book is, however, implicit—to have explicitly challenged Popper at each point in his interpretation would have credited his work with more importance than it deserves.

Although I am critical of existing commentaries on Hegel this does not mean that I have not learned a great deal from them. As the dedication of this volume implies, I am immensely in the debt of John Findlay. However much he will disapprove of the line taken in this book, he cannot avoid the responsibility of having interested me in Hegel and his work during a memorable series of lectures in 1965–6 when I was a student of his in the University of London. I am also deeply grateful to my friend and colleague, Geraint Parry, both for inviting me to write the book in the first place and for constant advice and encouragement. The historical, contextual approach adopted in the book owes a good deal to the stimulation of Professor W. H. Greenleaf and to Dr Bikhu Parekh, both of whom were involved in the supervision of my graduate work. Earlier drafts of chapters of this book were given as lectures to members of the Socialist Society in the University of Manchester, and I must record with thanks the interest and the tolerance which they showed in the lectures given both by and on a philosopher neither of whom they could have found very congenial. My erstwhile colleagues, Anthony Arblaster and Dick Atkinson, attended these talks and made helpful comments on them. Finally, my thanks are due to my parents who enabled me to have an academic career, and to my wife, Katherine, and son Nicholas, for providing an environment within which I could happily pursue my work.

RAYMOND PLANT

November 1971

CONTENTS

A Note on the Texts

Quotations in the book are given with reference to the Glockner Jubilee edition of Hegel's works, departures from this practice being necessitated by the non-inclusion of relevant material in the Glockner edition, particularly *Hegels Theologische Jugendschriften*, ed. Nohl; *Jenenser Logik, Metaphysik und Naturphilosophie*, ed. Lasson; *Jenenser Realphilosophie* I and II, ed. Hoffmeister; and *Schriften zur Politik und Rechtsphilosophie*, ed. Lasson.

The following English translations have been consulted and in many cases used: T. M. Knox's translations of pieces in the *Theologische Jugendschriften* in *Hegel's Early Theological Writings*; Knox's version of *Grundlinien der Philosophie des Rechts* in *Hegel's Philosophy of Right*; Knox's translations of pieces from *Schriften zur Politik und Rechtsphilosophie* in *Hegel's Political Writings*. My use of such translations is here very gratefully acknowledged, but is not explicitly acknowledged in the text. Knox's translations of the early theological writings and of Hegel's occasional writings on politics do not cover *all* the material which I have wanted to use and to sometimes cite the German original and at other times the English translation would have made already long footnotes extremely tedious and complicated. Passages quoted in the book may, however, be easily identified in the English translations: references to the *Theologische Jugendschriften* may be identified in Knox's *Hegel's Early Theological Writings* because Knox includes in the body of the English text the pagination of the German original and the same is true of his version of parts of *Schriften zur Politik und Rechtsphilosophie* in *Hegel's Political Writings*. My references to the Glockner edition of *Grundlinien der Philosophie des Rechts* includes a citation of the *paragraphs* which are the same as in the Hoffmeister edition of the work on which Knox based his *Hegel's Philosophy of Right* and are included in his translation.

A select bibliography is included at the end of the volume and full details of the works cited in this note may be found there.

Chapter I

Civil Theology
and Political Culture

*Our ideal should not be a contracted, disembodied, abstract being;
our ideal should be the complete and whole man, perfectly and fully
formed.*

L. Feuerbach

Hegel's mature philosophy can best be seen in terms of a response to
certain problems in social, political and religious experience which
preoccupied him for most of his life.[1] His initial inability to provide
solutions to these problems drove him on to philosophy and to a
particular conception of the purpose and character of philosophical
explanation. In a letter to Schelling, his friend from their days at the
Tübingen theological seminary, Hegel himself drew attention to the
way in which his later philosophical position had grown out of earlier,
non-philosophical concerns:

> In my scientific development which began with the more subordinate
> needs of men, I was compelled towards philosophy and the ideal of
> my youth had been transformed into a system.[2]

Any attempt to come to terms with Hegel's mature thought must start
with an endeavour to understand the problems which it was designed
to solve and out of which it grew. Initially this attempt requires a
discussion of the early, that is to say pre-1800 writings of Hegel, the
unsatisfactory nature of which led him on to philosophy. In advocating
this approach to the understanding of Hegel's mature thought, I must
record my profound disagreement with Professor J. N. Findlay who, in

[1] For a general rationale of this kind of approach to a text see R. G. Collingwood, *An Autobiography*, Oxford 1939, p. 31.
[2] Letter to Schelling 11 November 1800 in *Briefe von und an Hegel*, ed.
J. Hoffmeister, Hamburg 1952, vol. 1, p. 59.

a foreword to a recently published translation of *Hegel's Philosophy of Nature*, argues that:

> It may further be wondered whether the concern for Hegel's development displayed by many writers is not excessive, especially in a situation where there are no reliable and detailed commentaries on his major works. The Juvenilia of Berne and Frankfurt have been studied exhaustively for many decades and have thrown very little light on any major notion or position in Hegel's mature works. . . . . It is even arguable that the great interest in these Juvenilia stems in part from an unwillingness to scale the main crags of his system: men linger in the foothills because they resemble the lower-lying territories in which they feel best able to work and think.[1]

The whole argument of the present book will be contrary to the one advanced in this passage. It is intended to show that Hegel's mature philosophical position can be greatly illuminated by considering his own acknowledged failure to solve the problems in both personal and social experience which he diagnosed in his early writings. Consequently an attempt will be made in this chapter to reconstruct the original *Problemstellungen* of Hegel's philosophical work in order to make clear why, in the words of the letter cited above, the ideals of his youth had to be transformed into a philosophical system. To describe and to characterize these ideals must, of course, be a precondition of providing answers to the questions of why and how the transformation occurred.

Hegel's early ideals were part and parcel of the thought and feeling of his own and, indeed, the preceding generation of German intellectuals. To restore the harmony of personal experience and to recreate a closely-knit community in contrast to the fragmentation of the person and growing social divisions were the two basic aims of members of this generation. Goethe, Schiller, Hamann, Hölderlin and Hegel shared these two basic and interrelated ideals, although of course they differed profoundly both in the ways in which they articulated these ideals and in the paths by which they thought their respective visions might be achieved. Three factors led to these values being central to the consciousness of sensitive minds in Germany during this period. In the first place the idealization of Greek and particularly Athenian social and political experience gave them a paradigm in terms of which they could look at what they regarded, in contrast, to be the enervated and atrophied nature of personal and social relationships in the Germany and, indeed,

[1] *Hegel's Philosophy of Nature*, translated by A. V. Miller, Oxford 1970, pp. vii–viii.

the Europe of their time. Secondly, the depressed social, political and religious situation in Germany gave them an impetus to look for and to hold fast to ideals which were very far removed from the reality of German life. Finally the growing awareness, after about 1770, of the great works of the thinkers of the Scottish Enlightenment on the development of commercial society, particularly the writings of Adam Ferguson[1] and John Millar,[2] provided them with a diagnosis of the contemporary malaise and made them more aware than they had been previously of the difficulties involved in any attempt to reform the situation. These factors, crucial to the *Gedankenwelt* into which Hegel was born, will now be discussed more thoroughly.

Greece: Social and Personal Harmony

The idealization of Greek social and personal experience was very largely the result of the quite remarkable influence which the researches of Winckelmann into Greek art, particularly sculpture, had on German intellectuals during this period. From their understanding of Greek culture men of the generation prior to that of Hegel, the *Stürmer* and *Dränger*, developed the idea and vision of a harmoniously developed individual, and they took this vision to be a paradigm of human development and achievement, a model of *Humanität*. From a distance of 2,000 years, the inhabitants of Athens appeared to them to have developed their human capacities and powers in an all-round way, in a fashion which was denied to the contemporary European. As Schiller pointed out in his sixth letter in his *Ästhetische Briefe*, the Greek individual was able in a quite remarkable way to encompass the totality of experience available to him in his society and, as it were, to represent the whole ethos of his society in his own person. In the letter he asks:

Why was it that the individual Greek was able to be the representative

---

[1] Particularly *An Essay on the History of Civil Society*, by Adam Ferguson, Edinburgh 1767, translated into German by Christoph Garve in 1768. Herder, as will be shown below, was very much influenced by Ferguson, as was Schiller (see *Schiller*, by R. Buchwald, Wiesbaden 1953, pp. 213, 217, 224). Rosenkranz, in *Hegels Leben*, Berlin 1841, p. 14, says that Hegel read the works of Ferguson while a schoolboy in Stuttgart and traces of his influence may be seen in the essay 'Über einige Charakteristische Unterschiede der Alten Dichter' (1788) discussed below, pp. 28 ff. Ferguson was in his original way a disciple of Shaftesbury who in his *Charakteristiks* (1711) stressed the need for a person to develop the harmony of his powers. Shaftesbury also influenced Schiller: see 'Schiller and Shaftesbury' in *Publications of The English Goethe Society*, 1935.

[2] John Millar's *The Origin of the Distinction of Ranks* was translated into German in 1772 and was reviewed by Herder in *Frankfurter Gelehrte Anzeige* 1772 in *Sämtliche Werke*, ed. Suphan, Berlin 1877–1913, vol. 5, pp. 452–6.

of his age and why can no single modern man make a claim to be such ?[1]

Schiller's answer, at least so far as the first part of the question was concerned, was that Greek culture was homogeneous: there were no basic divisions or discrepancies between modes of experience and, in consequence, the individual was able to gain a perspective on and take part in the totality of experience in his society, thus becoming fully integrated into the culture into which he was born:

> In the fullness of form no less than of content, at the same time philosophical and creative, sensitive and vigorous, the Greeks combined the first youth of the imagination with the maturity of reason in a glorious manifestation.[2]

In contemporary European society on the other hand, culture had become fragmented and in the place of an all-round capacity there had developed narrow professional skills and expertize. The result of this cultural fragmentation was that man could no longer be aware of and share in the total experience available in modern society; consequently his inner harmony was shattered. In contrast to the Greek individual, Schiller argued that the average modern man had become enervated and narrow. Herder too, in *Auch eine Philosophie der Geschichte zur Bildung der Menschheit* (1774),[3] dwelt lovingly on the ways in which Greek forms of experience had enabled a man to maximize his potentialities and powers, to be a whole man. In contrast, his own times seemed to him to have lost sight of some of the most valuable of human qualities. He regarded Greek society as being the glorious youth of mankind; a fortunate geographical position had led to the development of trade and commerce, freedom and the law were in a state of balance, craftsmanship was still a mode of artistic endeavour and not a narrow specialism, and poetry and drama were intertwined with all the

---

[1] Schiller, *Briefe über die Ästhetische Erziehung der Menschen* in *Nationalausgabe*, 1962, vol. 20, p. 322.

[2] Schiller, op. cit., p. 321. This kind of argument, that the Greeks had attained the full development of their human powers and therefore constitute a paradigm of what it is to be human, is particularly clearly stated in von Humboldt's essay, 'Über das Studium des Altertums, und des Griechischen insbesondere' in *Werke*, ed. Leitzmann, Berlin 1903, vol. 1, esp. p. 274. For an even more romantic view see 'Hymne an die Genius Griechenlands' by Hölderlin in *Stuttgarter Ausgabe*, 1946, vol. 2, p. 125. This poem was written in 1793 when Hölderlin was in close contact with Hegel in Tübingen.

[3] *Werke*, op. cit., vol. 5.

activities of the community. In contrast, his picture of contemporary European society and culture was less than enthusiastic:

> Who reading this history will not often wonder what has become of the habits and values, of the honour and the freedom of these times, of their love of gallantry, their manners and their faithfulness ? Their depths have been silted up. Their foundations are merely bright shifting sands where nothing grows. However that may be, in some respects we would willingly take their devotion and superstition, their obscurity and their ignorance, their lack of order and coarse manners in exchange for our enlightenment and scepticism, our atrophied coldness and refinement, our philosophical exhaustion and our human misery . . . With all their philosophy and expertise how enervated are our men of the enlightenment in matters of life and common sense? In former times the philosophical disposition never existed merely for itself but pointed out towards affairs to shape them with the simple purpose of creating healthy and active minds, it now stands on its own and has become a specialism.[1]

Much the same type of argument is to be found in the work of Hegel's friend and contemporary in Tübingen, the poet Hölderlin. In *Hyperion* Hölderlin provided his contemporaries with a haunting image of their condition compared with the situation of the Greeks:

> These are hard sayings and yet I say them because they are the truth. I can think of no people as torn apart as the Germans. Craftsmen are to be seen, but no human beings . . . masters and men, but no human beings; young people and old, but no human beings. Is it not like a field of battle where hands and arms and other limbs lie scattered in pieces while the blood of life drains away into the soil ?[2]

Man's modern condition was not, however, regarded as being merely the result of the fragmentation of knowledge with the consequence that

---

[1] *Werke*, op. cit., vol. 5, p. 523. Similar points are to be found in his *Denkmal Johann Winckelmanns* in which Herder argued the need for a rebirth of the 'Greek spirit in Germany' in *Werke*, vol. 8, p. 476. Cf. also *Die Neuere Deutsche Literatur* (1767), *Werke*, vol. I. In his later *Briefe zur Beförderung der Humanität* (1793–7), Herder was again preoccupied with the relation between the present and the classical world. In these letters he argued that classical ideals should be taken as inspirational but not taken for mere slavish imitation, *Werke*, vol. 13, p. 80.

[2] Hölderlin, op. cit., vol. 3, p. 153. In fact, although *Hyperion* was not published until the late 1790s, Hölderlin had started to write the work before leaving the Tübingen *Stift* and it is therefore highly likely that he and Hegel discussed these matters. On their relationship during this period see J. Hoffmeister's *Hölderlin und Hegel*, Tübingen 1931.

only specialized human powers could be engaged. The position was regarded as being far more serious than this. The human person was envisaged as being deeply divided within himself; the central powers of the human mind were regarded as being in contradiction with one another. Nowhere was this felt dissonance given a more rigid and systematic expression than in Kant's philosophical anthropology.[1] In Kant's great works man appeared as an inwardly shattered being—a profound bifurcation existed, Kant argued, between reason and passion, duty and inclination, the autonomous and the heteronomous self, between the cognitive, conative and affective sides of man's nature. This influential philosophical justification and articulation of the divided structure of the human personality led an anguished Schiller to ask:

> What then becomes of grace and graciousness, of those moral deeds in which the *whole* man moves together than with clenched rigidity and *à contre coeur* ?[2]

Indeed, the whole point of Schiller's *Briefe Über die Ästhetische Erziehung der Menschen* was to show the possibility of reuniting through the *Spieltrieb* those aspects of human nature which Kant had so disastrously divided.

The ideal of the full and harmonious development of the individual personality was derived from the German's assessment of Greek experience and culture. Their culture was regarded as harmonious and in consequence, the individual was at home in all the modes of experience in his society. In addition, these modes of experience were regarded as being fundamentally different from modern ones in that they were thought of as being such as to engage all the faculties of the human mind. Greek religion, for example, was not rationalistic or cerebral like the Deism of contemporary Enlightened Europe but was thought to have appealed to the heart and to the imagination more than to the intellect. Their morality was not merely private and inward looking but was closely integrated into both the political and the religious life

---

[1] Kant was, of course, the author of *Die Streit der Facultäten*, in *Gesammelte Schriften*, Berlin 1955, vol. 7.

[2] Quoted in Wilkinson and Willoughby, *Schiller's Letters on the Aesthetic Education of Man*, Oxford 1967, p. xxv. For Hegel's reaction to Kant's anthropology see Nohl, *Hegels theologische Jugendschriften*, Tübingen 1907, p. 226. Indeed, much earlier in his M.A. thesis, Hegel had attempted to reconcile, or mediate, the Kantian dichotomy between sense and reason—'sensus cum ratione sic quasi coaluit, ut vis utraque unum constituat subjectum'. I am indebted to M. J. Petry's *Hegel's Philosophy of Nature*, London 1970, vol. 1, p. 70, for this reference.

of the community. However with the gradual development of specialization this homogeneity in culture had been lost. Schiller made this point particularly strongly:

> With the increase in empirical knowledge and more exact modes of thought deeper divisions between the sciences became inevitable and when the increasingly complicated machinery of the state entailed a more rigid separation of ranks and professions, then the inner harmony of human nature was disturbed and a disastrous conflict set the totality of its powers at variance.[1]

Thus the fragmentation of the personality came to be regarded as being very closely related to the growth of social divisions and the more socially aware members of the generation realized that the ideal of personal harmony, the achievement of the full potential of all the human powers could only be achieved satisfactorily if there was a corresponding renewal in *community*. This close connection between personal fragmentation and social division was also insisted upon by Herder when he wrote in *Vom Erkennen und Empfinden der menschlichen Seele*:

> Since together with the classes, ranks and professions, the inner faculties have unfortunately become separated . . . no single fragment partakes of the whole any more.[2]

This perception of the close relationship between social character and social situation was probably derived from Schiller and Herder's reading of Adam Ferguson's *An Essay on the History of Civil Society*.[3] Ferguson was interested primarily in tracing the history of mankind from 'primitive simplicity to complicated refinement' but at the same time he did not forget the effects which this complicated refinement had on the character of the individual through the division of labour. He pointed in the *Essay* to the human consequences of the development of specialism—the correlative of commercial society:

> Many mechanical arts succeed best under the total suppression of sentiment and reason; and ignorance is the mother of industry as well as superstition . . . Manufactures accordingly prosper most when the mind is least consulted, and where the workshop may, without any great effort, be considered as an engine, the parts of which are men . . .

[1] Schiller, op. cit., p. 322. [2] Herder, op. cit., vol. 8, p. 217.
[3] For the influence of Ferguson on Herder see Roy Pascal, 'Herder and the Scottish Historical School' in *Publications of the English Goethe Society*, 1938.

Thinking itself in this age of separations may become a particular craft.[1]

However the human consequences of the growing differentiation of function and the development of commercial society was not the *primary* interest of the Scottish historians and it was not until much later in the nineteenth century that the humanistic critique of industrial society implicit in the work of Ferguson and to a lesser extent in the, at that time, unpublished lectures of Smith,[2] was taken up by Coleridge, Carlyle, Morris and Arnold[3] in this country. It did however, touch a very deep chord among the Germans.[4] Imbued as they were with the ideal of the *whole* man derived from their idealized picture of Greek life and culture, it now seemed that the loss of a unified conception of the powers of the human mind could be seen to have been a consequence of wide-ranging social developments, particularly the division of labour. Schiller, for example, reacted to Ferguson's remarks in a much more morally concerned way than Ferguson himself. In a passage reminiscent of Marx he wrote:

Eternally tied to a single fragment of the whole, man himself develops into nothing but a fragment. Everlastingly in his ear is the monotonous sound of the wheel which he operates. He never develops the harmony of his being, and instead of stamping the imprint of

[1] *An Essay on the History of Civil Society*, Edinburgh 1767, pp. 182–3.

[2] I.e. *Lectures on Justice, Police, Revenue and Arms*, ed. Cannan, London 1896. These lectures were given in Glasgow in 1763 and contain significant criticisms of the 'commercial spirit'. It is even possible that Ferguson derived some of his views from hearing these lectures. There is an interesting discussion of these issues with particular reference to Ferguson in *Das Ideal des harmonischen Menschen in der bürgerlichen Ästhetik*, by Georgy Lukacs, Vienna 1952.

[3] Both Coleridge and Carlyle were profoundly influenced by German thought and Carlyle wrote a *Life of Schiller*, London 1845. See *The Prestige of Schiller in England 1788–1859*, Ewen, New York 1932.

[4] This fact needs to be accounted for. One would have expected this kind of critique of industrial society to have developed first of all in Britain where the industrial system had progressed furthest, rather than in Germany which was comparatively speaking industrially backward. It may have more to do with the general state of national morale rather than the iniquity of industrialism *per se*. The middle of the eighteenth century saw Britain at the height of its powers. It had acquired an extensive empire through the victories in the Seven Years War and had put down the possibility of internal strife in 1745. There was in consequence a good deal less motivation to look for a radical critique of the society. The situation was not so in Germany (see below, pp. 25 ff.). Of course Germany had factories—see Goethe's *Dichtung und Wahrheit*, Bk. 1, *Sämtliche Werke*, Berlin 1902, Vol. 24, for an impression of commercial and industrial activity in Frankfurt.

humanity upon nature he becomes no more than the imprint of his occupation and his specialized knowledge.[1]

How could this enervation of the individual's powers be arrested and something like the harmony of Greek experience be restored? More often than not, the earlier, pre-1770 writings of thinkers such as Goethe, Schiller, Hamann and Herder were passionate protests against the civilization which had imposed this fragmentation of the personality, but practical advice as to how to overcome the problem was in short supply, particularly during this earlier *Sturm und Drang* period when the social foundations of the problem were not much appreciated. Instead of proposals for the reform of society to make modes of experience more integrated and men more harmonious, works of this period tended to stop short at mere *cris de coeur*, or alternatively provided imaginary attempts to overcome the fragmentation of the person by some kind of Promethian act of will. A concrete example of such an attempt may be seen in the perverse and in many ways tragic life of J. G. Hamann,[2] of whom Goethe wrote in *Dichtung und Wahrheit*:

> All that a man undertakes whether it be by deed or word must spring from the totality of his unified powers. Everything isolated is harmful.[3]

Goethe went on to comment that although this was good advice, that the harmonious development of the human powers possessed great value, it was a difficult ideal to follow in practice. He showed how difficult in *Die Leiden des Jungen Werther*. It was difficult to follow in that the advice ignored the fact that the fragmentation of the personality was not just a *personal* failure but was rather a result of the structure of *society*. Consequently Werther's attempt to realize himself was nearly always frustrated by the narrow confines of bourgeois life. It was the very considerable merit of Hegel's thought from the very start that he considered the problem of personal fragmentation to be closely bound up with the structure of contemporary society. As will be seen below,[4] initially he saw the problem to be the result of religious developments and formulated the notion of a folk religion which would, at one and the same time, restore the homogeneity of culture and develop the wholeness of the individual personality. Later, after reading the works of Sir James Steuart, the Scottish political economist, he saw the problem far more in terms of economic changes and less in terms of

[1] Schiller, op. cit., p. 323.
[2] On Hamann see *J. G. Hamann* by R. Gregor Smith, London 1960.
[3] Goethe, op. cit., vol. 24, p. 81.
[4] See below, pp. 32 ff.

religious structures. But throughout he was committed to 'preserving the inner life of man within the commercial system'.[1]

The concentration, after the somewhat subjective *Sturm und Drang* period, on the social aspects of fragmentation, led fairly naturally to the view that not only was man in a state of dissonance, but society was also deeply divided. This perception of the loss of an integrated community became a cognate preoccupation of thinkers of Hegel's generation. Again the image of the ideal community was taken from their understanding of Greek, and more particularly Athenian, forms of social and political life in much the same way as they had turned to Greece for a paradigm of humanity and this image of political community was used to criticise the social and political culture of Germany. Periclean Athens was taken as an articulation of the very highest social and political ends in which no distinction could be drawn between man as a citizen and man as a private individual. A magnificent and influential paean to the social and political homogeneity of Greece was given to his generation in 'Die Götter Griechenlands'[2] in which Schiller stressed how closely political, social, family and religious obligations were interwoven. This contrast between the closely knit culture of the Greek *polis* and the fragmented state of German society became a very predominant feature of Hegel's thinking particularly in his early writings, although he was always very much alive to the difficulties in drawing such comparisons. Such was the influence of the Hellenic ideal on Hegel that, even as late as 1805, by which time the general Hellenic movement in Germany had lost a great deal of its impetus, Hegel was moved to call the Greek *polis* a work of art in that as no one part could be separated from the others, it was an ideal and harmonious entity.[3] As with the fragmentation of the human person, the breakdown of community in the modern world was attributed to the role of the division of labour, perhaps again under the influence of Ferguson who was not untainted by the idealization of Greek experience:

> To the ancient Greek . . . the individual was nothing, the public everything. To the modern in too many nations of Europe the individual is everything and the public nothing. . . . We in times more polished employ the calm we have gained not in fostering zeal for those laws and the constitution of government to which they owe their protection, but in practising apart and each for himself the several arts of personal advancement or profit.[4]

[1] K. Rosenkranz, *Hegels Leben*, Berlin 1844, p. 86.
[2] Schiller, op. cit., vol. II.
[3] Hegel, *Jenenser Realphilosophie II*, ed. J. Hoffmeister, Leipzig 1931, p. 251.
[4] Ferguson, op. cit., p. 55.

Rousseau, whom Hegel studied and was deeply influenced by as a student in Tübingen, perhaps summed up his view of the situation as well as any when he argued in his *Premier Discours sur les sciences et les arts*:

> We have among us physicians, geometers, chemists, astronomers, poets, musicians and painters, but no citizens.[1]

It was Hegel's achievement that he always kept in mind the social dimension of the problem of individual fragmentation. His ideal like that of most of his contemporaries was that of the *recreation of a whole man in an integrated, cohesive, political community*. Despite several changes in analysis and prescription, this humanistic moral and social concern was to remain at the very centre of his thought and constitutes the key to its identity.

The perception of the loss of political community and an homogeneous culture was not a merely intellectual appreciation on the part of German writers; it was immediately present to the eyes of any sensitive person in the latter part of the eighteenth century. Despite a shared language, Germany was very deeply divided on political and religious grounds, a division which in turn permeated the whole culture. At this period Germany was not, for example like France and Great Britain, a united, strong, national state, but in practice, if not in theory, a very loose confederation of states with badly defined boundaries and without clearly delineated areas of authority. Consequently it is in a sense misleading to even speak of 'Germany' as if it were the name of a coherent political entity. Indeed, particularism (*Kleinstaaterei*) was of the very essence of German political life of the period. The Holy Roman Empire, by the eighteenth century had developed into a loose confederation of states with no real political centre of gravity. It consisted of monarchies such as Prussia which were able to play a European role, but also of miniscule states such as the small Bishopric of Osnabrück. There were ninety-four spiritual and lay princes, 103 counts and forty prelates presiding over virtually sovereign states in addition to fifty-one free towns—altogether some 300 separate territories, each pursuing its own particular and isolated interests. Attempts to introduce some kind of cohesion by the Emperor, the *Reichskammergericht* for example, failed because most territories refused to accept such an institution as a final court of appeal in disputes. There was therefore no shared political tradition in Germany and, given this situation, it is not surprising that the Grecian *polis* with its ideal of community predicated upon a shared political culture should make

---

[1] *Oeuvres Complètes*, Paris 1964, vol. 4, p. 26.

such a wide appeal. Certainly Hegel always connected together the pursuit of harmony and coherence with the regeneration of Germany.

In addition the political fragmentation in Germany led to economic stagnation. With such dissipated political authority it was very difficult for services such as roads and bridges to be effectively constructed and this failure had an important effect on the economy, making it very backward relative to Britain and France, although underlying factors in the structure of the German economy were favourable and might have been developed had the machinery of economic management been there.[1] Thinkers of Hegel's generation had learned from the Scottish historians and political economists how crucial economic factors were in structuring the character of national life and this in turn became a preoccupation of Hegel,[2] particularly in the Jena period.

The other factor making for the fragmentation of German society was religious. Greek city states had a common, homogeneous religious life. As Schiller had shown in 'Die Götter Griechenlands', Greek religion contributed in a very real way to the homogeneity of the community; it provided a core of common culture to weld the society into a community. The religious context facing writers of Hegel's generation was very far from being like this: it was sectarian and encouraged particularism. The Treaty of Westphalia (1648), concluding the disastrous thirty years of religious civil war, formalized the religious divisions of the country on the *cuius regio, eius religio* principle.[3]

There were, in addition, very deep cultural divisions outside of religious activity. These divisions were of two kinds: a lack of communication between classes and a lack of a common or shared culture between individual states and territories. In his book *Germany in the Eighteenth Century*,[4] Bruford notes that there was in Germany at this time no cultural form which could appeal to all sections of society as could the Greek drama, or for that matter the works of Shakespeare in Britain. Herder pointed this contrast very clearly when he wrote about Greece in contrast with Germany:

[1] See G. Schmoller, *The Mercantile System*, trans. Ashley, London 1884:
'Germany had a good start in processes, traffic, even foreign trade, but no authority to take advantage of it. . . . Everywhere economic bodies were becoming political except in Germany where the advantages it had enjoyed before 1620 were being lost . . . the lack of politico-economic organization . . . caused Germany's decay.'
[2] See *Jenenser Realphilosophie I*, ed. J. Hoffmeister, Leipzig 1932, and *Jenenser Realphilosophie II*, op. cit., both of which are fully discussed below.
[3] That each state should take on itself the religion of its prince.
[4] W. H. Bruford, *Germany in the Eighteenth Century*, 2nd ed., Cambridge 1965.

The Greek language was spoken by all the children, understood by everyone and sung in the street by both poets and fools. The gods were the gods of the people, even of the rabble. History and heroic deeds were things cherished and possessed by all the people.[1]

In contemporary Germany there was a profound split between the consciousness of the educated classes and those who lacked education and in consequence no cultural form could appeal to both. Hegel was very well aware of this and his very first essay on these topics[2] indicated that he saw the central problem of both the individual and society in terms of the relationship between classes and the cultural forms available in society. This cultural divisiveness was not merely to be found in the relationships between classes *within* the community, but also *between* the different German territories. Such depths of particularism had been reached that Justus Möser who far from disapproved of the general fragmentation of German society[3] was moved to complain in his *Patriotische Phantasien*[4] that Germans were even forced to swear in French because there were no national oaths! Bruford interprets the situation thus:

> Goethe speaks more than once of a lack of 'general culture' in Germany contrasting it unfavourably with France and England. It was one of the difficulties that the writers of his age, with their new ambition to reach a national public felt most.[5]

It is precisely at this point in the outline of the *Gedankenwelt* that we can take up Hegel's work because in one of his very earliest essays he draws together in a quite remarkable way many of the complexities of the problem.

Hegel at Stuttgart: Greece and Germany Compared

We communicate, but being abstract and second-hand, the words of our communication do not achieve community.[6]

While still a schoolboy at the Stuttgart Gymnasium, Hegel began to grapple with the problems described. During this period he both read

[1] Herder, op. cit., vol. 4, p. 401.
[2] Discussed below, pp. 28 ff.
[3] See G. B. Parry, 'Enlightened Government and Its Critics in Eighteenth Century Germany', *Historical Journal*, 1963, p. 189.
[4] J. Möser, *Sämtliche Werke*, vol. 1, Berlin 1842–3.
[5] Bruford, op. cit., p. 45.
[6] George Steiner, *Language and Silence*, London 1967.

HEGEL

and commented upon a great many classical texts[1] and one outcome of this study was his essay 'Über einige Charakteristische Unterschiede der Alten Dichter' dated 7 August 1788, that is to say, a week or two before Hegel's eighteenth birthday.[2] In the essay Hegel draws a very sharp contrast between the situation of the Greek poet and the contemporary German writer in terms of the cultural homogeneity of the writer's audience. It is in this essay that the twin themes of personal fragmentation and social division, the two keys to the identity of Hegel's thought, make their appearance for the first time. The essay is largely diagnostic rather than prescriptive; he is more concerned to describe and analyse the problems affecting German culture in contrast to that of the Greeks, rather than to propose solutions to them.

Hegel argues that a very profound disassociation exists between the German people and their history. The German poet, unlike the Greek cannot assume on the part of the public any real understanding of the forces which have moulded the history of the society, nor of its traditions, its heroes and its martyrs:

> The heroic deeds of our ancestors and those of modern Germans are not intrinsically fixed into our conceptions, nor is their memory preserved in oral tradition.[3]

As there is no shared and common acquaintance on the part of the people with the traditions of society, an external and divisive view of those traditions is obtained. The acquaintance is external for the educated classes in that it is derived from reading history books which, as Hegel points out, are often written by foreigners; the relationship with tradition is distorted for those who are uneducated because history is for them merely a matter of superstition. These superstitions do not cohere with the religious beliefs of the very same people, nor do they bear any relationship to empirical fact. Because of these two different and quite inadequate perceptions of history, one discursive and external, the other immediate but distorted, acquaintance with history becomes socially divisive. Different classes have different relationships to the history of the society of which they form a part. Instead of history and tradition forming a core of common culture which would weld an

[1] Rosenkranz in *Hegels Leben*, op. cit., lists the following work by Hegel on classical texts: A study of the *Iliad*; Longinus, *On the Sublime*; Euripides; Aristotle's *Nicomachean Ethics*; Sophocles, *Oedipus at Colonus*. Cf. also *Zur Chronologie von Hegels Jugendschriften*, in *Hegel Studien*, Bonn 1963, pp. 111–60.
[2] The essay is printed in *Dokumente zu Hegels Entwicklung*, ed. J. Hoffmeister, Stuttgart 1936, pp. 48–51.
[3] Hoffmeister, op. cit., p. 49.

28

atomized society into an homogeneous community it is rather a divisive force:

> The ideas and culture of the classes are too distinct for a poet in our times to be read and universally understood.[1]

This lack of a shared culture, leads, Hegel argues, to a complete breakdown in communication. Such would not have been the case he comments 'If our public relationships had been Greek'. The Greeks, in his view, shared a literary culture which enabled them to produce universal works of art, works which did not have to be directed towards just one section of the community if they were to be intelligible.[2] Hegel had no doubt learned from Herder how far the cohesion of a culture depended upon its language, and the whole tenor of Hegel's argument in the essay is very reminiscent of the passage cited from Herder above.[3]

The second contrast which Hegel draws between the Greek and German artistic public is in terms of the different relationships between the individual and his experience and the language through which the experience is described and communicated. The Greek writer, Hegel argues, confronts and describes his experience in a direct manner in a language which was very closely tied to the experiences which it describes:

[1] Hoffmeister, op. cit., p. 49. Hegel returns to this point a bit later in 'Die Positivität der christlichen Religion', Nohl, op. cit., p. 216.

. . . the imagination of our more educated classes has an entirely different ambit from that of the mass of the people, for the latter do not understand in the least the characters and scenes of those authors and artists who cater for the former. On the other hand, the Athenian citizen who, because of his poverty was deprived of a vote in the public assembly or even had to sell himself as a slave, still knew as well as did Pericles and Alcibiades, who Agamemnon and Oedipus were when Sophocles or Euripides brought them onto the stage as noble types of beautiful and sublime humanity or when Phidias or Apelles exhibited them as pure models of physical beauty.

The Greeks had a shared literary culture which made the basis for some kind of shared and reciprocating community life.

[2] It is interesting in this context to consider the argument advanced by Goethe in his essay 'Literarischer Sansculottismus', written seven years after Hegel's youthful piece. In the essay Goethe examines the presuppositions of the appearance of a national literature or a national author:

. . . if the history of his nation furnishes him with a happy and significant system of great events and their consequences; if his fellow countrymen show him examples of high thinking, deep emotion and bold and enduring actions; if he himself, filled with the spirit of the nation, feels he has genius enough within him to share sympathetically its past and present life. . .'

In these circumstances a national literature might appear but, the situation being as it was, Germany could not produce such work.

[3] See above, p. 27.

One principally remarkable quality of the works of the ancients is simplicity, a feature which we can feel rather than distinguish. Simplicity consists really in this: that the poets give us a faithful picture of the subject. They do not try to make it more interesting by adding fine shading or learned artifices, or more splendid or more fascinating by a straight deviation from the truth such as we demand today.[1]

Hegel stresses how close Greek writing was to the situations and to the realities which it described, and because of this it was more widely intelligible. Unlike the German language and literature—full of artifice and sophistication—which, by removing the literature from the life experiences of the mass of the people, makes literature at once remote from them and at the same time a divisive force:

> The entire system of education and culture was constituted so that each acquired his ideals and experience for himself so that they were able to speak about their experiences, how, where and why they had them and were not acquainted with cold learning which implants only dead signs in the head.[2]

Such a situation contrasts very sharply with German experience where, Hegel argues, 'words stay in the mind without activity and without employment'. The kind of situation Hegel has in mind in this early essay may best be elucidated with reference to a later work—*Vorlesungen über Ästhetik*—in which he stresses how close Greek language was to practical activity, activity which all members of the society pursued, unlike German literature which is sophisticated, artificial and

---

[1] Hoffmeister, op. cit., p. 49. Cf. Bruford's description of Goethe's conversations with Eckermann, op. cit., p. 302:

German style he argued was spoiled by too much philosophical speculation . . . they (the writers) have both the strength and the weakness resulting from not writing for a clearly defined public. They lacked the tug from reality that even the most unworldly French or English authors constantly experienced.

[2] Hoffmeister, op. cit., p. 49. Cf. also Herder, op. cit., vol. IV, p. 365:

A proper school of language instruction will not teach a pupil a word which he cannot grasp from the content of his own experience. Turn through a German Dictionary and consider how much of our language we do learn in this way; go through a foreign language—it will be a thousand times less. This is where our age so badly fails.

Hegel's point is more general—the condition of a literature written in a language which at the very best is related to the experience of a few.

philosophical and therefore restricted in scope. Describing the work of Homer he argues:

> Everything is in its home and in its place; in everything a man discovers the energy of his own muscles, the ability of his own hand . . . Agamemnon's sceptre which his ancestor shaped from a block of wood and left it as an heirloom to his descendants. Odysseus put together the mighty bed which he shared with Penelope.[1]

The growth of science and what Hegel was later to call abstract labour, that is labour in manufacturing industry, has made modern man less bound up with the world, less closely related to it in practical activity. This estranged relationship is shown in the lack of vivacity of the German language compared with the Greek. Divorced from the world language becomes an end in itself—descriptive writing is embellished with all kinds of sophisticated contrivances with the result that it fails to connect with the experience of the vast majority of men.[2]

This early insight of Hegel's into the failure of the German language to be an adequate vehicle for community is of enormous importance for understanding his later development. It became one of his major preoccupations that conventional discourse has become abstract and one dimensional to the extent that life has begun to outrun thought. The task of philosophy, as he later came to see it, was to make thought adequate to reality, to develop a conceptual framework which would be capable of encapsulating the life of society, a framework which once shared would enable men to live at home in the world and with one another.[3]

During the next few years, however, Hegel devoted himself to a close examination of the causes of the social and cultural fragmentation which he had described in the early essay. He became particularly interested in the role of *religion* in bringing about the decline in closely-knit community life and the consequent fragmentation of the personality. This religious exploration of the roots of the contemporary crisis and

[1] Hegel, *Sämtliche Werke*, ed. H. Glockner, Stuttgart 1927–40, vol. XII, p. 382.
[2] Another characteristic is that the (Greek) writers describe the particular phenomenon based upon sense impression—the phenomenon of visible nature with which they are intimately familiar; whereas we are better informed about the internal play of forces and know the causes of things better than we know their appearances.
Hoffmeister, op. cit., p. 49.
[3] See J. Hyppolite, 'Life and Consciousness of Life in the Jena Philosophy', *Studies on Marx and Hegel*, London 1969, p. 4.

the search for a theological solution to it became Hegel's primary intellectual concern until the late 1790s.

Hegel at Tübingen 1788–93: the search for a social theology

Aber Freund! wir kommen zu spät. Zwar leben die Götter Aber über dem Haupt droben in anderer Welt.[1]

During the period in which he studied theology and philosophy in the Protestant theological seminary in the University of Tübingen, Hegel's attention turned towards the differences between the folk religion of the Greeks and contemporary Christianity and between the effect of each type of religious practice upon the social structures of Greece and Germany and upon the psychology of the individual as he participated in these very different patterns of religious experience, one integrated into the life of the community, the other creating deep social divisions. The task, as he considers it at this time, is to explore the characteristics of folk religion in order to derive some indication of the sort of religious reforms which it would be necessary to carry out in Germany in order to recapture anything resembling the wholeness of Greek life. It must be emphasized at the very outset of this discussion of Hegel's views on the social and indeed political dimensions of religious belief that he is not concerned with the truth or falsity of Greek folk religion or of contemporary Christianity, but is far more interested in their respective effects upon social and political culture—the way in which each tends or tended to promote communal ties. He is concerned with what might be called *civil theology*, to follow St Augustine's usage,[2] or with what Oakeshott considers to be the effect of such theology:

. . . not so much belief as practice, not with viable religious truths but with social peace.[3]

The pieces on these topics written by Hegel as a student in Tübingen have been collected together by Nohl in five major fragments[4] and

[1] Hölderlin, *Brot und Wein*. ('But my friend we have come too late. It is true that the Gods are alive but above our heads and in a different world.')
[2] St Augustine, *De Civitate Dei*, Bk. VI, London 1871.
[3] M. Oakeshott, ed., *Leviathan*, Oxford 1955, p. lxi. The fact that Hegel is not concerned with the problem of truth tests in theology but with the cultural effects of religious belief does not justify Lukacs who in his *Der junge Hegel*, Vienna 1949, argues that the attribution of a theological phase to Hegel is a 'reactionary legend'. Nor does it for that matter justify Kaufmann's claim in 'Hegel's Early Antitheological Phase', *Philosophical Review*, 1954, that Hegel's early works should be retitled *Early Antitheological Writings*. Hegel's works belong to a recognizable theological *genre*, namely civil or social theology.
[4] Nohl, op. cit., pp. 1–69.

although an adequate system of dating has been worked out[1] they will be taken as a whole for the purposes of this thesis. In the fragments, Hegel formulates his views around two sets of contrasts: objective and subjective religion on the one hand and private and folk religion on the other.

Hegel's concern with the difference between objective and subjective religion is motivated by what was described earlier in this chapter as the awareness on the part of men of his generation of the fragmentation of the individual personality. Hegel is concerned in drawing the contrast between the harmony of the individual's personality as he participates in a subjective religious practice and the bifurcation of his personality involved in objective religious activity. A subjective religion is one which appeals to the *whole* man so that religion becomes an affair of the heart, a matter of emotion and imagination[2] as well as reason and intellect. The claims of such a religion, he argues, would be accepted by the integrated powers of the human mind and would not appeal to the operation of one faculty alone. Objective religion, by which Hegel seems to mean a religion based upon truths about man and God discerned by the light of reason alone, is a religion which pays no attention to the conative and affective sides of man's nature.[3] As he participates in the two different religious practices, man appears differently. In a subjective religious practice, the 'whole man moves together', in Schiller's phrase; in an objective religious practice, the conative and affective sides of human nature become enervated. Not only is an objective religion personally divisive, it also leads to social fragmentation in that it leaves a gap between religious belief and social morality. The task of any religion in Hegel's view is that of fostering social morality,[4] but an objective religion cannot fulfil this role because, in Hegel's view, the impulse to morality is not, *pace* Kant, primarily intellectual. Reason by itself cannot move a man to action. To act morally a man must act as a total being, with all his powers engaged. In a passage reminiscent of Hume, Hegel argues:

[1] G. Schüler, '*Zur Chronologie von Hegels Jugendschriften*', *Hegel Studien*, 1963.

[2] Nohl, loc. cit., p. 9.

[3] Hegel would without doubt have sympathized with the *cri de coeur* of J. H. Merck, the Paymaster General of Hesse Damstadt, in *Teutscher Merkur* 1779:

> Now we have got the freedom of believing in public nothing but what can be rationally demonstrated. They have deprived religion of its sensuous elements, that is of all its relish. They have carved it into parts without colour and light.

[4] The highest end of man, Hegel argues, is morality, and the religious disposition is crucial for the living of the moral life. See Nohl, op. cit., p. 16.

33

The understanding serves only objective religion. By purifying principles and by representing them in their purity, the understanding has borne splendid fruit. But the understanding can never turn principles into practice. The understanding is a courtier who obeys his master's moods. . . . Enlightenment of the understanding makes men more clever but not better.[1]

Both the harmony of the person and social relations are destroyed by an objective religion and it is clear that what Hegel has in mind is Christian practice when it is permeated by rationalism. A subjective religion on the other hand, because it involves the totality of the human powers, can promote both inner harmony and social morality. At this stage, however, the whole conception of subjective religion is left rather vague and is subsumed into that of folk religion, the religion of the people or the nation.

The distinction between private and folk religion is basically the distinction between what Hegel takes to be the central features of the religious life of the Greeks and contemporary Christian practice. Again in these fragments Hegel insists upon the social and, indeed, the political dimension of the religious life of a people:

The spirit of the people, its history, its religion, its degree of political freedom cannot be considered in isolation by their separate characteristics. They are woven together in an indissoluble fashion.[2]

Greek folk religion was, in Hegel's view, the central determinant of the harmony and totality which he considered to be the distinguishing mark of Greek society; Christianity, on the other hand, he saw as a private religion which, far from encouraging social solidarity, in fact taught the individual to look beyond and outside the social order in which he lived to find his ideals and values. In so doing Christianity undermined social commitment.[3] Christianity was, in Hegel's view, a private religion because its stress is solely upon personal salvation through the private worship of a transcendent God, remote from the community[4] and its conventional morality. In consequence Christianity

[1] Nohl, op. cit., p. 12. [2] Nohl, op. cit., p. 27.

[3] Similar views are still held: see Erich Fromm, *The Sane Society*. On p. 349 of this work, Fromm argues that among other things religious changes are needed to alter the atomistic nature of contemporary society, changes which are similar in principle to those which Hegel goes on to advocate.

[4] In stressing in an almost Barthian fashion the remoteness of God from the world, the total division between finite and infinite, Hegel was probably reflecting the kind of theology disseminated in Tübingen at this time. Flatt and Storr, his two professors, used the Kantian distinction between the realm of phenomena and the realm of noumena along with his assertion that the noumenal

encouraged the neglect of social and political obligations, the morality present in society. Christianity had, therefore, contributed in very large measure to the loss of community by stressing inward and private ends as opposed to civic and communal ties:

> Our religion wishes to educate men to be citizens of heaven who always look on high and this makes them strangers to human feeling.[1]

It is probable that Hegel developed his views on the anticommunitarian spirit of Christianity from his reading of Rousseau's *Social Contract*[2] in which Rousseau was perhaps even more scathing than Hegel about the way in which Christianity had driven a wedge between man *qua* citizen and man *qua* child of God.[3] Instead of building up a harmonious, reciprocating community as Greek folk religion had done, the ends and values in human life were seen by the contemporary Christian in a totally a-social fashion and Hegel points out very explicitly the sharp contrast between the social effects of the religious forms of life:

> Private religion forms the morality of the individual man but the religion of the people as well as the political circumstances forms the spirit of the people.[4]

Christianity has, in Hegel's view, made man so unconcerned, at least in so far as his political outlook is concerned, that for example in

world is beyond human knowledge, in order to argue that the noumenal God is known only through supernatural revelation. This obviousy had the effect of making God appear very remote indeed. (See O. Pfleiderer, *The Development of Theology in Germany since Kant*, trans. Smith, London 1883.) It is perhaps no accident in view of this relationship between dogmatic theology and the work of Kant that Barth should have devoted a great deal of his time before the writing of his *Römerbrief* to the study of Kant's work.

[1] Nohl, op. cit., p. 27. The final part of the German runs: '. . . menschliche Empfindungen fremd'—this is the first time that Hegel uses the word 'fremd' which constantly occurs later in his work with reference to the idea of alienation.

[2] See J. Hoffmeister, *Dokumente zu Hegels Entwicklung*, op. cit., p. 430, in which he quotes from Leutwein, one of Hegel's contemporaries in Tübingen:

> At least metaphysics was not Hegel's special interest the four years when I knew him. His hero was Rousseau.

[3] J. J. Rousseau, op. cit., pp. 465–7. The basic argument here had been implicit in the work of theologians such as Augustine and Aquinas. It is implicit in Augustine's two loves for the two cities (see *De Civitate Dei*, op. cit.) and in the work of Aquinas on social and political theology:

> Man does not belong to the political community with the whole of his being (*secundum se totum*) nor with all that is his (*nec secundum tota sua*).

Summa Theologica II(a) 21, 4. Cf. St Peter, chap. 2 v. ii.
For Aquinas the human state was part of the road to the membership of the heavenly city. These issues in medieval social and political theology are dealt with by Fr Thomas Gilby in *Between Community and Society*, London 1953.

[4] Nohl, op. cit., p. 28.

Goethe's *Wilhelm Meisters Lehrjahre*, Werner was able to encapsulate the feelings of man formed in this tradition when he confessed to Lothario:

I can assure you that in my life I have never thought of the state.[1]

It is Hegel's strongly urged view in the fragments on folk religion that only something akin to Greek folk religion could recapture social and political homogeneity. He argues that a folk religion is necessary to replace Christianity in the hope that it would permeate society and so remove the dissonance and fragmentation which he regards as characteristic of his age. Such an effect could only be achieved by the creation of a folk religion which would find its gods, its symbolism and its ritual in the history and the traditions of the people and thus provide a core of common culture.[2]

It seems probable that two influences were at work on Hegel's mind so far as his rather vague formulation of these positive proposals were concerned. The social and political importance of a folk or civic religion was probably derived once again from Hegel's reading of Rousseau and his specific conception of Greek folk religion from Schiller's poem 'Die Götter Griechenlands'.[3] The whole distinction between private and folk religion seems to be taken over more or less directly from Rousseau's *Le Contrat Social*. In chapter five of that work Rousseau explicitly distinguishes between private and national or civic religion:

Religion considered with reference to society which is either general or particular may likewise be divided into two species, the private and the civic. The former . . . limited to a purely interior cult of an omnipotent God and the external duties of morality . . . is the pure and simple religion of the gospels. The second, limited to a single country, gives that country its special patrons and tutelary deities.[4]

Rousseau went on to recommend, and here Hegel seems to follow him

[1] Goethe, *Wilhelm Meisters Lehrjahre*, Book 8, ch. 2.

[2] Eventually Hegel was to argue that the whole bifurcation between the infinite life of God and the finite world of man was radically misconceived and that the philosopher could provide a conceptual grasp of the activity of God, realizing himself in the world, through the activities of men and thus doing away with any ultimate division between the mode and character of the being of God and that of his creatures. (See below, p. 80.)

[3] Although it is equally possible that Herder's influence was paramount. See *Ideen zur Philosophischen Geschichte der Menschheit*, in *Werke*, op. cit., vol. XIII. If therefore you would produce a new Greece in images of Gods, give a people again this mythological superstition.

[4] Rousseau, op. cit., p. 467.

closely, that what was needed in contemporary society was the development of a civic religion as a means of promoting communal ties:

> There is therefore a simple profession of faith whose articles the sovereign is competent to determine, not precisely as religious dogmas, but as sentiments of sociability without which it is impossible to be either a good citizen or a faithful subject.[1]

Given Leutwein's evidence, it seems reasonable to conclude that Hegel saw the contemporary situation in Germany very much through the eyes of Rousseau.[2]

So far as his particular conception of the style, content and effect of Greek folk religion is concerned, there is considerable likeness between it and Schiller's paean to the Greeks and their religion in 'Die Götter Griechenlands'. In this poem Schiller stresses the extent to which the harmony of the individual Greek and of his society was a function of religion. The Greeks were, in Schiller's view, aware of the divine in every aspect of their existence, both in the social and the natural worlds. The sun, for example, was not a mere ball of fire fixed in the void of space, but Helios mounted upon his golden chariot;[3] Dryads inhabited the woods, Naiads the streams.[4] Their gods were not transcendent and remote from the community but beings capable of being encountered in it.[5] Because the divine entered every aspect of their life, they were deeply at home in the natural world and the pervasiveness of their divinities gave a unity to their social lives—marriages were dedicated to Hymen,[6] feasting to Dionysus,[7] and stories from history and tradition helped to form morality.[8] As a result of the growth of natural science, however, Schiller argues, the golden age has fled from the world; natural phenomena have been robbed of mystery and social life has

---

[1] Rousseau, ibid., p. 469.
[2] See also G. A. Kelly, *Idealism, Politics and History*, Cambridge 1969, p. 324.
[3] Schiller, op. cit., vol. II, ll. 16–20.   [4] Ibid., ll. 22–5.
[5] Ibid., ll. 191–2.   [6] Ibid., ll. 69–70.   [7] Ibid., ll. 73–80.
[8] Ibid., ll. 137 ff. This point of course links up with Hegel's thesis in 'Über einige Charakteristische Unterschiede der Alten Dichter'. (Discussed above, pp. 28 ff.) Of course Schiller's view of Greece and its religious life is rather exaggerated. Not everyone regarded the sun, for example, in such a romantic fashion. The 'disenchantment' of the world began of course with Thales but it was left to Anaxagoras to make the observation that the sun was a red hot stone as large as the Peloponnese—a far cry from Helios riding through the heavens! It is also true that the Germans seriously overestimated the unity of Greek religious experience. They failed to take account of such secret cults as the Orphic cults which flourished at the sort of period which the Germans tended to idealise. I am grateful to Professor C. Lejewski for pointing this out to me.

become disenchanted.[1] Whereas Hegel at this time saw the solution to contemporary problems in terms of the recreation of a folk religion, Schiller argues that new forms of harmony and coherence have to be worked out to meet the fundamental changes in the human condition; there can be no return to outmoded types of social practice ignoring the changes which science and the division of labour have produced, nor the positive gains which had arisen from these changes.[2] Schiller devoted himself to this in his *Ästhetische Briefe*. According to Schiller the Greeks were at home in the world, had roots in and identified themselves with their social and cultural experience because they held this naive, intuitive religious faith in the divinity of natural phenomena. This intuitive relationship with the world has, however, broken down, men have become reflective, critical, more conscious of themselves and their power over nature. In place of the naive, unmediated *sinnliche Harmonie* which the Greeks had to their social and natural worlds, a new type of harmony will have to be developed to take account of the fundamental change in the human condition, a state of *moralische Harmonie*. In this state men would come to accept the values and traditions of their community freely and after reflection. Such a state could only be generated, according to Schiller, by aesthetic education. Only the operation of the *play impulse* could unite the powers of the human mind and from a restoration of the harmony of men's private capacities eventually social harmony would flow:

> Taste alone brings harmony into society because it fosters harmony in the individual. All other forms of perception divide a man because they are exclusively founded upon the sensuous or spiritual parts of his being. Only the aesthetic type of perception unites his being . . .[3]

[1] Schiller's views had an influence on Max Weber which can best be seen in his notion of rationalisation. See *From Max Weber*, ed. H. Gerth and C. Wright Mills, London 1948, p. 51.

[2] Some incorrigible romantics still see the solution to the problems of mass industrial society with its personal divisiveness and social fragmentation in terms of a retreat to more primitive relations with nature. See D. H. Lawrence, *A Propos of Lady Chatterley's Lover*, London 1930, p. 54:

> The universe is dead for us and how is it to come alive again? 'Knowledge' has killed the sun, making it a ball of gas with spots; 'knowledge' has killed the moon—it is a dead little earth fretted with extinct volcanoes . . . the machine has killed the earth for us. . . . How are we to get back to Apollo, Attis, Demeter, Persephone and the halls of Dis?

[3] Schiller, op. cit., p. 410. On Schiller's views here, see R. Pascal in '*Bildung* and the Division of Labour' in *German Studies, Essays in Honour of W. H. Bruford*, London 1962, p. 12:

> The best of German ethical thought is here, the recognition of absolute responsibility for the fulfilment of the whole self. And the fault of this type

The ancient Greek was naturally at home in the world; the modern man must bring himself to terms with it through arduous intellectual effort.

In the long run, Hegel came to agree with this view and his mature philosophy can be seen to be an attempt to bring about a reflective, *moralische Harmonie* between man and the world. At the time of the Tübingen fragments on folk religion he is, however, far too much imbued with the Hellenic ideal to adopt such a view, although towards the end of the fragments one can perhaps detect the first sign of †pessimism over the enterprise as he at this time envisages it. His attitude towards Greek culture, already one of nostalgia, becomes one of regret, based upon a fear that it will not be easy to recover it:

> We do not know any more about the spirit of the Greeks than we know by hearsay and it is left to us to contemplate with love and admiration certain of its characteristics in the copies that remain to us. They excite in us a burning and sorrowful desire for the original. . . . It has disappeared from the face of the earth.[1]

This combination of pessimism tinged with nostalgia was to become very much more pronounced but at this stage in his thought it was only just beginning to take hold, perhaps under the influence of his great friend Hölderlin who bemoaned the passing of Greece and its ideals in an elegy written in 1793 during the very period when Hegel was writing his more prosaic religious studies:

> Attika, die Heldin ist gefallen;
> Wo die alten Göttersöhne ruhn,
> In Ruin der schönen Marmorhallen
> Steht der Kranich einsam trauernd nun;

of approach is also evident. The objective is sought in the existential sphere only; social relations and obligations are put in the background or ignored.

[1] Nohl, op. cit., p. 29. This passage may be an echo of Hegel's reading of Winckelmann:

> Just as a woman on the shores of the sea follows her departing lover with tear-filled eyes without the hope of ever seeing him again and thinks she sees in the distant sail the image of her loved one, like such a woman we have as it were only a silhouette of the object of our desires but this awakens all the greater longing for that which we have lost.

J. J. Winckelmann, *Sämtliche Werke*, ed. J. Eiselin, 1825–9, vol. VI, p. 365. It is interesting to recall in this context Hegel's mature criticism of those full of nostalgia, e.g. in *Sämtliche Werke*, ed. H. Glockner, vol. 19, p. 641.

Lächelnd kehrt der holde Frühling wieder,
Doch er findet sein Bruder nie
In Ilissus heilgem Thale wieder—
Unter Schutt und Domen schlummern sie.[1]

[1] Hölderlin, op. cit., vol. 1, p. 180.

Chapter II

Folk Religion
and Political Analysis

*We are without any religious imagery which is home grown or
linked with our history and we are without any political imagery
whatever; all that we have is the remains of an imagery of our own,
lurking amid the common people under the name of superstition.*
Hegel

Ye are as aliens in a foreign land.
St. Peter

During his period in Berne as tutor to the Steiger von Tschugg family,
Hegel became increasingly pessimistic about the possibility of a
religious solution to the problems which preoccupied him. Indeed, the
scepticism noted at the very end of the previous chapter became out-
right in a work of this period, 'Die Positivität der christlichen Religion',
written during 1795. In this work Hegel moves away from a purely
religious diagnosis and prescription for the contemporary malaise
towards a politico-religious analysis. However, his first extended study
of the Berne period fits very closely into the pattern of development
hitherto discerned. This claim might, on the face of it, appear somewhat paradoxical, because many critics have found the work, 'Das
Leben Jesu', very difficult to fit into Hegel's development. Some
consider it to be a slight essay, and tend to adopt a dismissive attitude
towards it and as a consequence do not give any indication of its
significance.[1] They fail to answer the question as to why Hegel should
have devoted himself to the study, given the pattern of his preoccupations at Tübingen and indeed earlier in Stuttgart. Others see in
the work merely an attempt to depict Jesus as a mouthpiece for certain
Kantian positions.[2] Such an approach does not however explain the

[1] Lukacs, in *Der junge Hegel*, op. cit., fails to mention the work and T. M.
Knox in his translation of Nohl, op. cit., *Hegel's Early Theological Writings* does
not include a translation of the work.
[2] See L. Dupré, *The Philosophical Foundations of Marxism*, New York 1966,
p. 8.

paradox which arises from accepting it—namely why, after so much time criticizing Christianity in Tübingen and attempting to delineate a conception of folk religion which would revitalize the life of Germany, he should suddenly be concerned to interpret the life of Jesus at all, particularly in Kantian terms which, as his M.A. thesis shows, he regarded as the embodiment of a deep bifurcation between reason and nature. The paradox shows up in a very striking way if such reasons for writing 'Das Leben Jesu' are juxtaposed with his Tübingen view that religion is designed to foster morality and morality is not a Kantian intellectual activity predicated on struggle with the heteronomy of nature.[1] 'Das Leben Jesu' can best be seen contrary to both of these attitudes in terms of the requirements laid down for a folk religion in the hope that the interpretation of Jesus' message given in the work might lead to the development of a folk religion out of Christianity.[2]

Hegel's aim, as we have seen, was to develop a folk religion as a means of providing some non-divisive cultural form in Germany, a cultural form which would unite the powers of the human mind and unite divided and fragmented men into one society. This folk religion could not, however, be achieved by the external means of somehow reinvoking Greek mythology[3]—the whole notion of importing an alien religious tradition and superimposing it on the actual religious life of the community would seem to Hegel to be most implausible. Nor could a folk religion be created out of the ancient myths of the German people:

> The project of restoring to a nation the images once lost was always condemned to failure . . . the old German imagery has nothing in our time to connect or adapt itself to: it stands cut off from the whole circle of our opinions and beliefs and it is as strange to us as the imagery of Ossian or India.[4]

[1] See above, p. 33. Cf. Nohl, p. 389:
The need to unite subject with object, to unite feeling and feeling's demand for objects, with the intellect . . . is the supreme need of the human spirit *and the urge to religion.* (Author's italics.)
[2] Similar interpretations are provided by W. Kaufmann in 'Hegel's Early Antitheological Phase', op. cit., p. 62 and by Paul Asveld in *La Pensée religieuse du jeune Hegel,* Louvain 1953, pp. 50–9. Indeed, Knox now seems to accept it, see *A Layman's Quest,* London 1969, p. 77.
[3] Herder in his essay 'Iduma', in *Werke,* op. cit., vol. XVIII, pp. 453–502, advocated bringing back the old German Gods and the myths of the *Urvolk.*
[4] Nohl, op. cit., p. 217. This of course reflects what Hegel had said in the Stuttgart essay about the role of mythology among the uneducated classes. On the general point of this quotation it is interesting to compare his much later view:

Klopstock, no doubt, in his enthusiasm for everything concerning the father-

Two alternatives therefore faced Hegel: one was to give up the whole idea of developing a folk religion, but this would have been unthinkable because, at this time, he saw in folk religion the key to a common culture; the other alternative was to change people's perception of their actual religious practices so that these practices, once reinterpreted, could develop into a folk religion. 'Das Leben Jesu' is an attempt to interpret the life and teaching of Jesus in such a way that all transcendental, authoritarian elements in it would disappear in the hope that out of this demythologized, humanized teaching a folk or civic religion might grow.

Jesus loses all traits of transcendence on Hegel's interpretation. He becomes a figure comparable to Socrates, a point which he pursues more fully in 'Die Positivität der christlichen Religion'. He is born of earthly parents, his miracles are either disregarded or explained away and the essay ends with the death of Jesus—no mention is made of the resurrection. Throughout the essay Hegel treats Jesus as a purely moral teacher, concerned not so much to make claims about the relation of man to God but rather with fostering human relations and morality.[1] This emphasis upon the moral dimension of Jesus' teaching as opposed to the propagation of the directives of a transcendent God obviously squares with one of the central requirements which Hegel makes about the nature of folk religion—that it must be concerned primarily with moral and social relationships, the specifically religious dimension of such a religion being regarded by him as valuable only as an impetus to the moral message. In the Tübingen fragment upon objective religion Jesus had rejected at least the conventional, institutionalized form of Christianity because it was based upon dogma and doctrine and could not therefore provide such an impetus to the development of morality. In the cognate fragments dealing with private religion he rejected Christianity because it demanded service to a transcendent deity. In 'Das Leben Jesu' both doctrine and transcendence disappear. No doubt

land was prompted to substitute his Scandinavian Gods for those of Hellenic mythology; but, despite his zeal, Wotan, Valhalla and Freja remain mere names to us . . .

Vorlesungen über die Ästhetik in *Sämtliche Werke*, op. cit., vol. XII, p. 367.

[1] This contrast between the teaching of Jesus, primarily moral and the authority of Christ, primarily religious, was almost a commonplace at the time at which Hegel was writing. In Germany the contrast was perhaps most popularly made by Wieland in *Agathodonian*, *Werke*, Leipzig 1799, vol. XXXII —Jesus, according to Wieland, made the Jewish national God humane and argues that if Christian ethics were practised then earth would become heaven. Jesus was not interested in founding religious institutions or in propounding dogma although both developed as a result of his teaching. See also G. E. Lessing's *Die Religion Christi* in *Theologischen Nachlass* and G. Pons, *G. E. Lessing et le Christianisme*, Paris 1966.

HEGEL

the essay does appear to be very Kantian, stressing the reasonableness of Christian claims—so it is, but this dimension is built into the essay for very un-Kantian reasons. Kant was concerned to find a role for religion within the bounds set by the *Kritik der reinen Vernunft* and was thus concerned to eliminate transcendence from religious claims.[1] Such was not Hegel's aim. He was not led to remove the transcendental elements of Jesus' teaching for either metaphysical or epistemological reasons but rather for social and cultural considerations. The worship of a transcendent God could well set problems for the metaphysician but, more importantly in Hegel's view, it poses a grave threat to the harmonious moral life of the community[2] and to the integrity and harmony of the person. 'Das Leben Jesu' therefore is not an attempt to change the meaning of the Christian message for epistemological or metaphysical purposes but rather to change people's perception of their religious experience and thus alter its social effects. The teaching of Jesus is recast by Hegel so that the response of Christians to the gospel might be altered and so changed that the contemporary divisive type of Christianity practised in Europe could develop into a folk religion which would make for both social cohesion and personal integration.

To sum up the views of Hegel at this time: Jesus was the teacher of a non-transcendent, non-authoritarian moral religion whose accreditation was not to be found in divine sanction but in its appeal to the reasonableness of men. Religious beliefs have to be within the bounds of reason in order to exorcise the transcendent, that metaphysical threat to social harmony. The function of 'Das Leben Jesu' is to change people's perception of their own religion but, interestingly enough, it was not published during this period, or indeed during his lifetime. Yet surely publication, widespread dissemination and universal acceptance were the very preconditions of achieving the implicit aim of the work. This seeming paradox is explained by reference to other writings of the Berne period. In his next specifically religious study, 'Die Positivität der christlichen Religion' and in his correspondence and occasional writings on politics it is clear that soon after completing

[1] See Kant, *Religion innerhalb der Grenzen der blossen Vernunft*, ed. cit., vol. VI.
[2] See Nohl, op. cit., p. 333:

The community has need of a God who is the God of the community, in whom there is manifested just that exclusive love which is the community's character and the tie between one member and another; this must be manifested in God . . . not as a personification of a subjective entity for in such a personification the worshipper would become conscious of a cleavage between the subjective entity and its objective manifestation.

It is this cleavage, Hegel argues, which has destroyed community.

'Das Leben Jesu', Hegel begins to move from a totally religious analysis of the contemporary malaise to one which unites his religious pre-occupations with an analysis in wholly secular terms of German social and political conditions. He does not disregard religion but appears to begin to take more seriously the implication of his comment in Tübingen that:

> . . . the religion of the people as well as the political circumstances forms the spirit of the people.[1]

In a sense therefore 'Das Leben Jesu' was outmoded almost as soon as it was written in that it seemed to presuppose that a folk religion could be seen as the total solution to the problem.

It is to the analysis of these political circumstances along with his further studies on the role of the Christian religion in the development of the contemporary European crisis that he now turns. As the title would indicate, 'Die Positivität der christlichen Religion' is concerned largely with analysing further the social dimensions of Christian practice in the modern world but, at the same time, a new dimension enters the work in that the explanation of this social dimension is not wholly pursued in religious terms. Political and economic considerations now, for the first time, begin to play a part in Hegel's thought. In the essay Hegel is concerned to answer the question of how it had come about that Jesus' teaching, which as 'Das Leben Jesu' makes clear, Hegel regards as moral and humanistic, had become so distorted in the contemporary world so that it was now authoritarian, transcendentally accredited and socially divisive.

In Hegel's view, the positive element in Christianity grew up as a result of a number of factors, some religious, some psychological and some of a political and economic nature. The teaching of Jesus, he argues, had to contain a contingent amount of positive material in order for him to have gained an audience with the Jews at all, consequently, the transcendental and dogmatic parts of his message could be explained away by reference to the religious situation which confronted him. These elements were not crucial to his message but rather pedagogic devices. The Jews possessed an authoritarian faith, based upon revelation, consequently, if Jesus was to be able effectively to challenge the Jewish understanding of God as the infinite lord of the universe, totally divorced from the world, demanding service from his creatures, then he had, in a sense, to match their standards of authority. Merely to present a moral message of love, harmony and reconciliation without any divine warrant, without invoking divine authority, would have

[1] Nohl, op. cit., p. 28.

45

been a pointless enterprise.[1] These elements were taken by his disciples and eventually the Christian churches to be fundamental to his message and the faith of Jesus became a dogmatic, transcendentally related creed. Both the performance of miracles[2] and the character of the initial disciples[3] were other factors making for the development of a positive religious faith. Hegel points out that the crucial question about miracles is not whether they were performed but rather what followed, so far as practice was concerned, from the fact that they were believed to have been performed. Because Jesus was regarded by his followers as being able to intervene in the course of nature his powers were accordingly transcendentally accredited. This accreditation, Hegel argues, came easily to the disciples who were Jews, reared in the traditions of a positive faith. Naturally they interpreted Jesus' claims and his powers at their face value and did not see them as devices to gain a hearing in an unsympathetic religious environment. 'Die Positivität der christlichen Religion' therefore goes further than 'Das Leben Jesu': it still presents the same account of the core of Jesus' message but insists that the humanistic and moral heart of that message was distorted by a mis-interpretation of aspects of Jesus' message which were used as a means of delivering the message rather than as central parts of it.

The religious dimension of the explanation does not however, exhaust the discussion of the roots of the contemporary crisis. His interest in the essay moves towards the relationship between Christianity and its original social and economic context, namely the declining Graeco-Roman world. He explains the development of institutionalized Christianity with its positive character in terms of a response to certain problems posed by that wider social environment. In his discussion of how Christianity, with all its divisiveness, had supplanted paganism, Hegel once more shows his enthusiasm for a folk religion:

> How could a religion have been supplanted in states for centuries and intimately connected with their constitutions? What can have caused the cessation of belief in gods to whom cities and empires ascribe their origin, to whom people make daily offering, whose blessings are invoked on every task undertaken, under whose aegis the armies had conquered, who had received thanks for victories, who received songs of joy and conscientious prayers. . . . How could the faith in Gods have been torn from the web of human life into which it had been woven by a thousand strands? How strong the opposite must have been to overcome the mental habit which was not

[1] Nohl, op. cit., pp. 159–60.   [2] Ibid., pp. 161–2.
[3] Ibid., pp. 162 ff.

isolated as our religion frequently is today but is interwoven in all directions with all of men's capacities.[1]

Such a form of religious experience was succeeded by what Hegel considers, in contrast, to be an isolated, private and positive religion, one which weans a man away from the settled and common life of his community. This fact seems to have so amazed Hegel that he gives an ingenious socio-political explanation. In the first place though he dismisses the conventional view of the enlightened *philosophe*, namely that such a change is intelligible in terms of the passage from darkness into light, that the sheer intellectual difficulty in believing in the Olympian panoply is sufficient to explain the decline in folk religion. Hegel argues that a religion so closely tied up with the life of a people could never have been defeated intellectually:

... religion, particularly imaginative religion cannot be torn from the whole life and heart of a people by cold syllogisms constructed in a study.[2]

Rather, Hegel argues, reference should be made less to explicit intellectual factors and more to the general social and political conditions of the time. This recognition had a twofold effect on Hegel's thought. He realized that schemes for reform in contemporary society based solely upon some intellectually-founded attempt to change contemporary religious experience would come to nothing without correlative changes in general social and political conditions. Secondly, a more methodological point, which had been implicit in some of his general statements in Tübingen but which becomes explicit in these pages on developments in Christianity, was that religion does not play a uniquely determining role in structuring social and political culture. Rather it has to be considered among a complex of other social factors. In Tübingen he argued:

The spirit of the people, its history, its religion, the degree of its political freedom cannot be considered by their separate characteristics. They are woven together in an indissoluble fashion.[3]

This assertion begins to be taken seriously in 'Die Positivität der christlichen Religion'.

The actual explanation which Hegel gives of the interaction between general social and political conditions, the decline in folk religion and the rise of Christianity, is complicated and far from flattering to the spirit of Christianity. Hegel argues that the military might of Rome had

[1] Nohl, op. cit., p. 220.   [2] Ibid., p. 221.   [3] Ibid., p. 27.

47

led to the development of an aristocratic elite, whose support was both military and financial. This might enabled this class to exert considerable domination over the rest of the community. The domination, which they could not achieve solely in terms of the respect which their fortunes and military might engendered, they secured through corruption. Eventually power was voluntarily given by the masses to the aristocrats and so their *de facto* exercise of power was thus recognized *de jure*. These developments however led to disastrous social and personal consequences. Men began to feel estranged from the state. Previously there had been:

> The freedom to obey self-given laws, to follow self-chosen leaders in peace time and self-chosen generals in war, to carry out plans in whose formulation one had had one's share.[1]

With the rise of an aristocratic oligarchy this conception of the state and the citizen's integration into it through his participation vanished. Previously the state had been a work of art[2] in which a man could see the reflection of his own personality:

> The picture of the state as the product of his own energies disappeared from the citizen's soul. The care and oversight of the whole rested upon one man or a few. . . . Each man's allotted part in the congeries which formed the whole was so inconsiderable in relation to the whole that the individual did not need to realize this relation, or keep it in view. . . . All activity and every purpose now had a bearing on something individual—activity was no longer for the sake of the whole or the ideal.[3]

This change in social and political culture had a very profound effect upon the religious sensibilities of the Romans. All sense of harmony with society had vanished, the public was split from the private.

The folk religion of the Greeks and the Romans could not adapt to this changed situation. Folk religion was predicated upon a feeling of close identification with and integration into the community. With the breakdown of this integration in the political sphere, folk religion had to decline. It could not adapt itself to the isolation of the individual, private person which the political changes had produced. Christianity fortuitously filled this gap:

> In this situation men were offered a religion which either was already adapted to the needs of the age, since it had arisen in a people

[1] Nohl, op. cit., p. 223.
[2] Hoffmeister, *Jenenser Realphilosophie*, op. cit., p. 251.
[3] Nohl, op. cit., p. 223. See also his strictures on the modern state in *Erstes System programm des Deutschen Idealismus*, in Dok ed. Hoffmeister, p. 220.

characterized by a similar degeneracy and a similar, though differently coloured emptiness and deficiency[1] or else was one out of which men could form what their needs demanded and what they could then adhere to.[2]

Christianity therefore arose out of the unhappy consciousness generated by the lack of political *community* in Rome. Because men were now estranged from their modes of social experience, they beat a retreat into the inner citadel. When men could no longer find fulfilment in participation in the social life of the community, in the public world, they projected their ideals either into a purely private world or into a world over and beyond the community, into the Kingdom of Heaven:

> Practical principles, the absolute and self subsistent reality, now showed themselves in the deity proffered by the Christian religion, a deity beyond the reach of our powers and will, but not of our supplications and prayers. Thus the realization of a moral ideal could no longer be willed, but only wished for[3] since what we wish for we cannot achieve of ourselves, but expect to acquire without our co-operation.[4]

The Christian religion was therefore for Hegel now not so much a cause of human estrangement but a *symptom* of it or a *projection* of it. The distinction between public and private was not produced by Christianity 'making men strangers to human feeling' rather it reinforced and encapsulated in a series of images the deep bifurcations produced in Roman social experience, bifurcations which were to grow as time went on.[5] Hitherto Hegel's aim had been to recreate a folk religion as the crucial factor making for the general rejuvenation of social and political culture but his study of the social and political changes of the Roman world seem to have convinced him that religion was certainly

[1] Of course Hegel means the Jews and he develops his unfavourable views on Jewish life in 'Der Geist des Christentums und sein Schicksal', Nohl, op. cit., pp. 242-342. See below pp. 56 ff.

[2] Nohl, op. cit., p. 224.

[3] I.e. the Greek or the Roman prior to this period found his moral ideals and aims in the intimations present in the moral practices of his community; with the loss of integration in the community went a loss of confidence that the social world could generate moral insights.

[4] Nohl, op. cit., p. 224.

[5] Cf. von Humbolt among the Germans perhaps drew attention to the private/public dichotomy in the modern world more insistently than any one else in the generation prior to Hegel. The public world was the world of *Pflicht* and *Notwendigkeit* totally dislocated from the private world of the individual. See *Briefe an eine Freundin, Werke*, op. cit., vol. 1, p. 60. Cf. also p. 388.

not the only and not the most crucial determinant of the social and political character of a people. A purely religious attempt to overcome the problem of personal and social fragmentation began therefore to look less and less plausible. Hegel echoed this sentiment in a comment in the essay relating to the work of Klopstock the poet. Klopstock had strongly disapproved of the tendency among German intellectuals to look to the example of Greece for solutions to their problems and he was moved to ask:

Is Achea then the Teuton's fatherland?

Hegel, in contrast to those whom Klopstock criticizes, had argued that the problems could be solved only by a change in the conventional interpretation of Christianity. However his study of Rome seems to have suggested to him that Christianity was too closely woven into the very description of these problems to be demythologized as a solution to them. He therefore echoes Klopstock when he says:

Is Judea then the Teuton's fatherland?[1]

Christianity appeared as a projection, a symbolization of a deep social and political malaise; as such it was inappropriate as a solution. Because of this wider appreciation of the problem during this period in his development, Hegel moved towards purely political analysis and it is interesting that during the period he was writing 'Die Positivität der christlichen Religion' he also wrote several pieces of secular political and social criticism. These were very much *pièces de circonstance* and do not add up to anything remotely resembling a political philosophy. But their problematic is much the same, the fragmentation of the community and the enervation of the human person within such an environment as he had hitherto described in religious terms.

Hegel's earliest recorded political views, as would befit the son of a minor bureaucratic official in the service of an autocrat, were entirely reactionary. At the age of fifteen he reacted to a mild manifestation of peasant unrest in the Duchy of Wurtemberg with some fervour:

Oh dear! bad news from Hohenheim. The peasants are at it again. They are an accursed lot. They have broken all the windows in the Duke's castle at Scharnhausen.[2]

However, by the time he had reached university in 1788, or perhaps immediately afterwards, under the influence of both his reading and of

[1] Nohl, op. cit., p. 217.
[2] Hoffmeister (ed.), *Dokumente zu Hegels Entwicklung*, op. cit., p. 9.

Hölderlin[1] and Schelling, Hegel apparently became a committed supporter of the French Revolution. The evidence for this is somewhat oblique: letters written a few years later, his friendship with Hölderlin and Schelling, both convinced of the righteousness of the French struggle, the respect in which he held the Revolution even after the 'conservative' reaction in his thought.[2] Leon, in his book *Fichte et son temps*, has described the political situation in the University of Tübingen thus:

> A bust to Liberty was placed upon a balcony between busts of Brutus and Demosthenes; the room resounded with patriotic speeches. Two young students, members of the club,[3] left to go to the outskirts of the town to plant a liberty tree: they were called Schelling and Hegel.[4]

The evidence for this is somewhat obscure, but given his radical religious views with their implied social and political dimension, his admiration for the Greeks and their social and political achievements, it is more than likely that he would be in full support of the French Revolution which was widely regarded at the time as an attempt to restore a closely-knit community on the Greek model. Indeed such an attitude to the Revolution is implicit in the first sentence of Leon's above: liberty was commemorated by placing a bust in between two classical defenders of freedom. Even in Tübingen, therefore, it seems likely that Hegel kept before his mind the need for social and political reform to complement his express belief in the necessity of a fundamental change in the religious practices of Germany and, indeed, Europe generally, in order to secure his ideal of a harmonious human being in an integrated political community.

Certainly there is no doubt about his political attitudes in Berne where he became positively concerned not merely to criticize society

---

[1] G. Lukacs argues with a good deal of plausibility in the essay on 'Hyperion' in *Goethe und seine Zeit*, op. cit., that Hölderlin was in sympathy with the Jacobins.

[2] To the end of his life Hegel celebrated the fall of the Bastille; J. Ritter, *Hegel und die französische Revolution*, Cologne 1957, p. 18.

[3] Leon reports that 'They constituted a political club in which parliamentary debates were held.'

[4] *Fichte et son temps*, vol. 1, p. 173, Paris 1922. Cf. Dilthey:

It was during those years 1788–93 which Hegel spent in Tübingen that there occurred the two world historical events which brought the age of Enlightenment to an end and opened up the gates of the new era: Kant completed the recasting of his thought and the Revolution in France destroyed the old state and undertook the establishment of a new order. . . . Hegel himself was considered to be one of the most zealous spokesmen for freedom and equality. *Die Jugendgeschichte Hegels*, Berlin 1905, pp. 13–14.

from a religious standpoint but to go on to concrete political analysis. In his occasional writings on politics Hegel reveals that he has a sharp eye for social problems and is continually groping his way towards solutions of a revolutionary sort. For example, in a letter to Schelling on 16 April 1795, Hegel very severely criticizes the social and political structure of Berne and advocates drastic reforms. It seems that Hegel's strictures upon the nature of oligarchical and aristocratic government in Rome and the implication of Christianity in that situation may have their roots in his experiences in Berne during this period. It is clear that Hegel is impatient for reform and he stresses the role which new political ideas will have:

> Because of the propagation of these ideas which show how things ought to be, the indolence of those who confer eternity on everything that is will be swept away.[1]

Philosophy, he argues, will demonstrate the rights of man and the political order will not be able to withstand the onslaught of new ideas. He states quite categorically:

> I await a revolution in Germany.[2]

A similar attitude is to be found in the fact of his translation of the *Letters* of Cart, a Girondin exile, concerning the state of the people of the Vaud.[3] Hegel's revolutionary attitudes manifest themselves in several different ways in and through this translation. In the first place, the very fact that Hegel saw fit to translate these letters, originally published in Paris and extremely critical of the corrupt nature of German rule in the Vaud, suggests that Hegel had some interest in seeing the situation reformed, otherwise the letters might well have languished in untranslated obscurity. Secondly, as Rosenzweig has shown,[4] Hegel does not merely translate, but adapts Cart's letters and was thus concerned to translate them not for merely academic interest, but to use them for his own purposes. Again this purpose seems to be that of embarrassing an aristocratic and oligarchic government, accusing it of suppression and injustice. In the Preface Hegel points out that, between the completion of the translation and the publication of the

[1] *Briefe*, ed. Hoffmeister, op. cit., p. 24. [2] Ibid., p. 23.
[3] *Vertrauliche Briefe über das vormalige staatsrechtliche Verhältnis des Waadtlandes zur Stadt Bern: Aus dem Französischen eines verstorbenen Schweizers.* I have relied throughout on Rosenzweig, *Hegel und der Staat*, Berlin 1902, vol. 1, for information about these letters. The Preface, however, is published in Hoffmeister (ed.), *Dokumente zu Hegels Entwicklung*, pp. 247–8.
[4] Rosenzweig, loc. cit., p. 51.

letters, French troops had liberated the region, a development from which he is concerned to draw a general conclusion:

> But the events speak loudly enough, all that remains to be done is to learn from them in their entirety.
> They cry aloud over the earth
> 'Discite justitiam moniti'
> and the deaf will be hard smitten by their fate.[1]

It seems that Hegel's ideal of a truly human community begins to take shape in these occasional writings when they are considered in relation to his specifically religious works. He is committed to a view of social and political life which is radically democratic, praising a constitution which allows men to:

> . . . obey self-given laws, to follow self-chosen leaders in peace time and self-chosen generals in war, to carry out plans in whose formulation one had had one's share.[2]

Such a constitution would overcome the deep bifurcation between the public and private, between private interest and the realm of right. In addition, such a community to be a truly adequate environment for human beings, would have to be bound together by shared religious practices, activities which would not postulate the supreme ends of human life as beyond society in the private worship of a transcendent god, and which would be such as could engage all the powers of the human mind. In this way his 'Das Leben Jesu' links up very closely with his sustained attack during this period on oligarchic and elitist government. In a circuitous fashion this aim remains throughout Hegel's intellectual life. Even in his very latest work he was concerned to show that the constitutional arrangements of the modern state were such as to allow the type and the amount of participation necessary for modern men, given their emphasis on private self-seeking in the economic sphere. At the same time he took very great pains to demonstrate that the Christian religion and the Christian God once correctly, i.e. philosophically, understood were not inimical to the harmony of society. Finally, he saw it as the role of philosophy to provide man with an interconnected view of his experience so that his personal fragmentation was overcome. A full understanding of Hegel's early work is therefore, on this reading, a key to the identity of his later philosophy.

Hegel's attack on inhuman political and social conditions is carried further in his essay 'Über die neuesten innern Verhältnisse Württem-

[1] Hoffmeister (ed.), *Dokumente zu Hegels Entwicklung*, op. cit., p. 248.
[2] Nohl, op. cit., p. 223.

HEGEL

bergs besonders über die Gebrechen der Magistratsverfassung',[1] an
essay which interestingly enough was originally given the title, 'Town
Councillors ought to be elected by the People'. The essay was again
occasioned by an exercise in despotic power on the part of Duke
Frederick of Wurtemberg. The Duke held absolute power except in so
far as the treasury of the province was in the hands of the *Permanent
Committee* of the *Provincial Diet* which at this particular time was pro-
French in attitude. The Duke, adopting a foreign policy at variance
with the views of this committee, called the Estates of the province
together as the Diet. Eventually the Diet was dissolved, again as a result
of the personal exercise of power on the part of the Duke. Hegel's
essay was written at the beginning of this process during which time,
consistent with his whole attitude outlined above, he saw great possibilities for democratization in the calling together of the Estates.
Unfortunately most of the detail of the essay is missing. That which
remains is rather an abstract but highly committed radical tract—but
for the purpose of fixing more accurately at this time over the exact
nature of an adequate political constitution the detail of the essay
would have been invaluable. There is, however, a summary of the
work in Haym *Hegel und seine Zeit*[2] and this will be utilized to specify
Hegel's attitude at this important stage of his development. Haym
points out that Hegel unequivocally condemns the attitude of the Duke
in summoning the Estates as the Diet for the first time in a generation
and only then with the aim of using them for his own purposes. At the
same time he condemns the bureaucratic rigidity of the Permanent
Committee of the Diet. The conflict between the Duke and this committee is, in Hegel's view, a conflict between two oligarchic forces,
remote from the people. The Estates, however, are more closely related
to the people, but at the same time are not elected by popular vote. The
implication of this would seem to be that Hegel would advocate popular
election to the Estates with the Estates exercising some degree of
control over the Duke. This, however, is not the case. Hegel argues
that there would be considerable danger in suddenly granting the vote
to people who, having lived under a despotism, have become apathetic
and malleable. This point is of considerable importance. Up to this
time he had argued the need for a direct political democracy woven
together by some kind of demythologized Christianity; now he begins
to see the difficulties involved in direct democracy in the modern
world, perhaps as a result of developments in France. There is evidence

[1] Only part of the essay is extant and is published in Lasson (ed.), *Schriften
zur Politik und Rechtsphilosophie*, second ed., Leipzig 1923, pp. 150-3.
[2] Berlin 1867, p. 67.

54

that at this time Hegel was becoming disillusioned with the French Revolution.[1] It may have been the French experience during the terror which led him away from his support for a direct participating democracy and to search for a more appropriate means of political representation in the modern world. He confesses in the essay that he has not found out a way in which the demand for representation, which, as we have seen, is closely linked in Hegel's mind with the ideal of the whole man in an harmonious political community, could be linked with a recognition of the very considerable problems, perhaps shown by the French experience, in giving any kind of cash value to such an idea in the modern world. This search for a contemporary image of political community, together with a non-bifurcating interpretation of Christianity began to dominate the whole of his thought.

[1] See below, pp. 72 ff.

Chapter III

Towards a Perspective on History

That at that time ye were without Christ, being aliens from the commonwealth of Israel, and strangers from the covenant of promise, having no hope and without God in the world. But now in Christ Jesus ye who sometimes were far off are made nigh by the blood of Christ. . . . Now therefore ye are no more strangers and foreigners but fellow citizens with the saints in the household of God.

St Paul

Hegel completed 'Die Positivität der christlichen Religion' in the summer of 1796 and, after a few months with his family in Stuttgart, he moved to Frankfurt as tutor to the Gogel family, resuming his friendship with Hölderlin[1] which had been interrupted after their departure from the Tübingen faculty. His work during this period is vital for understanding the remarkable change which his thought underwent during the final years of the century—the change from socio-religious reformism with an emphasis upon the desirability of the foundation of a political community of free, self-directing, active, participating individuals held together by common values predicated upon a non-transcendental interpretation of Christianity, to a philosophically-based understanding of the contemporary world. Early in 1797, Hegel began preliminary studies for his essay 'Der Geist des Christentums und sein Schicksal' in which he once again returns to an attempt to understand the religious dimension of the social malaise affecting the German and, indeed, the wider European world. In this essay he is apparently most concerned with the relationship between Christianity and Judaism, and the latter's role in shaping the meaning of the Christian message. However, it is arguable that there is far more

---

[1] Hölderlin, in fact, arranged the post for him. He had been very unhappy in Berne; see *Briefe*, op. cit., p. 41.

to the essay than this.[1] According to Rosenkranz,[2] Hegel's first bio-grapher, during 1799 Hegel wrote extensive notes on *An Inquiry into the Principles of Political Economy*[3] by Sir James Steuart, a somewhat maverick figure of the Scottish enlightenment. This work was translated into German in two editions, one by J. von Pauli, the other by Christoph Schott, between 1769 and 1772. According to Rosenkranz, after reading the work Hegel put forward 'many magisterial views on both politics and history', which unfortunately are no longer extant. 'Unfortunately' is the operative word in this context for it is possible that these views and, indeed, the notes which Hegel made on Steuart's work represent an essential link in Hegel's development and may be crucial to making intelligible the transition mentioned above—from socio-religious reform to philosophical comprehension. It is, however, possible to discern in a fragmented way the influence of Steuart in 'Der Geist des Christentums und sein Schicksal' in so far as this essay shows something which has hitherto been lacking in Hegel's thought, namely the notion of a rationally discernible *development* in history, a develop-ment which, once comprehended, would change the attitude of people towards their social environment. In particular this perspective on history could and did lead in Hegel's own case to a revaluation of the role of Christianity in world history. Consequently the essay may perhaps be read in two dimensions, neither of which is exclusive of the other. It may be read as an essay in the genre of many of Hegel's early works, that of social theology as an attempt to discern the relationship between the Jewish religious context and Christian doctrine and hence its social dimension; or it may be read as an essay on the social and economic history of the Jews, a history which is in turn predicated

[1] My interpretation here is very heavily indebted to Professor P. Chamley's work, particularly *Economie politique chez Steuart et Hegel*, Paris 1963; *Documents relatifs à Sir James Steuart*, Paris 1965; 'La Doctrine économique du Hegel et la conception Hegelienne du travail', *Hegel Studien*, 1965; 'Les origines de la pensée économique de Hegel', *Hegel Studien* 1967, and 'Notes de lecture relatives à Smith, Steuart et Hegel', *Revue d'économie politique*, Paris 1967. I am much indebted to Professor Chamley for providing me with copies of these works. My conclusions, based largely on Chamley's evidence, are somewhat different from his.

[2] Rosenkranz, op. cit., p. 86.

[3] *An Inquiry into the Principles of Political Economy, Being an Essay on the Science of the Domestic Policy in Free Nations in which are particularly considered Population, Agriculture, Trade, Industry, Money, Coin, Interest, Circulation, Banks, Exchange, Public Credit and Taxes*, first published in 1767 in London; republished in 1805 in *The Works Political, Metaphysical and Chronological of Sir James Steuart Bart.*, ed. General Sir James Steuart, London, vol. 1. A new edition has recently been published by A. Skinner, London 1966. All quotations are from the 1966 edition.

upon at least a tentative philosophy of history, on the pattern of historical development. This interpretation of the role of the essay in Hegel's thought is somewhat unfashionable. Walter Kaufmann, for example, in his widely influential book on Hegel, gives it rather a damning dismissal:

> ... the essay has little originality or importance. While Schelling, as Hegel was to put it later, carried on his education in public, issuing book after book, sometimes several in one year, Hegel filed his latest attempt in a desk drawer, where it belonged.[1]

It is lucky that Hegel did file it away and did not dispose of it altogether because it may be the crucial text in attempting to make intelligible the profound change which his thought underwent in 1800.

The religious reading of the essay would see it as fitting into the pattern of development so far discerned in Hegel's thought. In the essay Hegel is concerned with exploring the historical background of the situation which confronted Jesus, who brought a message of reconciliation, love and harmony to the deeply divided life of the Jews; in so far as the background against which Jesus taught influenced the reception, interpretation and subsequent transmission of his message and given Hegel's view about the importance of understanding the role of institutionalized Christianity in understanding the bifurcations of contemporary social life, it may be considered as yet a further attempt to discern the religious roots of the modern European crisis.

The essay is very much preoccupied with the Jewish background of the Christian message and could equally as well have been called 'Der Geist des Judentums und sein Schicksal'. Hegel sees in the figure and history of Abraham a paradigm of the divisiveness of the Jewish character, the source of its conception of the infinite otherness of God, and the Jews' exclusiveness as a race. Hegel's description of Abraham and his role in the formation of Jewish religious conceptions has a certain sardonic brilliance and, because of its importance to both the religious reading of the essay and also to the socio-economic reading, it will be quoted and discussed at some length.

First of all Hegel stresses that Abraham's very first adult action, one which was to have very profound symbolic importance to the Jewish race and their conception of themselves, was one which involved the brutal snapping of communal ties and an assertion of his rights and privileges as a private person:

Abraham, born in Chaldea, had in youth already left the fatherland

---

[1] Kaufmann, op. cit., p. 64.

in his father's company, now in the plains of Mesopotamia tore himself free from his family in order to be a self subsistent independent man, an overlord unto himself. . . . The first act which made. Abraham the progenitor of a nation is a disseverance which snaps the bonds of communal life and love.[1]

Hegel then goes on to stress the extent to which this independence and rejection of communal ties guided his relationships with other races during the rest of his life:

The same spirit which led Abraham away from his kin led him through his encounters with foreign people during the rest of his life: this was the spirit of self maintenance in strict opposition to everything.[2]

This type of attitude also had its metaphysical dimension, according to Hegel. Not only did Abraham feel estranged from his fellow men but also from the natural world; a world which Abraham regarded as infinite and hostile, according to Hegel:

. . . with his herds Abraham wandered hither and thither over a boundless territory without bringing parts of it any nearer to him by cultivating and improving them. . . . He was a stranger on earth, a stranger to soil and men alike.[3]

Circumcision was also interpreted by Hegel to be a mark setting off one man from another, one community from another:

He steadily persisted in cutting himself off from others and made this conspicuous by a physical peculiarity imposed upon himself and his posterity.[4]

Abraham's conception of God was also involved in deep bifurcation. His God was not, like the deities of Greece, involved in the world and in the human community but, rather, infinitely far off, demanding blind obedience and abject worship:

The whole world Abraham regarded as his opposite; if he did not take it to be a nullity he looked upon it as sustained by a God who

[1] Nohl, op. cit., p. 245. Cf. Genesis, xii. 6:

Now the Lord had said unto Abraham, Get thee out of thy country and from thy kindred and from thy father's house . . .

[2] Ibid., p. 245.   [3] Ibid., p. 246. Cf. Genesis, xii. 8–9.

[4] Ibid., p. 246. Cf. Genesis, xvii. 14:

And the uncircumcized man child whose flesh of his foreskin is not circumcized, that soul shall be cut off from his people.

was alien to it. Nothing in nature was supposed to have any part in God; everything was simply under God's mastery.[1]

This terrible God demanded the kind of obedience which could have involved the sacrifice of Abraham's own son.

Abraham, the founder of the Jewish people and chief moulder of their religious tradition, exhibited, therefore, a profound divisiveness throughout his life, from his home, from his native land, from his people, from nature, and he lived his life in bondage to an alien and jealous God. His religious and social life is implicitly contrasted throughout with the tolerance, happiness and harmonious relationship with both the social, natural and divine world of the Greeks. One might here recall the relationship which Hegel considered the Greeks had to the world in the Tübingen fragments and Schiller's views in 'Die Götter Griechenlands'. Hegel argued earlier that the Greek found himself bound by *der Bedürfnisse an die Muttererde*,[2] whereas for Abraham the world was both hostile and alien. Instead of the Gods being part of the community, the Jewish God was infinitely other and, if anything, hostile to communal ties.[3]

Understood in these terms, the social experience of the Jews bore a considerable resemblance to the situation which Hegel had been concerned to describe in Germany. Alienation from God who transcends the community, estrangement from other men and from nature were not only central features of Jewish religious life but also elements in the cultural situation which confronted him in Germany. This point is not merely conjectural. In the essay 'Die Verfassung Deutschlands' which Hegel began to write in 1799[4] he points to this very comparison. Although the Germans were not in quite such a desperate situation as the Jews, they were still a people involved in a very deep social tragedy:

Once a man's social instincts are distorted and he is forced to throw himself into interests peculiarly his own, his nature becomes so deeply perverted that it now spends its strength on variance from others, and in the course of maintaining its separation it sinks into madness, for madness is simply the separation of the individual from his kind. The German people may be incapable of intensifying its obstinate adherence to particularism to that point of madness reached by the Jewish people—a people incapable of uniting in a common social life with any other. The German people may not be able to carry separation to such a pitch of frenzy . . .[5]

[1] Nohl, op. cit., p. 246.   [2] Ibid., p. 28.
[3] See above, Genesis xii. 1.   [4] See G. Schüler, op. cit., p. 133.
[5] Lasson (ed.), *Schriften zur Politik und Rechtsphilosophie*, op. cit., p. 136.

In this sort of situation in which Hegel saw an analogy between the German situation and the Jewish it is obvious that Jesus, who came, as Hegel has continuously argued in 'Das Leben Jesu' and in 'Die Positivität der christlichen Religion', as the bearer of reconciliation and community, must have exercised a special fascination over Hegel's mind. Hegel must in a small way have seen his own role in a similar light. Hegel's understanding of the way in which Jesus approached the diremptions of Jewish life and the correct understanding of his message are therefore important for comprehending Hegel's own attitude to the contemporary situation. So too his reflections on what he regarded as the failure of Jesus fundamentally to reform the experience of the Jews may be important in understanding his own change of attitude.

It is not necessary to discuss in detail Hegel's characterization of the teaching of Jesus in order to establish the importance of the essay. Rather, specific attention will be paid to one aspect of Jesus' message, namely his teaching on man's relationship to God. This was, in Hegel's view, the crucial diremption in Jewish life which exercised a baneful, ineradicable influence on the whole social and personal experience of the Jews.[1] The crucial element in the Jewish conception of the relationship between man and God was that it was thought of on the analogy of the master/slave relationship. Jesus sought to substitute for this image of the relationship one based upon love, of God as father and not as the remote, infinite lord of the Universe.

Hegel pays particular attention to the puzzling claim of Jesus that he was both the son of God and the son of man. He argues that the phrase 'son of God' describes not a mere conceptual, abstract unity between Jesus and his father:

... on the contrary, it is a living relation of living beings, a likeness of life. Father and son are simply modifications of the same life.[2]

Since Jesus as son of God stands as a modification of the life of God and, *mutatis mutandis*, as son of man, a modification of the life of man, it follows that both God and men stand in a very close bond which is given a living embodiment in the life of Jesus.

This recognition of the divine *within* life, within the social world, obviously links up crucially with Hegel's preoccupation with the fragmentation of the community. He points out the inadequacy of the Jewish conception of God which led to their baneful diremptive experiences of diremption. Their divinity was outside of them, unseen unfelt;[3] whereas the life of Jesus makes articulate in a particular case

---

[1] Nohl, op. cit., p. 302.   Ibid., pp. 309–10.   [3] Ibid., p. 252.

that visible, tangible relationship to God which must exist if a harmonious community of believers is ever to be established:

> If the divine is to appear, the invisible spirit must be united with something visible so that the whole may be unified . . . so that there may be a complete synthesis, a perfected harmony. Otherwise there remains in relation to the whole of man's divisible nature a thirst too slight for the infinity of the world, too great for its objectivity, and it cannot be satisfied. There remains the quenchless unsatisfied thirst after God.[1]

Hegel's earlier religious views come out very clearly in this passage. Only if the infinite is brought down to and united with the finite can man live at home in the world and in community with his fellow men. If God remains transcending the community this is a recipe for the development of the unhappy consciousness, division from the world, from men, and the isolation of the religious dimension of the personality from the other powers of the human mind which can find fulfilment *within* society and its established ways. Jesus is therefore a paradigm of the correct relationship between infinite and finite life.

At the same time, in context he was a failure. Jesus made articulate in both his teaching and his life a conception of God which was unintelligible to the Jews and hence was cut off from the mainspring of their social experiences:

> How were they to recognize divinity in a man, poor things as they were, possessing only a consciousness of the depths of their servitude, of their opposition to the divine, of an impassable gulf between the being of God and the being of men. . . . The Jewish multitude was bound to destroy this attempt to give them consciousness of something divine, something great cannot make its home in a dung hill.[2]

The mission of Jesus therefore was on the horns of a dilemma, a fact which in Hegel's view accounted for its failure. On the one hand Jesus came to bring reconciliation between man and God into Jewish life, to restore community and human relations by attempting to enable them to see God as part of their normal human life; at the same time his message was so revolutionary that it was totally divorced from the social, religious and cultural experience of the Jews and, as such, it was, paradoxically, a further bifurcating force. Either he could ally himself with conventional Jewish experience and attempt to reform it from the inside or, alternatively, Jesus could remain outside the circle of their

[1] Nohl, op. cit., p. 333.   [2] Ibid., p. 312.

beliefs and confront it with a challenge. In the first place his message, Hegel argues, would be ineffectual because the stifling religious life of the Jews would have undermined it; in the second place it would be pointless because unintelligible to those towards whom the challenge was directed.[1]

In fact, Hegel argues, the second alternative was followed:

> Thus the earthly life of Jesus was separation from reality and flight into heaven: restoration in an ideal world of the life which has been dissipated in the void.[2]

Jesus' mission was, therefore, a failure. Although himself a paradigm of the reconciliation between man and God so crucial to the achievement of community, his message of reconciliation stood apart, dislocated from the on-going life of the Jews. Jesus became a beautiful soul with a pure message set against the entire fate of the Jewish people. This failure had profound consequences for the subsequent course of history in Hegel's view. Because of the inability of Jesus to secure a proper understanding of himself and his relationship to God, this relationship was misrepresented by those who have claimed to follow him so that the Christian community has always found itself predicated upon an essentially Jewish understanding of God, remote from the world. Unlike the ancient Greek who found his gods and his morality within his community it is the fate of Christianity:

> . . . that church and state, worship and life, piety and virtue, spiritual and worldly action cannot dissolve into one.[3]

A passage which sums up the whole circuitous route of the religious dimension of Hegel's early thought, the bifurcation in the community caused by the separation of finite and infinite. The example of Jesus seemed to imply that some kind of detached religious reformism, isolated from the religious traditions of the society could not work, a realization which must have had a profound effect upon Hegel, given the pattern of his preoccupations so far. During this period he comes to reject such proposals for reform and he eventually sees it as the task of philosophy to provide an interpretation of Christian experience which, though tied to conventional ways of understanding such experience, would in the end so transform it that its transcendental, infinite dimension would come within human comprehension and thus be eliminated as causes of communal fragmentation. Similarly it became the task of philosophy to provide an understanding of religious experience thus transformed which would fit it into an overall view of

[1] Nohl, op. cit., pp. 328–9.   [2] Ibid., p. 329.   [3] Ibid., p. 342.

modes of experience and their relation to human development, thus eliminating the fragmentation of the personality to which the transcendental elements in Christianity have given rise. The task of philosophy becomes that of the:

... self elevation of man, not from the finite to the infinite ... but from finite life to infinite life.[1]

Philosophy, therefore, as Hegel comes to conceive it, makes articulate the ideal of harmonious religious life as the basis of community which, 'Der Geist des Christentums und sein Schicksal' had convinced him, could not be achieved by the brand of religious reformism which he had hitherto advocated.

While the figure of Jesus is quite pivotal for understanding the change of attitude which Hegel underwent soon after the completion of 'Der Geist des Christentums und sein Schicksal', it would be wrong to interpret the change solely in these terms. Hegel's reading of Sir James Steuart's *Inquiry Concerning the Principles of Political Economy* also had an effect upon his attitude both to the ideals which he formerly held and to contemporary social reality. However, before discussing in detail the influence of Steuart on his work, a seeming paradox must first be resolved. All that is known with relative certainty is that Hegel was concerned with Steuart's work from 19 February 1799 to 16 May in the same year and the product of this work was a no longer extant commentary on Steuart's work.[2] 'Der Geist des Christentums und sein Schicksal', which, arguably, presupposes a Steuart view of historical development, was composed *before* this date. The only answer which can be offered to this apparent inconsistency is that, although Hegel produced his commentary on Steuart during this period, it does not entail that this was his first acquaintance with the work. Of course, it may have been but the sheer weight of the evidence cited from 'Der Geist des Christentums und sein Schicksal' does seem to imply that it was not. Indeed it is probable that Hegel would not have been moved to produce an extensive commentary on Steuart's work had he not already been acquainted with it and pondered deeply on its implications for his views. However, the main answer to the apparent paradox is to be found in the evidence to be gained by comparing the central theses of Steuart's work with the view of historical development presupposed in Hegel's discussion of Jewish social and economic history in 'Der Geist des Christentums und sein Schicksal'.

The major general influence of Steuart's work was that it gave Hegel the notion of *historical evolution* or *development*. This assertion requires

[1] Nohl, op. cit., p. 347.   [2] Rosenkranz, op. cit., p. 86.

some explanation given the almost total preoccupation on the part of Hegel with the historical background of the contemporary malaise in social and political experience. In the writings prior to 'Der Geist des Christentums und sein Schicksal' Hegel had not operated with any notion of progressive evolution in history. On the contrary, if his writings up to this point presuppose any general, overall view of history it seems to be that of *regression*, that the course of history from the decline of the Roman Republic may be seen as a process of degeneration, particularly so far as social and religious forms of life are concerned. The happy, socially-cohesive folk religion had been replaced by a misinterpreted Christianity which had both helped to destroy the community and symbolize the plight of man in such a situation of loss; the active, participating, republican political communities of Rome and Greece had been replaced in the modern world by inefficient monarchical institutions with a corresponding enervation of the public responsibilities of citizens. After reading Steuart's works Hegel began to revise this picture. The modern world was no longer seen in such a jaundiced light but was regarded by Hegel as embodying certain values and principles and actualizing certain human powers and capacities which could not find realization in the Ancient world. The present began to be looked upon as part of man's *fate*: there could be no sense in trying to go back to more ancient types of social, political and religious organization—these were predicated upon quite different circumstances. What was required was some comprehensive grasp of the values, principles and human powers actualized in the modern world, how these were worked out in the modes of experience to hand in society and how they were related to other, earlier, different and less developed societies. The modern world was no longer to be condemned as irrational because it failed to correspond to a paradigm taken from the ancient world; rather, the rationality which the contemporary world had needed to be grasped. Only then could men find a home in it and be satisfied with the forms of community which it offered.

In his major work Steuart expounds an evolutionary theory of society and in particular of its economic structure which he takes in some sense as basic. He explicitly states it to be part of his task to trace:

. . . the regular progress of mankind from perfect simplicity to complicated refinement.[1]

The word 'regular' in this context seems to imply that Steuart saw the course of history not as a mere 'tissue of contingencies', but as having some rationally discernible form. The key to the understanding of this

[1] Skinner (ed.), op. cit., vol. 1, p. 28.

'regular development' was, in his view, the economic structure of society, the development of which was in turn explicable rationally in terms of certain postulates about human nature. These postulates are two in number: that man is dominated by sexual desire, the consequence of which is to push up the population to the available supply of food;[1] the second postulate was that men are also motivated by self-interest or self-love.[2] Using these assumptions he is able to explain the particular form of a given society and why each society is forced eventually to change its economic organization and with it its general culture and the conception of human nature presupposed in it. In Steuart's view there were three basic types of society, each a progression on the other; pre-agrarian pastoral societies, agrarian society, and the exchange economy of commercial society. These types and their interconnections will now be briefly discussed.

In a pastoral, pre-agrarian society, Steuart argued, men do not labour, rather they live on the spontaneous fruits of the earth, in which 'mankind may live in idleness'.[3] Such a form of life can never yield a standard of living much over a subsistence level and, because the ground is not cultivated in order to secure survival, men have to live a nomadic type of existence in such a society. Thus, urbanization comes much later. In this context, Steuart mentions the Tartars and Indians[4] as examples of surviving races at this primordial level of human personal and social experience. The political consequence of such a mode of economic life, if the word 'political' is not too strained in the circumstances is that each man conceives of himself as a free and independent being, 'remaining free from every constraint'.[5] He comments:

If we suppose all men idle and living upon the spontaneous fruits of the earth the plan for universal liberty becomes quite natural: because under such circumstances they can find no inducement to come under voluntary subordination.[6]

Steuart argued, however, that men could not long remain at this level of material existence and he explains the transition to a labouring agrarian society in terms of the twin motivating forces of sexual desire and self-love. The sexual drive leads to reproduction: self-love drives a man to provide the means of subsistence to his children. These two demands are incompatible with the maintenance of the pre-agrarian economy. The means of providing subsistence to children born in such a society, he argued, would be strictly limited by the amount of food

[1] Skinner, op. cit., p. 31.   [2] Ibid., p. 34.
[3] Ibid., p. 56.   [4] Ibid., p. 56.   [5] Ibid., p. 56.   [6] Ibid., p. 35.

available for spontaneous consumption.[1] As a consequence, he argued, those who had the physical power would be inclined to appropriate part of the land to themselves in order to work it to make it produce more.[2] The agrarian economy within which men labour with their hands on the earth to increase its productivity generates a decisive differentiation in social structure between those who have the physical power to labour and appropriate land and those who do not. These latter become servants and eventually slaves of the former.[3]

Again the influence of self-love explains a further complication of the human condition, the development of the exchange economy characteristic of modern commercial society. Labouring on the soil increases productivity beyond the level necessary for a subsistence level of consumption; the excess so produced is then used to barter for other commodities not produced by the labour of the individual concerned. The labouring process eventually generates its own momentum—men work harder to produce more and more surplus to barter or to sell for other goods which they do not themselves produce and in a sense, Steuart argues, men become slaves to their own wants.[4] These developments naturally lead over a long period of time to the development of trade and industry. One major social consequence of the development of commercial relations is that slavery becomes an outmoded form of working relationship. Slavery, Steuart argues, is incompatible with the free competition necessary for the full development of industry because the work of the slave is cheaper than that of the free man.[5] In place of the master/slave relationships characteristic of less developed societies men in an exchange economy come together into very intricate patterns of mutual interdependence. Such a society presupposes a system of needs and the means of their satisfaction, a society which:

... is a general, tacit contract from which reciprocal and proportional services result universally from those who compose it.[6]

The basic effect of the development of a commercial economy is the increasing urbanization of the community:

From the establishment of manufactures we see hamlets swell into villages and towns. . . . Sea ports owe their establishment to foreign trade. From one or other of these and similar principles are mankind gathered into hamlets, villages, towns and cities.[7]

The progressive development in the modern world is, therefore,

---

[1] Skinner, op. cit., p. 36.   [2] Ibid., p. 34.   [3] Ibid., pp. 34–5.
[4] Ibid., p. 51.   [5] Ibid., pp. 146–7.   [6] Ibid., p. 88.
[7] Ibid., p. 59.

according to Steuart, a drift from the land and the agrarian economy to urbanization and industrial society. It is at this point in the argument that Steuart makes a novel contribution and one which, as will be seen, affected Hegel profoundly. He argued that economic development requires the guidance of a *statesman*, the generic title for whatever person or body of persons is responsible for the formulation of public policy.[1] Within the exchange economy mere guidance is not sufficient, a measure of public control over economic life is required. Steuart argued that the social and personal consequences of the development of the exchange economy—increases and decreases in prices as a result of the operation of the market, the introduction of new techniques rendering old processes and operatives involved in them otiose—all required some degree of public control in order to mitigate socially harmful effects:

> It is hardly possible suddenly to introduce the smallest innovation into the political economy of the state, let it be ever so reasonable, nay ever so profitable without making some inconveniences. A room cannot be swept without making a dust, one cannot walk abroad without dirtying one's shoes neither can a machine which abridges the labour of men be introduced all at once into an extensive manufacture without throwing very many people into idleness. In treating every question of political economy I constantly suppose a statesman at the head of the government systematically conducting every part of it so as to prevent the vicissitudes of manners and innovations by their natural and immediate effects from hurting any interest in the commonwealth.[2]

This thesis had an enormous influence upon Hegel. He had been concerned in his development, as had many others in his generation, by the social and personal divisions of the modern world and here Steuart postulated a way of mitigating these problems. After reading Steuart's work Rosenkranz reports that Hegel was concerned to save 'the inner life of man within the (commercial) system'. Steuart had given at least some hints about how this might be done, hints which Hegel was soon to develop extensively.

However the task of this part of the chapter is not so much to trace the influence which Steuart's doctrine of the statesman had on Hegel[3] but rather to assess the extent to which Hegel at this time came under the influence of his general typology of human development. In much

[1] Skinner, op. cit., p. 16. [2] Ibid., p. 122.
[3] The influence of this thesis upon Hegel is discussed below, pp. 114 ff.

of 'Der Geist des Christentums und sein Schicksal' some of Steuart's typology is presupposed. The very first act which Abraham performed and which led eventually to the foundation of the Jewish race and fate was a *reversal* of the progressive change which Steuart had discerned in history. The way to progress for Steuart was from pastoral, unurbanized society, through agrarian society, to modern highly urbanized commercial societies. Abraham, in a sense, reversed this trend. He *left* an urban environment, however primitive, in Ur of the Chaldees and *reverted* to a nomadic, pastoral type of existence. Hegel describes this retrogressive process in a way reminiscent of Steuart. The latter had emphasized in the *Inquiry* that in pastoral contexts men are free and independent; only in agrarian and commercial societies do they come to be in patterns of dependence and interdependence. Hegel describes Abraham's departure from Ur in similar terms:

> Now in the plains of Mesopotamia, he tore himself away from his family as well in order to be a self-subsistent, independent man, to be an overlord himself.[1]

Steuart had very clearly brought out the connection which in his view existed between the lack of a settled existence, the lack of roots in the land, and liberty conceived in terms of self sufficiency:

> Where therefore the surface of the earth is not appropriated there the place producing the food determines the place of residence of everyone in society and there mankind may live in idleness free from every constraint.[2]

Similarly Hegel very clearly points to the connection: in discussing Abraham's freedom and independence, he refers to the social conditions which made this possible:

> With his herds Abraham wandered hither and thither over a boundless territory without bringing parts of it any nearer to him by cultivating and improving them . . .[3]

To maintain this independence Hegel argues that Abraham went to very great pains to avoid any kind of trading relationship with other tribes and peoples in the areas which he traversed:

> The country was so populated beforehand that in his travels he continually stumbled on men previously united in small tribes. He entered no such ties. He certainly required their corn but nonetheless

[1] Nohl, op. cit., p. 245.   [2] Skinner, op. cit., p. 56.
[3] Nohl, op. cit., p. 245.

he struggled against his fate, the fate which would have offered him a stationary communal life with others.[1]

This passage is of great importance in that Hegel calls Steuart's 'regular progress' 'fate', the implication being that the development of urban and eventually commercial society has to be considered as being in some sense necessary. He makes this point again later in the essay:

To the fate against which Abraham and hitherto Jacob also had struggled, i.e. the possession of an abiding dwelling place and attachment to a nation, Jacob finally succumbed.[2]

The divisiveness of the Jews, their exclusiveness and the profound diremptions of their religious experience could perhaps all be interpreted as attempts to fight against a fate to which they had eventually to succumb. Divisiveness Hegel considered to be a form of madness and, since in this essay he conceives divisiveness and alienation to be closely connected with an inability to live in terms of fate, the connection between this struggle and madness may be made. The appropriate attitude to have towards fate is not that of struggle, but acceptance and reconciliation. An attitude which in some way overcomes the brute externality of fate and history and makes it a necessary background to personal and social life and experience. As agrarian society, with its consequent patterns of mutual interdependence was part of the fate of Abraham, so modern commercial society in the contemporary world could be seen as part of man's fate. To be detached from the fate of one's community was, as the example of Jesus had shown, a disaster in that it led to the formation of the 'beautiful soul' standing above fate and disconnected from the on-going life of the community. Although Jesus brought a message of reconciliation, his relationship with his community was one of very profound estrangement. Similarly, Abraham's life and experience, so disastrous for the subsequent course and character of Jewish history, was also a case of a man defying fate and suffering the consequences. These two examples of the conse-

---

[1] Nohl, op. cit., p. 246.

[2] Ibid., p. 245. Of course, Hegel may well have exaggerated the extent to which the Jews were opposed to urban civilization. In Psalm 107, the psalmist, perhaps thinking of this period, praises God for having led man in the right way—towards an urban environment:

'They went astray in the wilderness out of the way; and found no city to dwell in;
Hungry and thirsty their soul fainted in them,
So they cried unto the Lord in their trouble; and he delivered them out of their distress.
He led them forth by the right way; that they might go to the city.' (4–7)

quences of the inability to overcome the estrangement of oneself from the concrete on-going life of the society to be found in the very same essay must have exercised a profound influence on Hegel. To stand apart from the modern commercial community with its own patterns of integration and to yearn for the closely-knit *polis* experience of the ancient world was to stand in an analogous relationship to the contemporary world as Abraham did to the agrarian society in Ur. He tried to recapture an earlier pattern of social experience and failed, producing at the same time a bifurcation in all the modes of his experience which Hegel was to call a form of madness. The point of the analogy was doubtless not lost on Hegel.

Reconciliation with fate manifested in the modern world in urban commercial society with its own differentiated, highly intricate patterns of human relationships in contrast with those of Greece gradually became Hegel's aim. This reconciliation with fate, as he came to develop his conception of it, was not some kind of brute acceptance of the world, but involved a profound grasp of the principles, the values and the patterns of human experience realized in the modern world. The ideal at the back of Hegel's mind in his development of this view seems to derive from a conception which he worked out in some of his earliest writings in Tübingen. In the Tübingen fragments he had argued that the Greek was at home in the world, reconciled with fate not as something merely *given*, but as assimilated and transformed:

> The Greek was chained to the earth with the iron band of necessity but with the aid of imagination and feeling so elaborated it and with the aid of the graces so entwined it with roses that he was satisfied with the fetter.[1]

Fate is seen as a necessary factor in life, which has to be accepted, but the mode of acceptance, Hegel seems to argue, transforms the very perception of the fate so that it becomes 'entwined with roses'; it was to become Hegel's view that the reconciliation of the modern man with the world was not to be achieved by the imagination, but by philosophy. As the Greek's perception of the world was changed by the reconciling and transforming power of imagination and feeling, so contemporary man's understanding of his world would be altered by philosophy. Imagination had enabled the Greeks to see the 'iron band of necessity' as 'intertwined with roses', so Hegel was to argue much later that contemporary man had to find his home in the world through reason and philosophy:

[1] Nohl, op. cit., p. 28.

71

> To recognize reason as the rose in the cross of the present and thereby to enjoy the present is the rational insight which reconciles us to the actual.[1]

Through reason, through a comprehensive philosophical grasp of contemporary experience man's attitude to it is changed:

> Philosophy is not a comfort; it is more; it reconciles, it transfigures the actual which seems unjust into the rational.[2]

Whereas imagination and feeling were sufficient for the Greek, in more reflective times man has to struggle to justify feeling at home in the world. His harmony with reality is no longer naïve, unmediated *sinnliche Harmonie* but *moralische Harmonie*, based upon intellectual effort, not upon immediate feeling.

The failure of Jesus to reform the religious life of the Jews, a failure which produced a profound split between Jesus' message of reconciliation and his life situation—his estrangement from Jewish experience, and the disastrous attempt of Abraham to turn his back on the pattern of historical development, as we shall see in detail later, profoundly altered Hegel's approach to the contemporary world. He now sought reconciliation with it and a grasp of the forces at work within it rather than a profound change in it, a change which would have to be based upon a decision to ignore its role in the pattern of human development. Other factors, too, may have had a role to play in Hegel's reorientation.

The other major influence on Hegel at this time was undoubtedly the unfolding pattern of events in France, particularly after 9 Thermidor 1794. Hegel, it was earlier argued, adopted the same kind of view of the French Revolution as many of his contemporaries, seeing in it an attempt to recapture something analogous to *polis* experience. However Hegel was soon disillusioned, at least with the methods of Robespierre. He wrote to Schelling thus:

> You will no doubt have heard that Carrier has been guillotined. Do you still read the French papers ? If my memory serves me correctly, they have been proscribed in Wurtemburg. This process is very important. It has revealed all the ignominy of Robespierre and his supporters.[3]

Similarly in a letter to Nanette Endel written from Frankfurt on 25 May 1798 he describes the desecration produced by the Revolutionary wars around Mainz where he had spent some time.[4] However,

---

[1] Glockner (ed.), *Sämtliche Werke*, vol. 7, p. 35.
[2] *Die Vernunft in der Geschichte*, ed. Hoffmeister, Hamburg 1955, pp. 77–8.
[3] *Briefe*, op. cit., p. 12.   [4] Ibid., p. 58.

it was not merely the methods of the Robespierrists which led to Hegel's change in attitude towards the Revolution, rather the changes in direction in the Revolution itself. It was impossible to claim after the Thermidorian reaction that something analogous to Greek social and political experience was being created in France. The outmoded institutions of *l'ancien régime* had been removed as being both an obstacle to freedom and offensive to reason, but in their place the closely-knit social and political unity characteristic of the Greek city state had not been generated.[1] On the contrary: in Hegel's view, made articulate some ten years later in *Die Phänomenologie des Geistes*, men had become more atomistic in their social relationships in that the rigid social functions to which most people had been tied during the pre-Revolutionary regime had disappeared and nothing comparable in social terms had taken their place. What had been created was not some kind of homogeneous social and political unit but rather an environment within which uncontrolled, undisciplined individualism could run riot.

In a sense it would of course be wrong to characterize this change in Hegel's attitude to the French Revolution as one of disillusionment because that would seem to entail that he could, at this later time, have envisaged its succeeding in recapturing the closely-knit social and political culture of the Greeks, or at least something analogous to it. By this time however, as we have seen, Hegel had become deeply sceptical about the feasibility of such idealism. The experience of the French Revolution would have confirmed in a concrete case the lesson which Hegel appears to have learned from Steuart, namely that there could be no return to anything remotely resembling Greek experience—the social, political and economic changes which had intervened made such an attempt impossible. The failure of the French Revolution to live up to the Tübingen ideals was, therefore, to be expected.

The other discernible intellectual influence on Hegel at this period, which, again, can only have influenced his move during the period from criticism of contemporary reality to the first attempts to comprehend it, was that of Schiller and in particular his *Ästhetische Briefe* which were published in 1795. It is known that Hegel had read, pondered and had been enormously impressed by Schiller's series of letters when they first appeared in *Die Hören*, the journal edited by Goethe and Schiller,[2] and these letters too involve a notion of historical development, a

---

[1] Cf. R. Garaudy, *Dieu est mort*, op. cit., pp. 44–9.
[2] *Briefe*, op. cit., p. 25:

'*Die Hören*—the first and second parts have filled me with great joy: the article on aesthetic education was a masterpiece.' Hegel to Schelling 16 April 1795.

typology of development which is not fundamentally different from that of Steuart, at least in general conception. Schiller, as we have seen, was as willing as any in his generation to idealize Greek experience and contrast some of the conditions of the modern world with Greek patterns of behaviour but, at the same time, he was very positive that the growth of commercial society, the division of labour and the concomitant sense of individualism had been an enormous gain:

> I readily admit that, little as individuals might have benefited from this fragmentation of their person there was no other way in which the species as a whole could have developed. . . . If the many capacities in man were to be developed there was no other way but to oppose them. The antagonism of the faculties and the functions is the great instrument of civilization.[1]

Greek life exhibited a naïve, unreflective harmony whose presupposition was no division of labour, no heterogeneous modes of experience. For that sort of society predicated on those kinds of conditions the Greeks constituted a paradigm which could not be expected to be improved upon. However, although a great achievement of the human spirit, if it was ever to be equalled it would have to be in quite different ways and upon quite different conditions. Schiller was confident that men in the contemporary world could develop new types of harmony and new types of community predicated upon new connections between the powers of the mind. This could not, however, be developed by ignoring the enormous changes which had overtaken society since the decline of the Greek city state. Schiller saw the long-term solution to the problem in terms of a programme of aesthetic education which, by uniting facets of personal experience, would lead eventually to the development of harmonious social experience. Schiller's typology of human development was, in a sense, therefore, triadic. It presupposed at the beginning of the historical world an undifferentiated society peopled by whole men whose capacities and powers had not been fragmented by the division of labour—such a society reached its zenith with the Greeks and has since declined as a result of the growth of science and the division of labour. These factors had led to the fragmentation of the community and of the person. The third stage of this process, which has yet to arrive in Schiller's view, was to be induced by aesthetic education, which would procure a regeneration of both the community and the individual personality appropriate to this change in the human condition. This typology of social change is not fundamentally unlike that of Steuart and it influenced Hegel greatly.

[1] Schiller, op. cit., p. 326.

He agreed that harmony in both the individual, personal sphere and in the social world would have to take a new form in the modern world; he also agreed that the solution to the problem lay in education, but he differed profoundly about the type of education involved. The need was, as Hegel began to see it at this time, for a comprehensive grasp of experience which, by enabling a man to have a very firm insight into the nature of the world confronting him, would change his view on that world so that it would no longer appear as a source of estrangement. This was to involve an understanding of modern political culture in an endeavour to show how the modern state did provide an adequate form of political environment for the modern man; an understanding of modern religious experience (which would, once grasped, remove its bifurcating effect on contemporary society) coupled with a comprehensive and total philosophical treatment of all the major modes of man's experience in modern society, showing their deep interrelations, obscured at the level of conventional description—a treatment which would overcome the fragmentation of the human personality. In this way Hegel's early aims became built in presuppositions of his later philosophy.

Chapter IV

Towards the Transfiguration of Politics

I can reconcile you to the human condition,
The condition to which some who have gone as far as you
Have succeeded in returning. They may remember the
Vision they had, but they cease to regret it.

T. S. Eliot

There can be little doubt that when Hegel arrived in Jena in January 1801, at the start of his university teaching career, he had emerged from a very difficult intellectual and emotional period. Between the years 1798 and 1800, he had seen all his hopes for reform, for promoting harmony and reconciliation in social and personal life, disappear and he had to make a complete intellectual readjustment. His preoccupations were still the same—to overcome the dissonance and fragmentation of experience—but these aims were now to be achieved not by structural reforms in the social world and in personal relationships but by a philosophical redescription of experience, a redescription which would 'transfigure' the world and enable men to live at home in it. However, at this time Hegel barely discerned this goal and had certainly not worked out in detail how it was to be achieved. There is a reasonable amount of evidence to suggest that his intellectual situation during this period caused him a good deal of personal distress and depression. Indeed, this mood may have begun in Berne where we learn from letters written to Hegel from Schelling[1] and Hölderlin[2] that he was both depressed and in a state of indecision. Although the reason for this is not stated and must remain conjectural it may well have been that his growing despair, evident in 'Die Positivität der christlichen Religion', about the possibility of recreating a folk religion out of Christianity

---

[1] *Briefe*, p. 37. [2] Ibid., p. 45.

induced this state. In Frankfurt the mood became very much more pronounced. In July 1797 he wrote to Nanette Endel that he sought to become 'reconciled both with himself and other men' and it is interesting to recall in this context that in 'Die Verfassung Deutschlands' Hegel should have linked up estrangement from others with madness and psychic disorder. Years later in a letter Hegel wrote of this period:

> From my own experience I know this mood of the mind or rather of the reason once it has entered with interest and with intimations into the chaos of appearance and yet, though inwardly sure of its goal, has not come through, has not attained the clarity and detailed grasp of the whole. I suffered for a few years from this hypochondria to the point at which I have been enervated by it. Indeed each person may have such a turning point in his life, the dark point of the contraction of his nature. . . .[1]

This letter sums up Hegel's situation at this period: he was inwardly sure of his goal—to overcome the fragmentation and dissonance in life and experience which had preoccupied him since he was a schoolboy, but at this time he was not at all sure of the way in which his goal could be attained. He came to see an inability to come to terms with the world, with the patterns of social and religious experience which it contained, as a pathological condition which could not be cured by taking up the attitude of a beautiful soul because such an attitude engendered, as was shown in the case of Jesus, a further cleavage between man and the on-going life of his community. No doubt Hegel's decision to abandon his radical line on reform and move towards an attempt to understand the nature of the values actualized in the contemporary world owed much, as we have seen, to the work of Steuart, Schiller and his own studies on Christianity, but the declining capacity of his friend Hölderlin may also have had an influence. Hölderlin was incapable of finding reconciliation in what he took to be an atrophied and enervated reality. In his great poem 'Hyperions Schicksalslied', written during the time Hegel was close to him in Frankfurt, Hölderlin articulated this failure to come to terms with the world in a very pronounced manner:

---

[1] *Briefe*, op. cit., p. 314. Letter to Windischmann, 27 May 1810. It is interesting to note in this context that Hamann who shared many of the same values as Hegel called his own restlessness of spirit 'hypochondria' although he was rather more tough-minded than Hegel and referred to it as 'holy'. It was for him a supreme mark of an intensely lived human life. See letter of 3 June 1781 to Herder in *Johann Georg Hamann Briefwechsel*, ed. W. Zeismer and A. Henkel, Wiesbaden 1955.

Doch uns ist gegeben
Auf keiner Stätte zu ruhn,
Es schwinden, es fallen
Die leidenden Menschen
Blindings von einer
Stund zur andern
Wie Wasser von Klippe
Zu Klippe geworfen
Jahrlang in Ungewisse hinab.[1]

Such was the fate which Hölderlin saw as the fate of the modern man and it was an experience which Hegel knew intimately, from the inside. At this time Hegel seemed to become concerned to extricate himself from this attitude. His studies had convinced him that the kinds of reforms which he had envisaged in his younger days could have no place in the modern world. The task which Hegel set himself was to enable man to feel at home in the world, to secure harmony and reconciliation not by changing the world in any fundamental manner but by providing a reinterpretation of experience which would change men's perception of their environment. It was the development of this philosophical approach to reconciliation which occupied Hegel from 1801–7 and it is to the discussion of the salient points of this development that we must now turn.

The change in Hegel's attitude is first explicitly recorded in the letter to Schelling of 2 November 1800 in which he points out that he feels impelled towards philosophy in order to realize his youthful ideals. This philosophical position did not appear fully fledged, but was worked out over a number of years, culminating in the publication of *Die Phänomenologie des Geistes* in 1807. The actual working out of his philosophical system is, however, of considerable interest to the student of politics because its development is very closely tied to social and political developments in Europe, developments which enabled Hegel to provide a plausible account of contemporary society as actualizing in its own way certain important human values and providing its own patterns of integration and community.

The first crucial work in Hegel's development is 'Differenz des Fichte'schen und Schelling'schen Systems der Philosophie'[2] for it is in this work that Hegel struggles to make articulate his own philosophical position against the background of the philosophy of Kant, Fichte and

[1] Hölderlin, op. cit., p. 265, 'But we are destined to find no resting place and suffering mortals dwindle and fall blindly from one hour to the next, hurled like water from ledge to ledge, downwards for years to the great abyss'.

[2] *Sämtliche Werke*, ed. Glockner, vol. 1. The essay was published in 1801.

Schelling. At the same time he deals with the presuppositions, the purpose and the character of philosophy.

The background of post-Kantian Idealism is today difficult, obscure and exceedingly esoteric, but at the same time some knowledge of the philosophical tradition, the *Gedankenwelt* within which Hegel was writing, is necessary to make intelligible his own conception of philosophy. Before briefly examining Hegel's attitude towards the philosophical achievements of his contemporaries, it is necessary first of all to deal with Hegel's view of the role of philosophy because it was against this that he assessed them. In this discussion Hegel very clearly brings to bear the preoccupations of his earlier writings. He sees in philosophy the need to reconcile what is opposed in conventional thought and description and to so philosophically interpret those activities from which man is estranged, which he is not able to grasp in a connected manner, that harmony between man and both the natural and the social worlds may be achieved:

> When we consider more closely the specific form which philosophy has we can see how it develops from the living originality of Spirit who in it has restored through itself the rent harmony and given structure to it through its own deed. . . . Bifurcation is the source of the need for philosophy.[1]

This passage is of considerable interest for several reasons. In the first place the final sentence links it with his preoccupations so far discerned. The solution to the problem of fragmentation and dissonance in the modern world is now seen to lie in philosophy whereas before he had looked for it in religious and political reform. Secondly, the process whereby division, fragmentation and dissonance are both developed and overcome is regarded by Hegel as having its source in the activity of *Spirit* (*Geist*), a concept which is not at this stage developed further. However, if some of the implications of Hegel's use of the term in this passage are unpacked, it seems that he is insisting on at least three things: that the development of fragmentation in the modern world is to be understood in some kind of teleological fashion, that its purpose in some way or other is to develop whatever is contained in the notion of Spirit; that in the modern world this fragmentation has implicitly been overcome; and, finally, that this has to be made explicit in philosophy, that in some way philosophy has to encompass this development-through-estrangement on the part of Spirit. This view that development involves opposition and bifurcation which are eventually done away in higher patterns of integration appropriate to the changed

[1] Glockner, op. cit., vol. I, p. 44.

context obviously owes a good deal to the writings of Steuart and
Schiller quoted in the previous chapter. But, interestingly enough,
Hegel links this idea up with that of the Crucifixion in another work of
this period, 'Glauben und Wissen'.[1] In this essay Hegel is concerned
with the relationship between God conceived as infinite, and the finite
world of men[2] and he argues that the Passion and Crucifixion were
necessary *developments* in the life of God. Taken as the infinite lord of
the universe God appears as totally other, but in the crucifixion this
otherness is negated, God's infinity becomes united to the concrete,
finite life of men and as such is quite crucial to God's own development.[3]
From one point of view the cross appears as an 'infinite grief', as the
very paradigm of division, dereliction and abandonment, but viewed
from a later standpoint it can be seen as a development in the richness
of the life of God. So, too, in other types of experience philosophy has
to comprehend how division and discord contribute to the development
of experience and at the same time how such divisions and discords are
overcome. Indeed in 'Glauben und Wissen' Hegel uses specifically
Christian images to characterize the philosophical tasks. Philosophy,
he argues,[4] has to endure a 'speculative Good Friday' but the cross is,
of course, entwined with roses. Bifurcation and discord are not merely
thought away by the philosopher, but have to be recognized by him as
important and central to human development, but at the same time,
grasped in such a way that the way in which they are overcome can also
be made clear. It has to comprehend how:

> The Absolute ever plays a moral tragedy with itself in which it ever
> gives birth to itself in the objective world, then in this form of itself
> gives itself over to suffering and death and then raises itself out of
> its ashes to glory.[5]

It was against this kind of approach to philosophy that Hegel began
to assess the achievement of his contemporaries. One of the most
general forms of bifurcation which Hegel had diagnosed was the general
estrangement between man and the world: the natural world was no
longer to be looked upon as *die Muttererde* but something from which
man was distanced and alienated; similarly social institutions appeared

[1] In Glockner, op cit., vol. 1.
[2] This aspect of the essay is discussed below, pp. 123 ff.
[3] Of course Hegel here revises in an important way the traditional Christian
understanding of God. In orthodox theology God was taken as self-complete.
For contemporary views, similar to those of Hegel but based upon a different
philosophical position, reference should be made to the 'process' theologians,
in particular Charles Hartshorne.
[4] Glockner, op. cit., p. 433. [5] Ibid., p. 500.

at best as necessary inconveniences and at worst as oppressive and a standing contradiction to man's freedom. Among philosophers Kant had provided the materials with which a philosophical solution to the problem could be provided, although he had not in Hegel's view solved the problem satisfactorily himself. Kant had argued, against the British empiricists in particular, that the mind is not some kind of passive organ which receives impressions from the external world, objects being constituted by some mechanism of association. On the contrary, in fact, Kant argued that objects and the experienced world are structured by the mind. The mind transforms and transposes the inchoate and chaotic manifold of sense impression into an intelligible world by intuition in the form of space and time and through the understanding by means of the categories such as causality, substantiality, reciprocity and so on. The experienced world in this sense is a human *creation*, the product of the activity of the human mind:

> The order and regularity in the appearances we entitle nature we ourselves introduce. We could not find them in appearances had not we ourselves or the nature of our minds put them there.[1]

The experienced could thus be seen as something embodying the creative activity of the ego and, as such, Kant's work postulated a very close, necessary, internal relationship between the human mind and the modes of experience available to human beings. Man could look upon the world of experience not as in some way alien and distanced from him but as something which was, at least in part, shot through with structuring principles which were expressive of the very make-up of his mind. So far Kant's metaphysic provided the groundwork, albeit in a very abstract fashion, on the basis of which the diremption between man and the modes of his experience could be overcome. At the very same time, however, Kant's theory had a very major drawback in that it left a residuum beyond experience, of *things in themselves* beyond the reach and outside the comprehension of the human mind. Such a realm, beyond possible experience, obviously posed a threat to the kind of interpretation of the relationship between man and his experience which Hegel had in mind. Furthermore Hegel was very antipathetic to Kant's conception of the mind which he considered divisive and incapable of doing justice to the conative and affective sides of man's nature. On the one hand things in themselves posed a threat to the integration of man and the world, on the other Kant's anthropology split man down the middle.

Because of his rejection of the Kantian notion of things in themselves,

[1] Kant, op. cit., vol. 4, p. 92.

Hegel regarded the work of Fichte as a considerable advance on that of Kant. Fichte, too, it seems appreciated the social dimension of a somewhat subtle epistemological argument when he wrote:

> My system is the first system of freedom. At the same time as this nation (France) has delivered humanity from material bondage, my system will deliver him from the yoke of the thing in itself.[1]

Fichte, the epistemological sansculotte, devoted his magnum opus, *Wissenschaftslehre*, to an attempt to exorcize the ghost of things in themselves from the palace of Idealism. The realm of appearance, the product of the human mind, became for Fichte the realm of true being and hence nothing was in principle incapable of being explained as a product of the structuring capacities of the human Ego. Fichte argued that the external world was initially posited by the pre-reflective, pre-conscious mind and because men, except philosophers, remain unaware of this the world takes on an external and alien character. The task of philosophy was to show how the conscious mind was able to reclaim the external world for its own in both theoretical and practical activity. The external world was in a sense created as a foil to the development of human self-consciousness. In attempting to overcome the otherness of the world men develop self-consciousness. Philosophy was to describe the general form of the relationship between man and this posited, but at the same time apparently alien world, demonstrating how, in specific modes of experience, self-consciousness could be seen to develop through the struggle, both practical and intellectual, to reduce this alien environment to Ego-dependence. At the same time Fichte believed that such struggle had no terminating point, that self-consciousness can never be fully and finally realized.

In his essay '*Differenz des Fichte'schen und Schelling'schen Systems der Philosophie*' Hegel rejects Fichte's views on two main grounds; on account of the unachieved character of the reconciliation between subject and object and the fact that, in a sense, any form of reconciliation on the Fichtean model has to possess a sham character about it, given the ambiguous nature of the external world on Fichte's theory.

Because the world of objects, though the posited product of the pre-reflective Ego, could not at any one time be totally reclaimed by consciousness, it followed in Hegel's view that Fichte's philosophy remained one of *sollen*, of what ought to be:

> The ideal is opposed to the real and the supreme spontaneous interaction of the self as subject-object is rendered impossible.[2]

[1] Leon, op. cit., vol. II, p. 288. [2] Glockner, op. cit., vol. i, p. 114.

The unachieved nature of the harmony between thought and the world as it appears in Fichte made his work, in Hegel's view, of a piece with the pining of the beautiful soul who merely wished that the world could be more rational. Fichte wished to show that the world and modes of experience could be shown to have a necessary connection with the development of the powers of the human mind, but in fact he was never able to offer such an explanation at least in the total fashion which Hegel required. This was a view of Fichte which Hegel was to hold all his life, a disagreement which he expressed very pithily in '*Vorlesungen über die Geschichte der Philosophie*' when he argued:

Fichte is stuck fast on an ought to be.[1]

In the essay Hegel also attacks what he takes to be the other major drawback in Fichte's theory about the relation between man and the world. He argues that even if reconciliation between subject and object could finally be achieved, given Fichte's premises, this would be a merely *soi-disant* reconciliation because Fichte takes one aspect of the subject-object relation, namely the subjective, as privileged. The world of objects has only a posited objectivity; it is in reality a philosophically discerned construction of the Ego in its primordial form. According to Hegel this means that reconciliation has been bought far too cheaply; it merely means that the object has been eliminated, not that a reconciliation between subject and object has been achieved:

. . . objects (for Fichte) are nothing in themselves; nature has substance only for consciousness.[2]

Such an approach was for Hegel the negation of the authentic philosophical approach which, as we have already seen, he insists must take seriously the objectivity of bifurcation and discord and not merely think it away by undermining the objectivity of one side of those things which are opposed.

Hegel's detailed criticism of Fichte is supplied in the section of the essay dealing with his writings on social and moral philosophy.[3] Instead of interpreting social experience in terms of an all-round development of self-consciousness, Fichte treats social experience generally, and political experience in particular, as a product of reason, of the autonomous self, a conception largely taken over from Kant with

[1] Glockner, vol. XIX, p. 635.
[2] Ibid., vol. I, p. 129. See also p. 76: 'Fichte's system is a subjective attempt to achieve a unity between subject and object.'
[3] Hegel particularly criticizes Fichte's *Grundlage des Naturechts* which he discusses in Glockner, ed. cit., vol. I, pp. 106 ff.

all the defects for which Hegel had already criticized Kant, namely its failure to take account of the conative and affective sides of the personality. Freedom was for Fichte, as it was for Kant, an attribute of the autonomous self, attainable only in so far as the heteronomy of passion, emotion and striving was kept in check. Fichte's theory of the state was therefore for Hegel predicated upon a fragmented understanding of the human personality and its powers:

> Because of the total opposition between pure impulse and natural impulse, natural right becomes a result of a concrete domination of reason and a suppression of life.[1]

Certainly Hegel's sympathies were very much with Fichte. He agreed that harmony between subject and object, or man and the world, could only be achieved in so far as the objective world, the world of experience, could be shown to be central to the development of self-consciousness and the powers of the human mind, but he rejected Fichte's particular theory of this relationship because he made the status of objects and modes of experience equivocal and because of the unachieved nature of the explanations of the subject/object relationship which Fichte thought that he could give. The philosophy of Schelling, on the other hand, although largely concerned with the relationship between man and the world of nature and less between the person and the cultural world, seemed to Hegel to avoid the drawbacks of Fichte. In his very earliest writings Schelling had been a disciple of Fichte; indeed, at the age of twenty he made important advances within the general Fichtean framework with his book *Vom Ich als Prinzip der Philosophie*. However Schelling very soon began to move a very long way indeed from this position. He took the view, with which, as we have seen, Hegel sympathized, that Fichte's system was far too subjective, in effect denying the objectivity of nature, giving it a merely *soi-disant* posited status. He rejected such a constructivist approach and argued that the Ego and Nature must both be taken as real, neither having a privileged position in the schema of explanation. At the same time he did not take the view that Nature and Ego were to be regarded as radically opposed. Nature was not for Schelling, as it was for example for Descartes, a mere amalgam of external, mechanically

---

[1] Glockner, op. cit., vol. I, p. 114. Hegel had earlier criticized Fichte on similar grounds in *Systemsfragment*, Nohl, op. cit., p. 351.

The opposition (i.e. between Ego and the world) would not be overcome in a beautiful union; the union would be frustrated and opposition would be a hovering of the Ego above all nature.

Here nature includes the heteronomous part of the self as well as the natural world.

related parts, governed by mechanical laws and counterpoised to the human mind, spiritual, dynamic and exempt from mechanistic explanation, nor did he take Fichte's view that its sole purpose was to act as a foil to the development of human self-consciousness; rather he considered that nature had a dynamism of its own. In *Ideen zu einer Philosophie der Natur*[1] Schelling argued that the essence of Nature or matter is force, while the essence of the Ego he took to be spirit. Both Nature and Ego were therefore basically dynamic and creative.[2] Both Nature and Ego thus shared a common ground and had a comparable ontological status, the crucial point, of course, where his theory began to diverge from that of Fichte. Schelling argues that:

> According to Fichte the Ego is everything but this is true only because everything is Ego.[3]

The common ground which both Nature and Ego share is called by Schelling 'the point of indifference'. This is Schelling's Absolute which appears in Spinozistic manner under two modes: in the spiritual creative activity of the Ego and as the system of natural phenomena with force as its vital principle.[4] At the same time, however, Schelling argues that the dynamic, spiritual side of Nature remains inarticulate until it is grasped and made explicit in the conscious activity of the Ego. The Ego does not construct Nature as its opposite but rather exists in reciprocal relation with it making explicit the spiritual principles operating in a blind kind of fashion in Nature. It is important to bear in mind when considering the philosophy of Schelling that he is not arguing the minimal thesis that we have to treat Nature as if it were an intelligible system, for such a view would not be very far from the Kantian position which asserts that the intelligibility of Nature is a 'regulative idea' but one which we cannot be sure applies to it in itself. Schelling commits himself to a far stronger position arguing that Nature in itself is dynamic, spiritual and teleological. On this point Hegel explicitly sides with Schelling as against Kant. The intelligibility of Nature is never for Hegel a merely regulative idea but something built into being itself. For Schelling this spiritual dimension of Nature is built into the natural world through the point of indifference which

---

[1] *Sämtliche Werke*, vol. I, Stuttgart and Augsburg 1856.
[2] Ibid., ch. 11, p. 56. It is of course arguable that Schelling's theories were much influenced by Spinoza. Indeed the work of Spinoza had a certain popularity during this period in Germany largely on account of Jacobi's translation of his letters.
[3] Ibid., ch. 15, p. 109.
[4] See *Werke*, ed. cit., vol. I, p. 13.

is discernible only through philosophical intuition. It is beyond rational comprehension, eluding capture in a net of concepts although crucial for understanding the reciprocity between subject and object, between man and the natural environment. The point of indifference objectifies itself in nature, becomes subjective in the life of man and becomes reconciled in philosophical reflexion.[1]

In his essay comparing Fichte and Schelling Hegel completely accepts the critique of the constructivism of Fichte and Kant which Schelling offers. He agrees with Schelling that the subject-object dualism, the bifurcation between man and the world, can be overcome only once one has accepted the reality of the division and the equal ontological status of the things so divided. At the same time there are indications that Hegel's thought is already moving away from close agreement with Schelling. Instead of using the notion of the point of indifference to denote the Absolute, that which secures the harmony between thought and being, man and the world, he uses and continues to use the word *Geist* (Spirit). The world is intelligible for Hegel because it is structured by Spirit, but at the same time Spirit is not for him something beyond rational comprehension and obviously could not be, given his philosophical aim to make men feel at home in the world. If the basic principle whereby reconciliation was to be achieved were to elude the grasp of the human mind then the thing in itself would re-emerge as a threat to human harmony. This point is made particularly strongly in Hegel's other major essay of this early period 'Glauben und Wissen'. In this essay he links up the metaphysical notion of Spirit, realizing itself both in nature and in human life with the activity of God in the world. At the same time he rejects the traditional understanding of God which places him infinitely beyond human comprehension, an understanding which, as we have already seen, Hegel regards as destructive of community. Hegel argues that God can be known, that the totality of his activity can be grasped by the human mind in philosophical reflection and description.[2] Whereas for Schelling the Absolute which secured the harmony between man and the world was beyond knowledge and amenable only to a private form of intuition, for Hegel Spirit, the structuring principle of the

[1] There is no easy way for the contemporary Anglo-Saxon reader to gain entry into Schelling's thought as it stands. One way of gaining perhaps an inkling of Schelling's view of nature is through the poetry of Wordsworth. Herbert Read has shown in *The True Voice of Feeling*, London 1963, the extent to which Schelling influenced Coleridge and no doubt this influence was transmitted via him to Wordsworth. 'Tintern Abbey' lines 90–100, are very Schellingian.

[2] See Glockner, ed. cit., vol. I, pp. 292–3.

world, showing itself both in nature and in human life and culture, can be known by reason—an intersubjective faculty. A shared, rational understanding of the development of Spirit both in nature and in culture would enable man to be reconciled with his world in a way that Schelling's system could not provide for with its esoteric emphasis upon the indefinability of the point of indifference. For Schelling the point of indifference was analogous to Wordsworth's

> dark
> Invisible workmanship that reconciles
> Discordant elements, and makes them move
> In one society.[1]

For Hegel the activity of Spirit could be neither dark nor invisible, but could be comprehended and described by the philosopher. Without such comprehension of the structuring power of spirit there would be at the heart of the world a residuum of transcendence. Transcendence as Hegel well knew was destructive of community.

To sum up Hegel's views so far: he rejected absolutely the constructivist approach to human experience advocated by Kant and more particularly by Fichte. Kant's constructivist approach left the residual thing in itself and was thus a threat to the reconciliation between man and the world; Fichte on the other hand gave both the natural and cultural worlds an ambivalent status and such reconciliation as he manages to achieve, through demonstrating the close link between the human Ego and modes of experience, was a sham. Hegel agreed with Schelling that the natural and social worlds could not be considered as constructions of the Ego and had therefore to be granted objectivity. At the same time however, to grant the objectivity of the external world did not entail that such a world was in some way alien from the nature of the human mind. On the contrary in fact even Nature, and more so the social and cultural worlds, embodied spiritual principles in such a way that the human mind could both encapsulate and find itself reflected in this external world. Hegel, however, disagreed fundamentally with Schelling about the way in which the spirituality of Nature was to be secured. According to Schelling both Nature and Ego had their ground in the point of indifference, accessible to intuition and beyond conceptual thought; for Hegel, on the contrary, this would leave reconciliation between man and the world at the mercy of the private intuition of a transcendent, even mystical entity. This final point leads the exposition back to the social dimension of these subtle arguments. Reconciliation and harmony, the two major social problems

[1] Wordsworth, *The Prelude* (1805 text), I, II, 322-5.

as Hegel saw them, could not be achieved as the result of some *private* intuitive activity, nor could they be predicated upon something inaccessible to the human mind, something transcendent and amenable only to intuition. Rather, reconciliation could be generated only through some kind of intersubjective activity whose results were communicable. Philosophy was this activity for Hegel and such was the key to community.

The task of philosophical explanation, geared as it was to the solution of the problem of alienation, of the unhappy consciousness, was to elucidate and describe how the human mind develops in self-consciousness by interaction with its environment—an environment both natural and social which is so structured that it provides the necessary means whereby this self-consciousness can be achieved. In doing so the philosopher will demonstrate the positive value of diremption and fragmentation, seeing in them necessary stages in the development of self-consciousness and as possessing within themselves the means of reconciliation and harmony. This task—to overcome the total problem of unhappy consciousness—would involve elucidating the development of various powers of the human mind in interaction with both the natural world and with all the modes of experience available in the cultural world. Within the confines of this book the emphasis will be placed upon Hegel's growing understanding of political experience in the development of the human mind. It must, however, be stressed that seen in the general terms argued so far in the book this constitutes only a part, although an important part, of Hegel's social and political concern. Because he saw the problems of social, personal and religious bifurcation as the central social and political difficulties of his age, it follows that in so far as he considered that philosophy, when taken as a whole, could provide solutions to these problems it can fairly be said that the *whole* of his philosophy, however abstract, is pervaded by this insistent and central social concern. Philosophy for Hegel, providing as it does a rational, intersubjective account of the development of the modern world in its totality, exorcising all transcendental elements and entities, highlighting conventionally-ignored patterns of integration, is the key to community. It provides the core of common culture, the common interpretation of experience which he regards as being central to the achievement of community.

In the case of the elucidation of social and political experience the task of philosophy is clear. It has to provide a rational grasp of political institutions and practices in terms of their ability to actualize and develop the various powers of the human mind and the development of self-consciousness. This is the universal element in any philosophical

88

explanation. At the same time, taken merely as such, this universal element is abstract and lifeless; the development of particular aspects of the human mind through political activity has to be shown in detail in specific cases. Philosophy has, therefore, a universal element and a specific and individual dimension, and an adequate philosophical explanation has to unite all three elements. Understood in this way political experience is not a construction of the Ego, nor a mere addendum to human life, a necessary convenience, it is rather a rationally intelligible structure whose function is to develop the consciousness of individuals. When grasped in this way a particular form of political life may be seen as making articulate a specific capacity or nexus of capacities of the human personality and providing its own patterns of relationship and integration. Hegel's view of politics is therefore teleological: politics is a goal-directed activity, particular forms of political life, practices and institutions leading to the development of human minds and self-consciousness. This goal Hegel regards as being 'built in' by Spirit, a crucial but ambiguous concept which will be discussed more fully as the concept itself develops in Hegel's own writings during this period.

The general character of a philosophical explanation of politics becomes clear and is given detailed expression in his two earliest essays of social and political philosophy: 'Über die wissenschaftlichen Behandlungsarten des Naturrechts'[1] and 'System der Sittlichkeit'.[2] The former was an article which Hegel originally published in *Kritisches Journal der Philosophie* in 1802 and the latter, unpublished by Hegel himself, comprises lecture notes on social and political philosophy for a course which he gave in the autumn in 1802. The essay on Natural Law criticizes philosophers who have failed to provide understandings of social and political experience according to the criteria implied by Hegel for an adequate philosophical treatment of politics; the other work gives in a seminal fashion Hegel's ideas on the detail of a correct analysis of the development of political experience and the correlative development of the human mind.

In the essay on Natural Law Hegel is concerned to criticize both the empirical approach to politics and what might be called the formal approach. His objections to both styles of theorizing are both methodological and substantive but both types of criticism are directed towards making the same point, namely a treatment of politics which links it with the development of the human mind and the failure of both the empiricist and the formalist to provide one. The empiricist approach

[1] Glockner, ed. cit., vol. 1, pp. 437–537.
[2] In Lasson, *Schriften zur Politik und Rechtsphilosophie*, ed. cit., pp. 415–99.

to the understanding of politics Hegel regards as either inadequate or self-contradictory. It is inadequate when true to itself because, *qua* empirical, the conclusions of any research within such presuppositions must be regarded as having a merely limited validity and cannot therefore provide the kind of universal link which, Hegel wishes to argue, holds between the development of consciousness and *any* form of social and political experience. On the other hand when the conclusions of such research are generalized they become more adequate from Hegel's point of view in that they have things to say about the relationship between men and political experience *per se*, but at the same time empiricism has transcended itself.

The arguments about formalism, by which Hegel implies the political philosophies of Kant and Fichte,[1] are a mirror image of the attack on empiricism. Whereas he had criticized empiricism for its inadequacy when bound purely by contingent and specific material, his criticism of formalism is that it operates at all too an ethereal level with a conception of the human mind and reason which is linked in an abstract way with social and political experience but which is never used in the explanation of detailed and specific circumstances. Because such approaches virtually exclude detailed empirical analysis, their conclusions, although they do postulate a close relationship between man and his experience, remain empty and insignificant. These critiques bear out the point made earlier, that an adequate philosophical explanation, one which will perform its reconciling role, must unite within itself the universal, namely that political experience embodies and makes articulate powers of the human mind, and at the same time must show in detailed and specific circumstances how and in what way. Hegel hints at this point in a general fashion in his essay comparing Fichte and Schelling when he argues that:

> The method (of philosophical science) is neither analytic nor synthetic.[2]

The connections which Hegel makes between politics and the development of the personality are not merely logical, being elucidations of the concept of reason, nor are they merely empirical. They rather unite in a complex fashion the metaphysical view that politics is connected with the articulation of the mind's capacities with empirical detail illustrating this general point.

Hegel's critique of the substantive conclusions of the empirical approach to politics involves in a more circuitous fashion much the

---

[1] Hegel particularly has in mind Fichte's *Grundlage des Naturrechts*, 1796–7.
[2] Glockner, op. cit., vol. 1, p. 72.

same point. The empiricist, Hegel argues,[1] tends to understand the development of society in general and political institutions in particular in terms of the consequences of man's asocial state—various difficulties in the state of nature lead to the formation of society and political institutions. Here again, however, the connections between man and his political experience is envisaged in merely contingent terms.[2] The social and political world appears to him an arbitrary if convenient construct. Nor is such a theory in the remotest sense rational in Hegel's view, for the description of the asocial state of man must rest not upon some kind of rational discernment, but rather on intuition or feeling. At the back of this argument probably lies the point which Hegel insisted upon very explicitly in a Preface to his essay 'Die Positivität der christlichen Religion', which he wrote at this time some six or seven years after the essay's completion. In this Preface Hegel argues that the concept of human nature, the description of the central powers of the human mind, cannot be separated from the social context within which minds are formed[3]—if so, there cannot be any universal conception of human nature in an asocial state which could then be used to explain the genesis of society. Indeed, Hegel's whole philosophical programme would have been thwarted if such a conception could have been so formed because he wants to connect up living in society and under political authority with becoming human in the full sense, that is to say of becoming conscious of oneself and attaining power and control over one's environment. Hegel makes his position clear in a comment on Montesquieu:

> That is why Montesquieu has founded his immortal work on the individual character of the various peoples. True enough he has not been able to raise himself to the fully living idea but at least he has interpreted the particular laws and institutions on the basis of the whole and its individuality . . . rather than deducing them from

[1] Hegel discusses empiricism in Lasson, op. cit., pp. 443 ff.

[2] In Nohl, op. cit., pp. 139 ff.

[3] Hegel is surely right here. There is no expertise which can elucidate the human powers in the void, outside a particular form of life. The only concepts which might be elucidated in this way are purely formal, for example that men are capable of reason, that they are able to act as well as acted upon, that they are rule-following animals and so on. This is about as far as can be gone in elucidating human potentialities outside a particular culture. They are formal as they stand and can be filled in only by reference to particular societies and the paradigms of human nature presupposed in those societies. The content of human nature, the patterns of human response, are by and large socially given. I have developed this argument in my book *Social and Moral Theory in Casework*, London 1970, ch. 3, 'Community and Mental Health'.

reason and abstracting them from experience and raising the latter to a certain universality.[1]

Whereas the empiricist had gone wrong in seeing the genesis of society in contingent terms, the consequence of the baneful asocial state of man, the formalist in Hegel's view had gone much too far in the opposite direction. Kant and Fichte deduced social and political experience from the pure Ego without connecting the powers of this Ego with the particular contingencies of a cultural situation. Fichte had argued that political institutions are necessary because there is more than one individual possessing a free and independent Ego, the role of the law being to safeguard the ability of the individual Ego to express itself in both thought and action. The state is only rational when ordered on such a basis. In fact such a view, according to Hegel, is inadequate, because based upon purely *a priori* considerations, ignoring the different ways in which the mind responds in different circumstances and the different types of freedom for which it strives. It does provide, as the empiricist view does not, a metaphysical deduction of politics, so that politics is not seen as something detachable in human life but, being disconnected from any close understanding of the relationship between the human mind and a particular form of political culture, it becomes inadequate for philosophical explanation. Again Hegel uses the critiques of empiricism and formalism to imply the structure of an adequate philosophical theory of politics.

Hegel's complementary essay 'System der Sittlichkeit' constitutes his first attempt at providing such a theory. He tries to show, albeit in somewhat sketchy fashion, how social and political life generally is correlated with the self-development of persons and as such this articulates the universal element in philosophical explanation; at the same time, however, he tries to show how different types of social and political organization are correlated with the development of particular human powers and this of course emphasizes the empirical element in his theory, an element which is historical in the sense that it traces a pattern of *development* through time.

Primeval social and political experience in Hegel's view involved a very close relationship between man, the natural world and the community. This level of undifferentiated social experience he calls *natürliche Sittlichkeit*,[2] to stress the fact that at this stage self-consciousness had not developed and men were incapable of distinguishing adequately between themselves and their environment, between their own activity and how they were acted upon. At such a level of social development

[1] Nohl, op. cit., p. 411.　　　　[2] Lasson, op. cit., pp. 417 ff.

there was no labour. Men consumed the natural fruits of the earth and lived in a naïve, *sinnliche Harmonie* with the natural world and with their community. At this level of experience, men had not learned to distinguish between themselves and their community, between themselves as private individuals and as members of a collectivity. At the same time this close, unmediated pattern of social integration must break down. As each man satisfies his desires by consuming the natural fruits of the earth, so his desires multiply. Once satisfied, the desires reappear, perhaps in the same form, perhaps differently. Consequently to satisfy his desire each man begins to labour and in labour a crucial change both in man and his environment is reached. Hitherto man has been a passive consumer and had not had to struggle, consequently his capacities and powers had remained dormant. With the development of labour, however, he begins to take up an active role, transforming the world, moulding it in such a way that it could satisfy his desires and in this process he becomes aware of himself as a person. With this realization the naïve unity of *natürliche Sittlichkeit* is forever broken. The close integration is replaced by a more external form, relationships based upon labour and co-operation in production. One type of such a relationship is to be found in the use of tools which demand co-operation to be used effectively and efficiently.[1]

In this argument may be seen the dominant trend of Hegel's thinking —apparent fragmentation, the collapse of the close-knit harmony of the primeval community is understood in terms of a development in self-consciousness, a development which at the same time leads to new patterns of integration, no doubt very different from earlier, less reflective ones, but still modes of integration and co-operation. Along with the development of labour with its correlative gain in self-consciousness and the emergence of new patterns of integration out of increasing differentiation goes the development of various types of social institution. As a man labours he produces more than he requires to meet his needs and this excess turns into private property. The role of property in society does not therefore have to be justified, but understood in the context of human development. Property, the result of labour, is thus, in a sense, the embodiment of the human personality and therefore of value and the emphasis upon its value leads to the development of a set of legal relationships to govern property and a system of specifications of crime. At a personal level the difference in the labouring capacities of various members of society leads to various types of domination and servitude. The labouring process leads eventually beyond the mere integration required by the co-operative

[1] See Lasson, op. cit., p. 427.

93

use of tools on to an extremely complex pattern of mutual inter-dependence. Each man labours initially to satisfy his own desires but he is incapable of satisfying the whole range of his desires through his own efforts and he acquires the fruits of the labour of others to satisfy those desires which he cannot fulfil. Other men stand in the same situation to him. This leads to an unwitting mutual interdependence in what Hegel calls a system of needs.[1] Men are no longer related to one another in a naïve and uncomplicated fashion but in more intricate, less easy to discern ways, but at the same time ways which are appropriate to the fundamental change in the human condition produced by the development of labour. With the increasing division of labour there develops, according to Hegel's argument, a system of class relationships. Classes he regards as being dominated by the type of consciousness generated in the kind of labour undertaken by the members of the class and, in the essay, he distinguishes three major classes in society, the agricultural or substantial class,[2] the acquisitive class[3] and the universal class,[4] the class of civil servants who attend to the needs of all in society and administer such institutions as have grown up.

The development of the mediated interdependence of the system of needs and the complex relations between classes in modern society cannot however, appear as something providing adequate integration because it appears arbitrary. Until such relationships are governed by rules and the implicit relationships, so naturally engendered between men, have been made explicit, the system appears as something deeply alien,[5] in which man cannot feel at home. Of course, here Hegel is talking about the kinds of relationships which the modern man in incipient industrialized society experiences, relationships which, as we have seen, were incisively criticized by many of Hegel's generation. Without some kind of control over the inter-relationships produced by the system of needs what regulates human relationships, Hegel argues, is:

The mindless, blind totality of needs and the means whereby they are satisfied.[6]

Men have to take control of this 'unconscious blind fate' as Hegel describes it and bring it under government control.[7] The development of the modern state is therefore shown by Hegel to be a rationally discernible development from human labour, which in turn is compre-hensible in terms of the need to satisfy a wide range of desires.

[1] Lasson, op. cit., p. 488.   [2] Ibid., p. 489.   [3] Ibid., p. 491.
[4] Ibid., p. 493.
[5] 'Es ist eine fremde Macht, über welche er nichts vermag, von welcher es abhängt.' Ibid., p. 489.   [6] Ibid., p. 489.   [7] Ibid., p. 489.

Hegel considers two major forms of government, the system of Justice (*System der Gerechtigkeit*)[1] and the system of Discipline (*System der Zucht*).[2] By the System of Justice Hegel seems to have in mind the classical liberal view of the state, as an umpire, *au-dessus de la mêlée* and non-interventionist. At the same time Hegel argues that such a form of government is self-contradictory in that it represents *particular* interests even though it poses as a *universal* force. The second kind of control which Hegel discusses is the System of Discipline, which includes the moral life of the community, the general system of law and order and a strong state based upon preparedness for war—a somewhat odd conception of the state and one which Hegel does not go on to amplify.

Obviously it would be wrong to consider at great length the argument of the essay for it is clearly a work in progress and was not meant for publication. No doubt its many obscurities would be elucidated in the lectures of which 'System der Sittlichkeit' is, after all, a set of notes. However, certain interesting features emerge from the argument, features which are both methodological and substantive. In the first place it articulates Hegel's aim to steer a course between the Scylla of analytic insignificance, disconnected from any real, empirically-based analysis, and the Charybdis of empirical restriction—philosophically valueless on account of its inability to generalize about political experience. The essay discusses the development of political experience in a universal manner, seeing in it ways and means in which powers of the human mind are actualized, at the same time exhibiting in some detail this point with reference to precise conditions, for example in the short discussion of labour and property. It also illustrates the methodological point that progress and development involve initial fragmentation but out of which new patterns of integration may be seen to emerge. In the essay, *natürliche Sittlichkeit* is seen as embodying a very close relationship both between man and his natural and social environment, but within which the individual had no conception of himself and his powers. The development of labour was crucial to the realization of consciousness, but at the same time as it was a gain in human development it led to a break-up of the older pattern of community. However, labour eventually leads to new types of relationship between men which have to be comprehended for what they are and not dismissed for not being of an earlier and thus inappropriate type.

At this stage in the argument there is some tension in the essay in that Hegel considers that the patterns of relationship produced by the system of needs and the division of labour have to be seen to be rational

---

[1] Lasson, op. cit., p. 495.　　　　　　　　　　　　[2] Ibid., p. 496.

and controlled, otherwise they will appear to those who live within them as a 'blind fate'. Such control, he argues, must come from the state,[1] regulating the economic life of the community. However his discussion of the state is brief and inconclusive and the reason for this is not difficult to see, for in 'Die Verfassung Deutschlands', written such a short time previously, he had lamented the absence of adequate state machinery in Germany. In consequence his philosophical position here may be taken as inconsistent with his dominant approach, namely that of providing a rational understanding of 'that which is' in order to reconcile men to their world and to the mediated patterns of integration manifested in it. Taken in a *European* rather than a merely German context however, the inconsistency is not extreme. In France during this period Napoleon was involved in building up a strong state structure designed to control and regulate a great many aspects of civil society and, considered against such a background, Hegel was perhaps drawing attention, albeit in a somewhat abstract fashion, to the developing role of the state in the modern world at least in so far as it was manifested in France. Such a state, devoid of philosophical comprehension, would appear as a merely arbitrary and oppressive imposition of the freedom of individuals to pursue their own interest. Given the philosophical deduction of 'System der Sittlichkeit' however this alien aspect of the progressive modern state would disappear and would be seen not as an imposition but a development of self-consciousness. By regulating and codifying many aspects of social practice, it gives to the modern world a rationality and a predictability which it would not otherwise possess and thus provides man with more insight and control over his social environment.

[1] The influence of Steuart's notion of the statesman appears to be important here. Cf. Steuart, in Skinner, op. cit., p. 122. Hegel now sees the solution to the problem of social and political fragmentation to lie in the state and the state's control of the system of needs, the relations involved in the progressive division of labour.

Chapter V

A System of
Philosophical Politics

*I am at home in the world when I know it, still more so when I
have understood it.*

Hegel

Despite the two essays discussed in the previous chapter, Hegel had no
settled view at this time in his development about the detail of the
philosophical explanations of political life and experience which he was
attempting to provide. The actual form of the deduction of human
society and its various modes was changed, at least at the level of detail,
until it reached its final form in the *Enzyklopädie*. To elucidate these
changes is a rewarding exercise which clarifies the purpose of philosophy
in its relationship to politics as Hegel saw it and reveals the very many
insights which he had into the operation and problems of developing
commercial society.

One objection which could be raised by the critic versed in Hegel's
philosophical aims against the sketchy treatment of politics provided in
'System der Sittlichkeit' is that the essay makes no deduction of human
life itself. *Natürliche Sittlichkeit*, the primeval human world, is taken as
a presupposition of the work and its genesis is not discussed. However
it might be argued that without some philosophical deduction of the
very development of human life itself, within the natural world, *before*
the development of culture and politics, the unhappy consciousness,
the sense of estrangement from one's environment could not be overcome. The essay, it might be maintained, could well explain man's role
in various modes of social and political experience, but without the
establishment of some philosophical connection between man and the
natural world, the individual could easily regard himself as living in, on
the whole, an alien environment. Without such a deduction a merely
political philosophy would be inadequate for solving the general social

97

problem of alienation and philosophy would not be able to provide the key to community in the modern world.

Such an objection would, however, prove entirely unfounded in that it was precisely at this period that Hegel began to work out a *system* of philosophy in which a discussion of social and political experience and its connection with the development of consciousness was to be fitted into an overall framework of philosophical explanation in which the existence of the human mind was not to be taken as an unargued datum but demonstrated as arising of necessity out of nature. The full and adequate philosophical explanation of the modern world, including its politics, could only be achieved by showing the necessary development of the human mind out of Nature. *Naturphilosophie* was not, therefore, for Hegel a detachable part of his philosophical enterprise but a necessary prerequisite of the sort of philosophical treatment of human experience demanded by the pervasive problem of human estrangement in the contemporary world.[1] However esoteric Hegel's work on *Naturphilosophie* may seem to the contemporary reader, it had an essential social dimension. In the same way as the Greek's relation to the natural world, admired by both Hegel and Schiller, was part and parcel of his general feeling of community, so too the modern man has to be given some philosophical explanation of his place in the natural world, for only by overcoming estrangement in all its forms could community be achieved.

Similarly with Hegel's logical writings: in his view the language of conventional discourse, and indeed of academic philosophy, involved bifurcation and discord. Consequently the philosopher, who sought to demonstrate that, in fact there were deep connections to be discerned between things, experiences and practices kept apart in conventional discourse, could not rely on such language for his philosophical writing, but had to revise conventional conceptions in the interest of the pursuit of coherence. Before an adequate philosophical description of the modern world in general and its politics in particular could be given the conventional structure of notions had to be philosophically revised and this Hegel attempted first of all in his lectures on logic given in 1802.

[1] Because of this Findlay seems to me to be wrong when he writes: 'Hegel, like many another young philosopher faced with a teaching situation and names like "metaphysics" and "logic" to channel his effort, matured overnight from the rather dreary lucubrations of his years of tutorship to the astounding writings of the Jena period.' Findlay in A. V. Miller, op. cit., p. viii. This makes Hegel's development into a systematic philosopher appear to be a result of the exigencies of the timetable and the courses in the University of Jena, whereas such an approach was vital if he was to overcome the problems diagnosed in his *Hauslehrer* period.

In the collected lecture notes of the Jena period, therefore, the overall structure of Hegel's thought may be seen for the first time and understood in the light of the considerations so far advanced. The collected lectures are *Jenenser Logik, Metaphysik und Naturphilosophie*, 1802;[1] *Jenenser Realphilosophie I*[2] of 1803–4, containing 'Naturphilosophie' and 'Philosophie des Geistes', and *Jenenser Realphilosophie II*[3] of 1805–6, containing 'Naturphilosophie' and 'Geistesphilosophie'. The merely formal pattern of the lectures reveals something of Hegel's intentions— prefacing all discussion with the *Logik*, designed to formulate the appropriate form of philosophical discourse, leading to a philosophy of the natural world tracing the development of mind from Nature, culminating in a philosophy of the cultural world including the world of political experience.

Hegel's *Jenenser Logik* is, in a sense, the basic text because it provides the concepts in and through which the philosopher is able to provide an harmonious and necessary grasp of both the natural and social worlds and thus provides in abstract form the means of achieving the reconciliation of man with the world. Such a grasp of experience has to be rational and communicable, unlike Schelling's description of experience based ultimately on the intuitive point of indifference, and must bring out in thought the necessary forms through which Spirit, the agent of change and development, passes. The *Logik* therefore shows up deep connections between concepts which are normally kept apart in conventional thought and description. At the same time because a philosophical grasp of experience must reconcile man with his world, the system of concepts through which this grasp is achieved must not be, as it were, wished on to reality by the philosophy, must not be regulative but must be shown in some way to be able to make articulate the development of being. If the philosopher was merely wishfully reinterpreting the world, he could achieve only a *soi-disant* grasp of it and at the same time would be indulging in a mystification of reality.[4] It is one thing to argue that Hegel was *in fact* guilty of purveying such a mystification, quite another to show that this was intentional. All the indications are that Hegel took his descriptions seriously.

[1] Ed. Lasson, Leipzig 1923.   [2] Ed. Hoffmeister, Leipzig 1932.
[3] Ed. Hoffmeister, Leipzig 1931.
None of the above three works is available in English which is in some ways unfortunate in that Hegel's discussion of politics in both *Realphilosophie I* and *II* is both instructive and interesting as will, hopefully, be shown below.
[4] This was, of course, the essence of Marx's criticism of Hegel's general position and of his social and political thought in particular. For Marx's criticism see *Kritik des Hegelschen Staatsrechts*, and *Die heilige Familie*.

The Jena lectures on logic are divided into three main sections: Simple Connection, Relation and Proportion. Each section deals with a particular set of concepts and the relation between the sections is in terms of ascending levels of adequacy so that eventually the general form of a judgement enabling a full conceptual grasp to be taken on reality is attained.

The section on Simple Connection[1] is divided into three main subsections: Quality, Quantity and Infinity. The first two concepts are related particularly to the qualitative and quantitative individuation of an object and, as such, the concepts cover, in generic form, the attitude of common sense towards experience, namely that one object may be differentiated from another by the enumeration of its specific qualities, e.g. 'This chair is wooden, painted white and upholstered with red leather'. A conceptual grasp of recurrent features of experience is to be attained at this level by picking out and enumerating the qualities of an object. At the same time, however, Hegel argues that a full, satisfying and total grasp of experience is impossible in terms of such a Humean schema because in his view the specification of the qualities of an object, essential to its individuation, can never be complete. He argues that the specification of a quality presupposes a background of qualities which the thing does not possess and the qualities which it does have make sense only when this background is presupposed. To say 'This chair is white' has sense only when this background is present, given that there are other colours which the chair could have been but in fact is not. The ascription of a quality to an object therefore depends on a contrast with other qualities which it does not possess and for individuation to be both secure and complete it is necessary in Hegel's view to make articulate these correlative qualities:

> A quality is related to what it shuts out, it does not itself exist in an absolute way for itself, but in such a manner that it is for itself only in so far as some other quality is not present.[2]

To attempt to grasp the world through a schema based upon the concepts of quality and quantity therefore leads to an impasse when its presuppositions are philosophically examined. On the one hand common sense presupposes that an object may be grasped in an isolated and disconnected way without any necessary reference to anything else, merely by listing its specific qualities but such an approach is predicated precisely on the connection between words denoting the specific qualities in question and other words denoting correlative but not

---

[1] Lasson, *Jenenser Logik*, op. cit., pp. 1–34.
[2] Ibid., p. 4.

possessed qualities. A grasp of an object at this level is both self-contradictory and elusive. Self-contradictory in that its presuppositions turn out to be so on philosophical analysis; elusive because the full specification of an object may never finally be achieved. Such a frustrated and frustrating attempt at individuating objects and thus comprehending the world Hegel regards as being involved in the *bad infinite* (*die schlechte Unendlichkeit*).[1] *Qua* infinite task, such a way of approaching experience has to be inadequate in that it cannot yield a complete grasp of experience, the *sine qua non* of man's being at home with the world. Obviously a critic might argue against Hegel that one might be willing to be satisfied with the *relative* specification of a thing but, against this, Hegel would object that so long as there is an aspect of experience which eludes comprehension, which remains inexplicit, then man's relation to the world must have a self-deceptive character. Only a fully-rounded comprehension of the world could overcome man's alienation from it. The way out of this impasse is indicated by Hegel's notion of the *true* or the *good infinite* (*die wahrhafte Unendlichkeit*).[2] Instead of a self-deceptive and self-defeating attempt to grasp something in isolation, the interrelatedness of objects and the correlative concepts for their individuation has to be admitted for it is necessary, Hegel argues, to understand that the identity of an object is parasitic upon its relationship to others. This is not just a matter of the correct attitude of mind towards reality; on the contrary, reality itself exemplifies such a relationship—a point which Hegel makes when he claims that an object in itself has to preserve its identity in and through its relation to the other. This insistence upon the interrelatedness both of things and concepts leads on to the next general section of the *Logik*, that on Relation (*Verhältnis*).[3]

One general point may perhaps be made at this juncture. Hegel has already tried to show that the usual isolated ways in which experience is grasped at the common sense level or at the level of conventional discourse is inadequate and it was of course this isolated comprehension of the world which had contributed to the fragmentation of experience. Consequently when Hegel talks of objects having necessary relations with one another, his point would apply equally well to whole modes of experience, for example science, art and politics. The *Logik* provides the tools for an interconnected grasp of experience and thus does away with its fragmentation into isolated and exclusive spheres, or at least does so when these tools are put to work in the task of explaining in detail a particular form of experience.

[1] Lasson, op. cit., pp. 26–30.
[2] Ibid., pp. 30–4.
[3] Ibid., pp. 34 ff.

The concepts which Hegel discusses in the section on Relation are: Substantial Relations;[1] Causal Relations;[2] and Reciprocity (*Wechselwirkung*).[3] These concepts allow a more adequate, because more integrated, grasp to be taken on experience. Whereas at the level of Simple Connection the isolated individuation of an object was the keynote, at the level of Relation the complete interrelation of things is able to be grasped in an increasing pattern of adequacy by one of the three concepts falling under the general section. This is true, for example, of the notion of substantial relation which asserts an interdependence between a substance and its qualities. A substance is defined through its qualities and at the same time the qualities are only the *qualities* which they are by their relation to a substance. Similarly cause and effect are so because of their relationship, one cannot be defined without the identification of the other. The most general form of these relationships is that of Reciprocity which merely makes explicit in a more general way the drift of the argument of this section of the *Logik*, namely that individual substances and objects exist as such only within the nexus of the relationships which define them. Considered in this light the notion of reciprocity is the crucial one in the move towards a more adequate conceptual structure. It has as its presupposition that experiences and things are interconnected and that the fragmentation of life and experience to be discerned in the modern world is something which at its deepest level does not reflect the structure of being. To make this explicit, however, Hegel sees the need to pass beyond the relations between things which have so far been discussed to the development of the proper form of *Judgement* which would be able to do justice to the integration of objects which has been insisted upon thus far in the argument. This form of judgement, suitable for a comprehensive, philosophical grasp of the object, is developed in the second part of the general section on relation, namely Relation of Thought (*Verhältnis des Denkens*).[4] The theory of adequate judgement advanced in this section of the *Logik* is quite crucial to understanding his mature and more philosophically structured works on political and social experience. For in this section Hegel is dealing with the general form of a judgement which will enable the philosopher to encapsulate a particular structure of experience.

The argument of the section is developed through a discussion of various types of judgement. These forms, listed as they appear in the *Logik* are as follows:

[1] Lasson, op. cit., pp. 36–40.
[2] Ibid., pp. 40–64.
[3] Ibid., pp. 64–76.
[4] Ibid., pp. 76–108.

1. Universal Judgement (*Allgemeines Urteil*)[1]
2. Particular, or specific Judgement (*Partikulares Urteil*)[2]
3. Singular or individual Judgement (*Singuläres Urteil*)[3]
4. Hypothetical Judgement (*Hypothetisches Urteil*)[4]
5. Negative Judgement (*Negatives Urteil*)[5]
6. Infinite Judgement (*Unendliches Urteil*)[6]
7. Disjunctive Judgement (*Disjunktives Urteil*)[7]
8. Accomplished Judgement (*Vollendetes Urteil*)[8]

The major point of importance in this section of the *Logik*, in so far as the argument of this book is concerned, is Hegel's distinction between a universal, a specific and an individual judgement. A grasp of experience might be recorded in a universal judgement so that all specific and individual aspects are obliterated and an example of such a judgement, important for our purpose, might be 'All experience develops self-consciousness'. The difficulty with a grasp of experience recorded in such a judgement is its totally abstract character and its restricted nature. The judgement would be abstract because it would exclude reference to the specific experience of an individual; it would be restricted in that the possible class of such judgements could not be large. In his criticism of the universal judgement taken as adequate on its own account for a grasp of reality Hegel probably had in mind his criticism of the formalism of both Kant and Fichte in their approaches to political experience which he put forward in his essay on Natural Law written at the same time as these logic lectures. Hegel would no doubt have regarded their judgements concerning the relationship between political experience and the human Ego as being merely universal and therefore inadequate.

A specific judgement to some extent escapes the strictures of Hegel upon a purely universal one, but again its major disadvantage is that it does not refer to the individual, detailed case. An example of a specific judgement might be 'Participation in the Assembly of Estates develops self-consciousness' but, without referring to the character of individual experience on the one hand and the universal character of experience on the other, it falls between two stools. Because it does not deal with individual experience it is abstract and thus suffers in a slightly less degree from the same disadvantage as the universal judgement; if it is not seen in relation to some higher order, more comprehensive judgement, it may itself appear as a type of universal assertion. The individual

[1] Lasson, op. cit., pp. 83–4.   [2] Ibid., pp. 84–5.
[3] Ibid., p. 85.   [4] Ibid., pp. 85–8.   [5] Ibid., pp. 88–9.
[6] Ibid., pp. 89–90.   [7] Ibid., pp. 91–2.   [8] Ibid., pp. 93–5.

judgement, on the other hand, steeped in the particularity of a specific perception of experience has the advantage of being concrete but at the same time not really significant for a comprehensive grasp of the character of experience, because it excludes any link with specific or universal judgements about experience. As Hegel probably had in mind his critique of formalism in passing his strictures on the value of the universal judgement, he very probably had in mind his assessment of empiricist approaches in his discussion of individual judgement.

Each form of judgement, therefore, taken on its own is inadequate to provide a comprehensive grasp of experience. The achieved or the accomplished judgement, however, is the one which is adequate for philosophical purposes in that it unites all three judgements, referring to the universal features of a situation or mode of experience along with its specific detail and individual peculiarities. A good example of such a judgement might be thought to be a definition, a concept which Hegel discusses in the *Logik*.[1] Classically, however, a definition would fall under Hegel's notion of a universal judgement and thus be too abstract for philosophical utility. He argues, however, that granted a definition must embody a statement of the universal qualities of a thing or a mode of experience, it must also unite with it detail concerning its specific and individual aspects. Consequently a definition has to be both metaphysical, the source of the universal dimension, and empirical and historical, at least in so far as a definition relevant to the cultural and political world is concerned, yielding the specific and individual element. A definition, therefore, cannot be given in a single proposition but has to be complex, relating the universal element to the detail of the specific and individual case. An example may make Hegel's point more clear. In the philosophical explanation of social and political experience, the universal element in Hegel's view is the development of consciousness through interaction with an intersubjectively perceived environment. But merely to *define* social and political experience in this way does not help to grasp the essence of a *particular* form of social and political experience and its individual character, and yet such a grasp, relevant for the modern world, is essential for the reconciliation of man with his environment. In fact, for all its complexity, Hegel's 'System der Sittlichkeit' was an attempt in this sense to provide a *definition* of politics, in the sense of trying to encapsulate in language the role of political experience with its specific institutions and practices within human life and experience. The *Logik* at this point presents in an extended form what was implied in Hegel's assertion in his essay on

[1] Lasson, op. cit., pp. 108–11.

Fichte and Schelling that his method was to be neither analytic (i.e. universal) nor synthetic (purely individual).

Philosophical thought can therefore grasp reality because it can comprehend the correct interrelations within reality and, of course, such a comprehensive grasp of experience is a gain in self-consciousness and a step forward in overcoming the estrangement of man from his environment. Men are no longer cast adrift in an alien world but rather they live in a milieu which, though not a product of their mind, contributes to the development of minds in a necessary and irreplaceable way and can be absolutely comprehended by the philosopher.

A change of emphasis at this point leads Hegel to his crucial insight, the metaphysical insight which enables him to secure the harmony between thought and being, the reconciliation between man and the world. If philosophical thought can comprehend reality and, when achieved, can constitute the full articulation of self-consciousness, then this possibility must have been immanent in the situation from the beginning so that both the natural and social worlds can be seen as having as their goal the comprehension of the way in which they develop the human mind. The world is, therefore, shot through with this end, having the *telos* of the achievement of self-consciousness built into it, this telos being made plain and intelligible in Hegel's own philosophy, through the comprehensive and total grasp of the relationship between the mind and its environment.[1] How this goal is actually structured into the fabric of the world will be discussed more fully in the next chapter but the answer has already been intimated in the whole discussion of Hegel's philosophy thus far. Spirit is for Hegel the agent in which the harmony between thought and reality is achieved, an achievement fully grasped in philosophy. The philosopher is able to describe the way in which Spirit develops in both the world of nature and in the social world and is able to discern in this development the crucial connection between such patterns of development and the realization of the central features of the human mind.

The *Logik*, as it stands, is formal and abstract, indicating the concepts in and through which a grasp may be taken on experience. But, at the

---

[1] Hegel's argument is, of course, circular. He presupposes that the world can be comprehended and develops a logic to show how reality can be caught in a particular net of concepts. When this logical system is worked out it is then used to justify the view that the possibility of this comprehension must be immanent in the world. There is no independent check on the congruence between the conceptual structure of the *Logik* and reality; nor could there possibly be. Hegel's assertion of the harmony between thought and being, despite his dialectical virtuosity in an attempt to prove the contrary, remains a presupposition which is neither rationally checkable nor disprovable.

same time, these conceptual tools have to be put to work in describing the development of experience in the world in such a way that its goal-directed nature is brought out, so that the individual can grasp his experience as being part of the realization of Spirit whose goal is the achievement of self-consciousness in the minds of men. Nature is the cradle of the development of consciousness and *Naturphilosophie* constitutes in both *Realphilosophie I* and *II* the next progressive section after the development of logic. Nature is not for Hegel a construction of the human mind but can be grasped philosophically as having the eventual emergence of mind as its aim and as such it is shot through with Spirit:

Nature exists in Spirit as such and it is its essence.[1]

Hegel's discussion of the relationship between human life and the natural world is a central part of his social concern and refers back to his earlier, somewhat romantic discussion of the Greeks' relation to nature. The Greeks stood in a naïve, intuitive, harmonious relationship to nature. The world was accepted by them as being a benign environment as the home of the divine. With the development of science and consequent technological changes the world had become disenchanted, with the result that men have come to feel less and less at home in it. In his lectures on *Naturphilosophie* Hegel attempted to show that even when the world is considered through the less romantic eyes of modern science it can be understood both in general and in detail as a milieu geared to the emergence of human life and the realization of consciousness. The natural world is not, therefore, a hostile environment, from which men ought to feel estranged; rather, the various natural modes can be seen as necessary presuppositions of conscious life in general and self-conscious life, attained in a philosophical grasp of this development, in particular. *Naturphilosophie*, therefore, has a social dimension because a conceptual grasp of the way in which Spirit realizes itself in Nature is a precondition of understanding the development of consciousness in human life and is in itself a way in which the general problem of estrangement between the person and the world is overcome.

In the sections on *Geistesphilosophie* in *Jenenser Realphilosophie I* and *II* Hegel attempts to provide a comprehensive, universal, specific and individual grasp of the relationship between the human mind as it has emerged from nature and how the various modes of experience confronting man develop in an intelligible manner his human powers.

---

[1] *Jenenser Realphilosophie I*, ed. Lasson, ed. cit., p. 191.

Although these two works differ from one another in some respects, these differences are of marginal importance and will be ignored for the purposes of this book and consequently the arguments will be taken together.

Following his position in 'System der Sittlichkeit' Hegel argues that the primordial form of human consciousness and human organization is not differentiated, not specific. There is no consciousness of individuality, only communal consciousness. This is the first primeval form in which consciousness exists after its emergence from nature. This communal consciousness becomes specific and individualized initially in the development of language. He argues that language gives some kind of power over the world—through it aspects of the world may be ordered and differentiated with the result that the world appears to become amenable to the activity of the human mind:

> The first act by which Adam constituted his domination over animals was to give them a name.[1]

He makes this point more succinctly in *Realphilosophie II* when he says:

> To give a name is the sign of majesty.[2]

At the same time language is not something merely 'fitted on' to reality. Hegel argues that in fact reality is such that its nature is to be comprehended linguistically—a point which he makes in a somewhat oblique way in the ambiguity of the German:

> Die Bildung der Welt zum Sprechen ist an sich vorhanden.[3]

This developing mastery of the external world through language leads to a correlative change in man's conception of himself. The individual becomes able through the use of language to distinguish his own experience from that of others and in such a way each person's conception of his individuality begins to take root. The use of language is, therefore, a gain in self-consciousness but at the same time this gain is possible only as a result of the fragmentation of the primeval pattern of social organization from which Hegel starts his analysis. Here again we see the preoccupation of Hegel in trying to grasp the educative role of fragmentation and dissonance in human life. From another angle, however, the fragmentation in personal relationships produced by language leads to the development of new patterns of integration in that language is *shared* by all members of the community. Language has a dual function, developing the consciousness of the individual and

[1] *Realphilosophie I*, ed. cit., p. 211.   [2] *Ibid., II*, ed. cit., p. 183.
[3] *Ibid., I*, ed. cit., p. 235.

uniting such individuals through their use of symbols. Hegel insists upon the social dimension of language when he says:

Language exists only as the language of the people.[1]

—a point which he re-emphasizes later in the same section when he argues:

Language is the means whereby a people expresses what is its essence and its being.[2]

Language is the first form of human experience wherein man begins to take control of his environment but even so the pattern of integration set up between man and the world through language is very formal. The world is certainly appropriated by thought, but at the same time it remains, in a sense, as it was. Language does not change the world—a point which Hegel makes when he says:

Language is only the ideal existence of consciousness.[3]

Self-consciousness in the sense of the control and manipulation of environment is achieved far more completely in labour and the use of tools.[4] Labour is the way *par excellence* through which a man moulds the world to his own patterns of meaning, transforming it to satisfy his own desires and is able to see in such transformations the reflection of his own personality. Labour lifts man above the animals because man *uses* his environment to satisfy his desires, whereas the animal is a merely passive consumer, annihilating it in appropriating it:

The simple satisfaction of desire is the obliteration of the object.[5]

In labour a man makes concrete his projects and intentions, moulding the world to his will:

The things which satisfy needs are *products* . . . Labour is the activity of making consciousness concrete.[6]

Again a mode of human activity in interaction with an environment, though not created by the activity but amenable to its development, is seen by Hegel to involve differentiation—men become more and more aware of their own individuality and thus old, naïve patterns of integration which cannot accommodate such conceptions break down. At the

[1] *Realphilosophie I*, ed. cit., p. 235.   [2] Ibid., p. 235.
[3] Ibid., p. 227.
[4] Ibid., pp. 235 ff., and *Realphilosophie II*, pp. 297 ff.
[5] *Realphilosophie II*, ed. cit., p. 197.   [6] Ibid., p. 214.

same time, however, the labouring process brings with it new patterns of relationship. The use of tools, Hegel argues, links one generation to another in that tools and working techniques endure over time and men of a later generation imitate and extend the experience of an earlier one.[1] More important, however, are family life and the foundations of property. Hegel argues that marriage, based on love, grows naturally out of man's consciousness of himself in the labouring process in that such consciousness is purely external, devoted to appropriating the external environment. There is no reciprocity between the world and man, it is in this sense, therefore, a one-sided relationship. There is a need for a relationship within which a man will find his own capacities and powers recognized by another of the same species, a relationship which finds expression in love and marriage. Along with the foundation of the family goes the possession of property for the family has to secure to itself whatever is necessary for its corporate existence. Labour, therefore, is at once an agent of differentiation, distancing one man from another, but at the same time other, mediated patterns of integration, marriage and the possession of property may be seen to develop naturally out of the labouring process.[2]

At the same time, however, it might be argued that after the dissolution of the primeval community mediated, differentiated forms of social integration have not gone very far. Although in marriage and the family individuals are united by bonds of love and obligation, such relationships are obviously restricted. No *overall* patterns of community have emerged to replace the close-knit life of the communal primeval situation. Indeed, the reverse is the case. Each family confronts similar families unrelated to one another through some higher level institutions. Society is an amalgam of molecular families. In such an isolated state each family needs to have its property secured by the recognition of its right to it by other such property-owning families. The recognition of this right is crucial for the development of self-consciousness because property is the result of labour and labour is the realization of consciousness in its external form. This struggle for recognition (*der Kampf des Annerkennens*)[3] is destructive without some higher order, rule-governed practice within which the title to property rights can be recognized. The struggle must be destructive because each side involved has to take it seriously in that its own self-consciousness is at stake. Considered in

[1] *Realphilosophie I*, p. 221.
[2] There is an interesting discussion of Hegel's teaching of the Jena period in Jürgen Habermas, 'Arbeit und Interaktion' in *Technik und Wissenschaft als Ideologie*, Frankfurt 1968.
[3] *Realphilosophie I*, pp. 226–32; *Realphilosophie II*, pp. 209–12.

this sense the struggle for recognition is a contradiction.[1] Recognition is crucial for self-consciousness but the severity of the struggle entails the obliteration of the consciousness of one side involved in the struggle. The realization of this contradiction leads to the development of a higher order dimension of social life within which the title to property and thus self-consciousness may be achieved. Such a dimension Hegel calls the Nation or *Volk* with its concrete interpersonal norms, its rule-governed standards and its political and juridical authority.[2]

Of course labour continues within such a political community. Indeed Hegel links up the character of the community, its spirit, with the labour performed within it:

> The spirit of the people has to change itself immediately in labour, that is to say in so much as it is always a spirit in development.[3]

However, although the character of the community is in this sense predicated upon the labour performed within it, this character transcends the labour of individuals:

> They produce this spirit but they venerate it as an entity which exists for itself.[4]

Again labour produces its own form of integration, this time a political and juridical order which is able to point a way out of the impasse involved in the struggle for recognition. The state has to concede the right of the individual to property, to protect such a right, and in so doing it concedes recognition, within a political framework of the character of the individual as a conscious, individual agent.

As labour develops so the patterns of integration become more and more complex. Wants multiply and means of satisfying such wants have to be produced and this leads to a progressive division of labour. A man no longer labours to satisfy his own needs, but those of others too. Consequently within the overall political community of the Nation a new complex type of interdependence is generated:

> The individual satisfies his needs by his labour but not by the particular product of his labour.[5]

Each man still labours to satisfy his needs but the relation between labour and his own personal needs is now a mediated one. He uses the products of his labour either to barter or secure money to satisfy his needs by acquiring the products of another's labour:

[1] *Realphilosophie I*, p. 230.
[2] Ibid., pp. 231 ff.; *Realphilosophie II*, pp. 212 ff.
[3] *Realphilosophie I*, p. 232.   [4] Ibid., p. 233.   [5] Ibid., p. 238.

Needs are multiplied. . . . Universal labour is also a division of labour. Each individual because he is an individual works to satisfy his needs. The content of his labour becomes something over and above his need. He labours to satisfy the needs of many and himself at the same time. Each therefore satisfies the needs of many and the satisfaction of the many particular needs is the labour of others.[1]

Again with the division of labour there is a development of self-consciousness, of differentiation, of individuality, of growing power over the natural world and again this seeming dissolution of bonds between men appears on reflection to involve complex patterns of mutual interdependence. Modern industrializing society is not merely a desert comprised of isolated individuals, enervated in their own powers by their concentration on one aspect of the labouring process, but a complicated system of relationship between one man and another through the system of needs. Hegel is, however, prepared to take up at this point his earlier critique of industrialism even though he can now see its positive value in developing the powers of the human person and in providing new patterns of mutual relationship.

The patterns of integration secured through the system of needs cannot be ignored; they do provide the basis of community appropriate to the modern world. But Hegel argues that the person within the system has no grasp of the way in which he is integrated into society. He has no perception of the complex exchange relationships which turn the pursuit of private satisfaction into a means of social integration. The system Hegel argues is one of 'incalculable, blind interdependence'. Whereas the Greek individual had felt an intuitive sense of belonging to his community, the modern man can become aware of it only at the cost of a great deal of intellectual effort and even those who had spent a great deal of time describing the underlying mechanism of integration into commercial society still found it exceedingly obscure. Adam Smith, for example, called it the 'hidden hand' and Mirabeau considered it to be a 'magical process'. In Hegel's view it is the role of the state in *regulating* the operation of commercial relationships which makes the system both calculable and rational and thus enables man to see within commercial society a mode of integration appropriate to the change in the human condition. He indicates the need for strong state regulation of economic relationships in the following passage:

Society becomes a vast system of community and mutual inter-dependence, a moving life of the dead. The system moves this way

---

[1] *Realphilosophie II*, pp. 214–15.

and that in a blind and elemental fashion and like a wild animal calls for permanent control and curbing.[1]

Only when such operations are rule-governed and such rules have been made explicit can a man have a rational grasp of his mode of integration into the community. A conceptual grasp of such integration could, therefore, only be fully developed in a society with sufficient state control of economic activity. The development of such political institutions was for Hegel the prerequisite for the solution of the problem of social fragmentation in the modern world. As will be seen below, Hegel saw in the state too the way of solving the personal dimension of the problem, the enervation of the human powers in the division of labour. Only within such a society with its economic structure regulated by the state could the philosopher provide the grasp of the situation, the recognition of which would reconcile men to their environment.

At this point it is arguable that there is a tension in Hegel's work if it is taken in a German rather than a European context. He had eschewed political reform in favour of philosophical comprehension and yet he had already committed himself to the view in 'Die Verfassung Deutschlands' that there was in Germany no such state control:

The German political edifice is nothing but the sum of the rights which the individual parts have wrested from the whole and the system of justice which carefully watches that no power is left over to the state is the essence of the Constitution.[2]

Taken in the German context Hegel's writing about the role of the state vis à vis economic activity appears, inconsistently, to be in the prescriptive mode. In a broader context, however, the objection has much less force because Napoleon was introducing into both France and Italy at this time modifications to the power of the political authorities to regulate, at least in some minimal fashion, the economic and commercial relationships of modern society. In his lectures Hegel appears to be trying to provide a philosophical grasp of the politico-economic role of the progressive modern state. Such an attitude towards the political reforms of Napoleon and perhaps an anticipation that they might be introduced into Germany goes a long way towards explaining Hegel's enthusiastic response to Napoleon's victory at the battle of Jena in 1806 when in a letter Hegel referred to him as the 'world soul'.[3]

Hegel's second reason for insisting upon the necessity of state

[1] *Realphilosophie I*, op. cit., p. 240. The description 'bürgerliche Gesellschaft' appears first in Hegel's work in Nohl, p. 44.
[2] Lasson, *Schriften zur Politik und Rechtsphilosophie*, ed. cit., p. 14.
[3] *Briefe*, ed. cit., p. 119.

regulation of the operation of commercial society was connected with the possible enervation of the powers of the individual within the system, predicated as it was upon the progressive division of labour. Hegel did not go so far as he had gone in his younger days in passing strictures upon this situation—his reading of Steuart and Schiller had convinced him that modern commercial society was both part of the fate of modern man and that it had also actualized some important human values and powers. At the same time he was still much concerned with the remaining baneful effects of the division of labour on the individual, effects which he saw as being mitigated in the structure of the modern state and its relationship both to the economic system and to the individual. In a passage reminiscent of his own earlier writings and of those of others of his generation cited earlier in this book Hegel argues that within the progressive division of labour:

> The faculties of the individual are restricted and the consciousness of (the factory worker) is degraded to the lowest level of dullness.[1]

Man becomes a spiritless enervated being. He is fragmented and his human powers are not fully utilized, a point which Hegel makes with reference to Adam Smith's description of a pin factory in *An Enquiry into the Nature and Causes of the Wealth of Nations*.[2] The poor position of the factory worker within the commercial system requires some degree of state regulation of the economic system:

> A mass of the population is condemned to the stupifying, unhealthy and insecure labour of the factories, manufactures, mines and so on. . . . Whole branches of industry which supported a large bulk of the population suddenly collapse because the model changes or because the value of the products fall on account of new inventions in other countries or for other reasons. Whole masses are therefore abandoned to helpless poverty . . . this inequality of wealth and poverty, this need and this necessity turn into the utmost dismemberment of the will, inner rebellion and hatred.[3]

This enervation of the human being constitutes Hegel's second argu-

---

[1] *Realphilosophie I*, p. 239. It is possible that Hegel's hitherto intellectual appreciation of this problem was made more concrete by his experience in Frankfurt. Frankfurt had a fairly well developed factory system; see Goethe, *Dichtung und Wahrheit*, ed. cit., Bk. 1.

[2] Hegel cites the discussion from p. 8 of the German translation of the work translated by Christoph Garve published in Breslau 1794–6. Hegel's discussion appears in *Realphilosophie I*, p. 238, and, as usual, he quotes incorrectly from memory.

[3] *Realphilosophie II*, pp. 232–3.

ment for state intervention and it is instructive to compare Hegel's argument with that of Steuart discussed earlier.[1] The arguments are so similar that surely Steuart's profound influence on Hegel's thinking about the role of the state *vis à vis* the economic dimension of society cannot be doubted. In Steuart's account the 'statesman' is 'the legislator and supreme power according to the form of government' and his theory does not entail any particular view of the desirable political character of the state—for example whether it should be monarchical, despotic, democratic or whatever. Its function was to regulate economic activity and as such his argument does not entail any view about the political complexion of such a government. Hegel, however, wished to argue that only state regulation of the economy by a political authority of a special kind could save the inner life of man within the commercial system. Only a state which provided some means of participation to the individual could help to overcome this enervation of the personality and enable him to pursue less private, less restricted ends. Hegel very clearly retained in his mind the picture of the alienation of man from the state in the post Greek world which he painted in 'Die Positivität der christlichen Religion':

> The picture of the state as the product of his own energies disappeared from the citizen's soul. The care and oversight of the whole rested upon one man or a few . . . the administration of the state machine was entrusted to a small number of citizens and they served only as cogs . . . the citizen lived in a polity with which no joy could be associated.[2]

Such an emphasis on the estranged character of the modern state was entirely lacking in Steuart. He was concerned merely to secure state

[1] See Steuart in Skinner, op. cit., p. 122. It is probable that Steuart, paradoxically enough in the circumstances, derived his point of view on state intervention from the writings of the Cameralists in Germany, particularly from Justi's *Staatswirtschaft, oder systematische Abhandlung aller Oekonomischen und Cameralwissenschaften*, 1755. Steuart had lived in Germany for a time and had been in contact with some professors from the University of Tübingen (see Skinner's introduction to his edition of Steuart's works). Certainly Steuart's argument for state intervention was very badly received by reviewers in this country—see the *Monthly Review*, vol. 36 (1767). Steuart made a reply to his critics which perhaps bears out the point about Cameralist influence:

'Can it be supposed that during an absence of near 20 years I should find my studies have been all the while modelling my speculations on the standard English notions?'

See Skinner, op. cit., p. 2. I have benefited much in the next few pages from many talks with Geraint Parry.

[2] Nohl, op. cit., p. 223.

regulation of commercial activity and was not concerned particularly about the character of such a state. Hegel wished to go much further than Steuart and his Cameralist mentors, a point which shows up particularly well in 'Die Verfassung Deutschlands'. The dominant image of the state in Cameralist thought was that of the state as a machine, a conception which appears particularly clearly in the work of Justi who argues that:

> A properly constituted state must be exactly analogous to a machine in which all the wheels and gears are precisely adjusted to one another; the ruler must be the foreman, the mainspring of the soul— if one may use the expression which sets everything in motion.[1]

The emphasis in Cameralist thought was upon administrative efficiency not upon the kind of political authority overseeing the administrative machine. Geraint Parry has made this point particularly clearly:

> The theory was fundamentally indifferent to constitutional issues, as Sonnenfels revealed by basing his *Über die Liebe des Vaterlands* explicitly on Pope's couplet:
>
> > For forms of Government let fools contest
> > Whate'er is best administered is best.[2]

In 'Die Verfassung Deutschlands' Hegel describes what may be the views of the Cameralists and by implication those of Steuart in a passage which reads very much like the quotation from Justi:

> In recent theories, carried partly into effect,[3] the fundamental presupposition is that a state is a machine with a single spring which imparts movement to the rest of the wheel in its infinite complexity and that all the institutions in the nature of society should proceed from the supreme public authority and be regulated, commanded and overseen by it.[4]

The function of the state in modern society, according to Hegel, is not merely to control and regulate commercial relationships, although such control is essential to a rational grasp of man's integration into the

[1] Justi, *Gesammelte Politische und Finanzschriften*, Copenhagen and Leipzig 1761, vol. III, pp. 86–7.
[2] G. B. Parry, 'Enlightened Government and its Critics in Eighteenth Century Germany', *Historical Journal*, vol. VI, no. 2, 1963, p. 183.
[3] The phrase 'partly put into effect' seems to imply that Hegel is thinking here of the Cameralists who were active in administration rather than for example, about Fichte's *Der geschlossene Handelstaat* of 1800.
[4] Lasson, *Schriften zur Politik und Rechtsphilosophie*, op. cit., p. 28. Cf. Dok. ed. Hoffmeister, p. 220.

modern world, but also to provide some means through institutions which would allow some individual participation in the state to overcome the enervation of the personality developed in the manufacturing processes of modern industry. Control of commercial relationships and efficient administration, Hegel argued, were not the only criteria of good government:

> The pedantic craving to determine every detail, the illiberal jealousy of any arrangements whereby an estate, a corporation, etc., adjusts and manages its own affairs, this means carping at any independent action of the citizens which would only have some public bearing and not a bearing on the public authority is clothed in the garb of rational principles. . . . This is not the place to argue at length that the centre as the public authority, i.e. the government, must leave to the freedom of citizens whatever is not necessary for its appointed function of organizing and maintaining authority and thus for its security at home and abroad. Nothing should be so sacrosanct to the government as facilitating and protecting the free activity of citizens in matters other than this . . . for the freedom of citizens is inherently sacrosanct.[1]

Hegel seems to be trying to steer a *via media* between non-intervention in the economic life of the community which would be disastrous for he regarded the state as the means of regulating and thus making rational the patterns of integration achieved in the system of needs, and too much intervention which was implicitly allowed in the theories of Steuart and the Cameralists. Too little intervention could make social life anarchic and further alienate modern man from it; too much intervention on the other hand would be dangerous in that individuals would not be able to pursue their own interests as private individuals and at the same time too oppressive a state would not allow any role for individual participation in government at a local or a national level. Yet Hegel saw in the possibility of such participation some way out of the baneful personal consequences of the division of labour. He makes the point about the role of involvement in government with reference to Prussia:

> But what life and what sterility reigns in another equally well regulated state, in the Prussian, strikes anyone who sets foot in the first town there or sees its complete lack of scientific or artistic genius.[2]

The state has to regulate commercial relationships, to secure the grasp

[1] Lasson, op. cit., pp. 28–9.   [2] Ibid., p. 31.

of the integration of modern man into his environment, but at the same time the state has both to allow unregulated activity, unstructured by political authority, and equally important, provide institutional means whereby men may be involved in government and thus be lifted out of the particularity of interest and their own private concerns. In 'Die Verfassung Deutschlands' he argues that modern states are far too large for direct democracy but contends that:

> Each estate, city, town, commune, etc., can itself enjoy freedom to do and to execute what lies in its area.[1]

It is quite possible that Hegel derived his perception of this aspect of the role of the modern state from Justus Möser, one of the most perceptive and trenchant critics of Cameralist thought in Germany. Certainly at this time Hegel sets more store by the role of the Estates as a means whereby individuals could come to have a role in politics and it was, among other things, the Estates on which Möser concentrated. Möser rejected what he called the academic, rationalistic theorizing of the Cameralists:

> The men of the central department would like, so it seems, to reduce everything to simple principles. If they had their way the state would permit herself to be governed by an academic theory.[2]

Möser rejected the view of administration and the relation between the state and society presupposed in Cameralist thought, because in imposing uniform laws on a pluralistic and variegated social order the Cameralists departed:

> from the true plan of nature which reveals her wealth in variety and we pave the way for a new despotism which forces everything to a few rules and thereby loses the wealth of variety.[3]

Hegel's conception of the role of the state at this and indeed all subsequent stages of his thinking is linked closely to the ideals which he had held as a youth, overcoming the fragmentation of society and the enervation of the person. At the same time the two dimensional nature of these ideals, one social and the other personal, leads him to a conception of the state which overcomes the polarities of political thinking present in his own intellectual context. He sees in the state regulation of commercial activity the precondition of providing a full

[1] Lasson, op. cit., p. 27.
[2] J. Möser, *Sämtliche Werke*, ed. Abeker, Berlin 1842–3, vol. II, p. 20.
[3] Ibid., vol. II, p. 21. Both of these references are taken from Geraint Parry's article.

and profound grasp of the means of integration and relationship available in modern society and as such the modern state could provide the basis of community life and solve the social dimension of Hegel's problem. Of course the state could only partially solve the problem; its role in regulating modern society had to be grasped philosophically before a full solution could be obtained. At the same time the personal dimension of the problem, the enervation of the person in industrial society, pulled Hegel towards the other polarity, namely that the state should allow the individual free rein to realize himself in other activities besides his labour and at the same time provide him with a role in the government of the community to lift him out of his particular and private pursuits. Only a state which could provide for both of these conditions could be adequate as the precondition of community in the modern world.

In *Realphilosophie II*, Hegel discusses the development of three main types of government and looks at them in conjunction with their appropriate social environment. The three types are Tyranny, Democracy and Hereditary Monarchy. Tyranny he regards as the lowest and least developed form of the state. Such a state is appropriate and possible within a social context in which there is very little social differentiation, in which man has not developed a conception of himself as an individual. Consequently the total domination of one man does no violence to this social and personal background. In modern society, however, Hegel argues, based upon the division of labour and the differentiation of function, with its correlative development of the human personality such a form of political authority is both outmoded and cannot exist without violence and oppression.

Democracy supersedes such a primitive form of authority *pari passu* with the development of labour and the realization of individuality on the part of men. Hegel speaks in this context of a total participatory *polis* democracy. Such a form of democracy, Hegel argues, can exist only when the split has not yet occurred between the individual as a citizen and as a private person, when there is a total identity of interest between personal interest and civic duty.[1] Obviously, given Hegel's link between developments in the labouring process and the realization of various aspects of consciousness, such a *polis* type democracy must presuppose a fairly restricted kind of economic and social infrastructure. Such a form of political organization, for precisely this reason, is however, inappropriate in modern society, with its progressive division of labour.

Hereditary monarchy Hegel sees as the natural and fitting form of

[1] *Realphilosophie II*, op. cit., p. 249.

political authority in the modern world, satisfying the two criteria of adequacy implied in 'Die Verfassung Deutschlands'. A monarch is in an ideal position to oversee the regulation of commercial relationships which would remove the blind and anarchic character of the latter. The monarch is able to be involved in this regulation *sine ira et studio* in that he stands outside of commercial relationships, he has not any particular interests, he belongs to no social class and to no occupational groups. An hereditary monarchy, complemented of course by advisers and councils, is able to fulfil the first role which Hegel saw for the modern state. The second role, overcoming the particularity of individual interest and giving man, enervated by his labour in the manufacturing system, some universal conceptions, is able to be fulfilled by some kind of representation through Estates. Direct participation as was implied in his discussion of democracy is impossible given the social and personal infrastructure of modern society, with the gap between private interest and the state's, between man as bourgeois and man as citizen. Hegel envisages three estates, the substantial estate, comprising the landed gentry, the acquisitive estate, representing business and commercial interests, and the universal estate of civil servants who attend to the needs of the community *per se*. Apart from the universal estate, members are envisaged as being elected and Hegel insists that each sphere within society, towns, guilds and other such organizations, should administer their own affairs so far as is consistent with the maintenance of the role of the monarch.[1] Considered in this way, therefore, such a state would satisfy the criteria laid down in 'Die Verfassung Deutschlands' for the political dimension to an adequate community in the modern world.

It might be objected to Hegel's argument that it is inconsistent with his professed aim, to grasp what is and to eschew theorizing in the prescriptive mode. Against this, a point tentatively asserted earlier in the book may be made with more confidence about this stage of Hegel's development, namely that he was attempting to grasp the European trend in political development and not the merely German. Napoleon had through his *Civil Code* introduced a good many regulations into the commercial sphere and in Italy after his conquest he introduced a political system which at one and the same time involved the acceptance of Napoleonic legislation concerning commercial relationships and also involved a measure of political representation through the three estates, the *possodenti*, the *merchanti* and the *dotti*. Small wonder in the circumstances that Hegel welcomed Napoleon's victory at the battle of Jena because he naturally had hoped that he would introduce similar reforms

[1] *Realphilosophie II*, op. cit., p. 251.

into Germany which Hegel very clearly regarded as a political back-water. In a letter to Niethammer, he brings out what has been implied that he saw—namely trend of political authority in the modern world going in the way in which Napoleon was directing it:

> The Emperor—this world soul—riding on horseback through the city to the review of his troops—it is indeed a wonderful feeling to see such a man.[1]

Indeed, Hegel's hopes were not disappointed. Either under Napoleon's direction or inspired by his example, major political reforms were undertaken in Germany during the period following the battle of Jena. Nowhere were these reforms taken further on the lines which Hegel envisaged than in Prussia at the instigation of Baron von Stein.[2] The major political reform which von Stein introduced was some measure of local and provincial government. He advocated revitalizing or establishing in places where they had not hitherto existed provincial diets to which members could be elected by their respective communities. Simon comments of Stein's reforms thus:

> Certainly the effect was to set a precedent both for active participation of provincial representative assemblies in provincial government and for limited extension of membership in such assemblies to classes other than the nobility. The free peasants, having assumed the same financial obligations as the noble landowners, were entitled to the same rights which included a voice in future disposition of the province's financial problems.[3]

Such changes in the political structure of Prussia fitted in very well indeed with Hegel's criterion of the maximum autonomy in government where possible. Indeed, Stein gave his own proposals an almost Hegelian justification when he wrote that he hoped that his reforms would lead to:

> the reawakening of a spirit of community and civic pride, the employment of dormant or misapplied energies and of unused knowledge.[4]

Another of Stein's reforms was the abolition of serfdom, which in Prussia almost amounted to slavery.[5] Again, Hegel could see in this the

---

[1] *Briefe*, op. cit., p. 119.
[2] On Stein, see Simon, *The Failure of the Prussian Reform Movement 1807–19*, Cornell, 1955.
[3] Simon, op. cit., p. 31.
[4] In Botzenhart (ed.), *Stein*, vol. II, p. 210, Berlin 1957.
[5] See Bruford, op. cit., pp. 108–9.

gradual percolation through the political and social system the conception of the rights and powers of the individual actualized in the labouring processes. At the same time Stein laboured to make the Prussian monarchy more constitutional by removing from Frederick William III most of his personal aides and secretaries who were able to influence policy without being responsible for it. These reforms, coupled with the already existing machinery for regulating commercial activities, made Prussia, given Hegel's principles, the most progressive state in Europe—a state which by combining the polarities of regulation of commercial aspects of society with some measure of self-government and participation in government where possible, provided the groundwork for the recovery of community in the modern world. How far Hegel considered the role of the modern state to be indebted to the perception of Napoleon is well revealed in one of his letters, written in 1807:

> In Berg the Diet still exists. When it was abolished in Wurtemberg Napoleon said severely to the Wurtembergian Minister 'I have made your master a sovereign, not a despot', German princes have not yet grasped the concept of a free monarchy or attempted its realization. Napoleon will have to organize it all.[1]

An hereditary monarchy, with regulations and administrative machinery to control the anarchy of commercial relations combined with some measure of mediated participation and as much local autonomy as possible provided the basis of the type of political community appropriate to the present stage in the human condition. Of course these features of the modern state and its relation to society have to be grasped by the philosopher both in terms of their development and their relation to the realization of self-consciousness, otherwise they would appear as merely arbitrary matters of convenience and not as essential features of human reconciliation and integration in the modern world. Understood in these terms, Kojève's comment on Hegel may seem appropriate:

> Is not this Hegel a thinker endowed with absolute knowledge because on the one hand he lives in Napoleon's time and on the other is the only one to understand him?[2]

[1] *Briefe*, op. cit., p. 185. In the letter Hegel calls Napoleon 'der grosse Staatsrechtslehrer'. In a letter of 11 February 1808 he goes further and says à propos of Germany, 'Nothing happens spontaneously and as a consequence of one's own judgement for where is it to be found?; and so Heaven's, that is to say the French Emperor's, will must decree it', p. 218.

[2] A. Kojève, *Introduction à la lecture de Hegel*, Paris 1947, p. 164.

Philosophy making explicit the form of political community implictly articulated in the modern state is, therefore, the key to community. In this way Hegel's political and social philosophy is shot through with his metaphysics. His social and political thought as we have seen it develop is not some detachable addendum to a metaphysic, rather that metaphysic is itself, however abstract, a very manifestation of this concern.

One aspect of Hegel's youthful diagnosis of the malaise of contemporary society which so far has not been seen to appear in his developing mature system is the divisive role of Christianity. It might well be argued that without some comprehensive treatment of Christianity and how it is reconciled to the emerging form of community in the modern world, Hegel's developing thought must be seen as incomplete. Certainly in his Jena lectures his discussions of religion are both abstract and incomplete, but sufficient pointers may be gained taking all the works of the Jena period, excluding *Die Phänomenologie des Geistes*, for us to be able to see the kind of solution which he saw to the divisive effect of Christianity which had so much preoccupied his thoughts earlier. Religion is not mentioned in *Realphilosophie I*, in fact the manuscript finishes after his demand for state intervention in a quite unsatisfactory manner, but in *Realphilosophie II* it is dealt with at some length but in a highly abstract and elusive manner, so much so that we have to go to his other works to gain some idea of the kind of interpretation of the religion of the modern world which Hegel has in mind. Hegel appears to assert that in some way religion is a totally social activity not inconsistent with the state, and in fact he goes much further than this:

. . . the state stands above all; it is Spirit which knows itself as the universal essence and reality. . . .

The state is the reality of the kingdom of heaven.[1] These are paradoxical and extravagant remarks. Particularly paradoxical in that Hegel had in his earlier days regarded Christianity as an anti-communitarian religion. Now he links up in an extraordinary fashion the Christian concept of the kingdom of God with membership of a modern state. Hegel gives no extended explanation of his view and his developing position has to be reconstructed from intimations in other works of the period. The key to the solution of the problem is the use of the word 'Spirit' in the quotation cited above. As was seen in his essay 'Glauben und Wissen' Hegel links up the metaphysical notion of Spirit realizing itself in nature and in human life with the activity of God in the world. His political and social philosophy articulated in both 'System der

---

[1] *Realphilosophie II*, op. cit., pp. 267 and 270.

Sittlichkeit' and in *Realphilosophie I* and *II* constituted an attempt to comprehend social and political experience as the way in which Spirit realizes itself in the world, or, given the link in 'Glauben und Wissen', as the way in which God realizes himself in the world. The modern state, providing the reality of political community when comprehended philosophically, could therefore be seen as the highest articulation of Spirit, or God in the contemporary world. Consequently religion, dealing in a different kind of way with the being and activity of God, cannot be inconsistent with the modern state when grasped philosophically because the state, when seen in this way, is a supreme manifestation of the activity of God in the world. The other aspect of the Christian bifurcation of experience was the remoteness and otherness of God, the infinite lord of the universe, totally divorced from the world and self complete. Again 'Glauben und Wissen' helps us to understand the way in which Hegel solved this threat to community. We saw earlier that Hegel took the view that, considered as merely infinite, the conception of God is inadequate, his infinite being has to be united to the finitude of worldly life and experience, a conception which provides a rationale for what appeared as the 'infinite grief of the crucifixion'. Considered as the concrete way in which God is united to the world, the crucifixion was, therefore, a stage in the development of the life of God in the world, a development which can be understood as he was later to say through *Vorstellungen* in religion but through *Begriffe* in philosophy. The activity of God in the world can be known and comprehended by the philosopher[1] and thus God no longer appears as remote and beyond the world but as the animating force in both nature and in human life and community, reaching the zenith of this activity in the creation of a new kind of political community in the modern world, appropriate to the changed condition of human experience, itself part of the realization of Spirit/God. Christianity still has to be reinterpreted before it can provide an adequate religious sense of community and in this sense Hegel's developing religious philosophy harks back to 'Das Leben Jesu'. In that essay, however, the reinterpretation was from very different presuppositions.

Within the lectures, essays and articles of the Jena period, therefore, we can see the intimations of his mature system in and through which his early ideals become satisfied. Certainly Hegel's philosophy has been criticized for its inhumane elements but it nevertheless has as its centre and as its presupposition that profoundly moral humanistic concern for the fate of man, his religion and his society in the modern world which characterized his very earliest work.

---

[1] Glockner, op. cit., vol. I, pp. 292–3.

Chapter VI

Reason, Reconciliation and Community

We shall not cease from exploration,
And the end of our exploring
Shall be to arrive where we started
And know the place for the first time.
T. S. Eliot

So far this book has concentrated upon Hegel's development but in this chapter an attempt will be made to outline the main features of his mature philosophical system, relating it to the pattern of his development discerned so far. His mature philosophical position will be treated in this chapter in a profoundly unhegelian way in that it will be discussed in both abridged and abstract terms, its detail, at least so far as social and political thought is concerned, being treated in the next chapter.[1] Such an attempt is unhegelian in that it presupposes what in fact he is concerned to deny, namely that there is a gap between form and content in philosophy and it would also seem to ignore Hegel's view that philosophy, uniting the universal with the individual and the specific, has both to be complex and incapable of being understood in an abstract fashion. The approach adopted in the chapter, however, has some justification in that, the above observations notwithstanding, Hegel does in fact discuss his philosophical programme in abstract terms particularly in the Preface to *Die Phänomenologie des Geistes*, a work which he regarded as an introduction to his philosophy as a whole. This programmatic approach is also adopted in other works.[2]

We have already seen throughout the argument of this book that the

[1] Victor Cousin once asked Hegel for a concise statement of his position and Hegel replied: 'Monsieur . . . ces choses ne se disent pas succinctement'. Stirling, *The Secret of Hegel*, London 1865.
[2] Particularly in the Introduction to the various editions of the *Enzyklopädie* and the Preface to *Grundlinien der Philosophie des Rechts*.

pursuit of coherence and the therapeutic value of such a pursuit lies at the very heart of Hegel's thinking. This is as true of his mature philosophy as of his earlier social and religious criticism. The lack of coherence was for Hegel a personal problem because, if taken to its extreme, could lead to madness and a social problem in that the fragmentation of experience had led to a decline in community. The 'happy peoples'[1] of history (the Greeks) could achieve 'a most perfect integration' because their life was not broken up by the division of labour and divisive religious practices. The contemporary world, however, has lost sight of such an integrated community and 'their highest pride must be to cling to separation and maintain the existence of the unit'.[2] Community could not be recaptured by political and religious reforms which ignored the great changes in society since the decline of the Greek *polis* and the corresponding gains in self-consciousness. At the personal level estrangement could be overcome only by having a home in the world, by seeing the world as it is as necessary to man in both its specificity and particularity as contributing to the realization of some of the most distinctive human capacities and powers. Similarly, community could be achieved only by an understanding of contemporary social and political institutions as embodying forms of integration and connection appropriate to both more complicated societies and more developed individuals. Both of these aspects of estrangement could be overcome only by philosophy, a point which he makes very strongly in his *Philosophie des Rechts*:

> I am at home in the world when I know it, still more so when I have understood it.[3]

Because of his approach to philosophy, Hegel was concerned to criticize those of his contemporaries who found in philosophy not an actual reconciliation between man and the world, but the pious hope that such a reconciliation might eventually be achieved, for whom reconciliation was a mere ideal. In his mature philosophical work, he constantly criticizes the work of Kant and Fichte as providing philosophical doctrines which make some kind of achieved harmony impossible. In *Die Phänomenologie des Geistes*, he says *à propos* of Kant's philosophy:

[1] Nohl, op. cit., p. 350.
[2] Ibid., p. 351. Such was the life of the unhappy peoples.
[3] Glockner, op. cit., vol. 7, paragraph 142, additions. In his essay 'L'Attitude Hegelienne devant l'existence', Franz Gregoire argues: 'This is I believe the fundamental existential experience of Hegel's system', in *Études Hegeliennes*, op. cit., p. 9. This is certainly true, but because he totally neglects Hegel's development he fails to provide a convincing account of why this experience should be fundamental.

The completion of harmony is therefore not reached as an individual fact: it is thought of rather as an absolute task or problem and one that remains a problem pure and simple.[1]

At the same time Hegel was both critical and contemptuous of the prophesying and utopianism of incomparably lesser figures such as Jacobi and Novalis.[2]

Against such philosophers who 'get stuck fast on an ought', Hegel counterposed his own philosophy. Whereas Kant, Fichte, Jacobi and Novalis all preserved the 'unhappy consciousness', however much they may have wished to overcome it, Hegel argues that it can be overcome only by demonstrating with close attention to detail that the world is intelligible, that any specific mode of experience within it may be interpreted as a stage in the development of human capacities and powers, that is to say in self-consciousness. The philosopher cannot achieve this aim by merely describing the world in conventional terms. If he could, he would be redundant because conventional descriptions and interpretations of experience would in that case embody harmony and reconciliation.[3] At the same time, however, the philosopher cannot dispense with traditional and conventional discourse, because that would involve a further bifurcation—he would be cut off from the on-going life of his community.[4] The philosopher can neither accept conventional ways of speaking as they stand because they embody diremption and discord; at the same time he has to avoid distancing himself from such forms of description. He has rather to acquire a philosophical perspective, that is to say a harmonious perspective, by *developing* conventional ways of speaking so that they come to encapsulate both the metaphysical and the historical dimensions of experience which are of crucial importance for philosophical comprehension. The actual mechanics of this process will be discussed below in the context of the notions of 'Understanding', 'Reason' and 'Dialectic'. Basically,

[1] Glockner, op. cit., vol. II, p. 465. Criticisms of Fichte may be found in Nohl, op. cit., p. 351, in Glockner, vol. I, pp. 33–168, and ibid., pp. 394 ff.

[2] For Hegel's criticism of Jacobi, see Glockner, vol. I, pp. 328 ff. ('Glauben und Wissen') and vol. II, pp. 505 ff. For Novalis, see Glockner, vol. II, pp. 506 ff.

[3] It was of course Hegel's thesis in his very earliest essay on these themes, 'Über einige Charakteristische Unterschiede der Alten Dichter', discussed above p. 27 that conventional discourse is divorced from the world and does not provide the symbolic basis of community life.

[4] Compare here the position of the philosopher *vis à vis* conventional descriptions of experience with Hegel's discussion of the relationship between Jesus and the on-going life of the Jewish community in 'Der Geist des Christentums und sein Schicksal', discussed above, p. 63.

however, Hegel's position is that the thought of the Understanding corresponds to the conventional level of thought which the philosopher has in some way to develop. The Dialectic is the name of the process through which these conventional notions are made richer, so that they come to embody the metaphysical and empirical emphasis referred to earlier. The level of Reason is attained when this dialectical enrichment of the thought of the understanding has been attained.

Hegel stresses the role of empirical material in his philosophical explanations of the world, material which, in the case of the social world, might be called in a broad sense of the word historical, but at the same time he is very concerned to insist upon the wide gulf which exists between the philosopher's approach to the past of a mode of experience, or a social practice and the historian's approach. An historical approach does not reveal the metaphysical element immanent in the subject matter, namely the progressive evolution of consciousness, or the realization of Spirit in and through such experience and such practices. The historian does not reveal Spirit as the structuring element in social life, the element which makes social experience in its various modes central to the development of self-conscious minds. Rather history is concerned merely to narrate the sequence of past events:

> History concerns the individual existent, the accidental and arbitrary side of those features which are not necessary.[1]

Although philosophy has an historical dimension, and this dimension is at the very centre of its concern to re-establish coherence in human thought and experience, its treatment of the past is not historical. Whereas history is in principle concerned with *all* of the past, with the accidental and the peripheral as well as what the philosopher considers to be the central and necessary, philosophy on the other hand is concerned only with those modes of past experience which enable us to see the present as a stage in a rational and necessary development, the progressive realizations of self-consciousness.[2] Considered in this way, therefore, the past is really considered from the standpoint of the

[1] Glockner, vol. II, p. 40.
[2] See Oakeshott, *Experience and Its Modes*, Cambridge 1933, p. 155:
A third conception of the 'philosophy of history' is to be found in the notion of the discovery and elucidation of the plan or plot of history . . . a selective simplification of history based upon some assumed notion of general significance.
Oakeshott notes that Hegel's work falls into this class and he goes on to comment:
. . . the plot or plan of history (taken in this sense) may possibly be philosophy, but has certainly nothing to do with history.
Ibid., p. 155. Hegel would of course have agreed. He first drew this distinction between philosophy and history in his diary. Vide Dok. ed. Hoffmeister, pp. 9–10.

present.[1] The philosopher looks at the past to discern those shapes of experience which have contributed in a significant fashion to the contemporary stage of conscious development. This does not entail, however, that the philosopher and the historian are in any sense in conflict. Indeed, the philosopher will depend upon first-order researches of historians to achieve his philosophical purposes. Only when the structure of past experience has been brought to light by the activity of the historian can the philosopher be in a position to discern within this structure those modes of past experience significant for comprehending the present.

Hegel's discussion of various modes of experience may seem to us today, in our situation, to be arbitrary, but from Hegel's point of view they constitute the background in terms of which his contemporary world could be made intelligible. Hegel is not concerned in his use of the past to justify this or that political principle, this or that social doctrine, a point which he explicitly rejected early on in the argument of *Vorlesungen über die Philosophie der Geschichte*;[2] his task *qua* philosopher was not justification, but comprehension, understanding the modern world, explaining it to be the result of a rationally discernible development and exemplifying this development, at least so far as the social and political worlds were concerned, with detailed attention to the past. Experience presents to the philosopher an 'infinite wealth of shapes and appearances' which the historian merely records, but which the philosopher seeks to penetrate, to find the 'inward pulse' within the complex process, this inward pulse being the development of self-consciousness in lives of men, or, the same point made more metaphysically, the self-realization of Spirit in the world in and through the lives of men to discern those events which are not merely *historisch* but also *geschichtlich*.

[1] Hegel's distinction between the historical approach to the past and an approach in terms of significance is paralleled in the work of two recent writers on the role of historical experience in human thought, Martin Heidegger and Michael Oakeshott. In *Sein und Zeit*, Heidegger draws the distinction between *Historie* and *Geschichte*, a distinction which he draws for philosophical purposes and does not reflect anything in ordinary German usage. In Heidegger's account *Historie* consists in history considered as the mere chronicle of events; *Geschichte* concerns the significance of those events for here and now existence. This distinction has also been influential in German theology. Theologians within that tradition often draw a distinction between history and 'salvation history' (*Heilsgeschichte*). For a skilful attempt to disentangle these usages, see Pannenberg, 'Redemptive Event and History' in *Basic Questions in Theology*, London 1970. In terms of Oakeshott's typology in 'The Activity of Being a Historian' in *Rationalism in Politics*, London 1962, Hegel adopts the practical approach to the past, reading the past backwards, in the light of the present.

[2] Glockner, op. cit., vol. XI, pp. 31–2.

It is at this point that a major controversy in the interpretation of Hegel arises. Most contemporary scholars argue that Hegel did not operate with a concept of *necessity* and furthermore that he did not mean to do so. The first part of this is certainly true—Hegel's explanations are not as a matter of fact necessary, a point which will be argued at length in the final chapter. But unless Hegel intended that they should be necessary it is difficult to see how he could maintain a coherent philosophical position. Kaufmann argues:

Hegel uses 'necessary' as an inclusive antonym for 'arbitrary' as if everything for which good reasons could be found and which was not therefore arbitrary could reasonably be called necessary.[1]

Frithjoff Bergman agrees with Kaufmann when he maintains:

Many commentators have felt that the possibility of alternative arrangements, which is of course evident, is inconsistent with the necessity of Hegel's system and therefore constitutes a refutation of Hegel's claim to it. . . . This is untenable once Hegel's conception of necessity is understood.[2]

Bergmann then goes on to give an account of Hegel's notion of necessity on the same lines as those of Kaufmann. If these arguments are accepted as accurate reflections of Hegel's purpose as opposed to his achievement, then it is difficult to see how his position could be coherent. His aim was the reconciliation of man to the world, to overcome alienation, to lead a man to find a home, as he puts it, in his environment. Merely to give a reason for something, however, does not necessarily lead someone to be reconciled to it—on the contrary, perhaps. In fact it might well be argued that to discern the reason for an institution having the character that it has might well be a prelude to a radical critique of that institution. This point is of course borne out in Hegel's own early work. For example, he tried to understand the *reasons* for Christianity having the character that it had in contemporary Europe, but at the same time, although obviously he did not think this character was wholly arbitrary, he still considered that it stood in need of both criticism and reform. The whole of Hegel's early writings could be considered as an attempt to look into the past to discern the reasons for the crisis in European consciousness, but as a basis not for reconciliation, but for reform or revolution. If Hegel held the conception of necessity attributed to him by both Kaufmann and Bergman, there would be no significant

[1] Kaufmann, op. cit., p. 85.
[2] 'The Purpose of Hegel's System', in *Journal of the History of Philosophy*, 1964, p. 20.

difference between Hegel's earlier writings and his later ones, whereas the difference is both striking and obvious. It was only towards the end of the Frankfurt period, with the growth in his mind of the idea of historical development and fate, that he found the key to the solution of the problem of estrangement and it was at that time that he moved on to philosophy. Nor was Hegel inexplicit in linking together the notion of reconciliation with that of necessity. Indeed, two passages separated by twenty years show the consistency of Hegel's thought on this matter. The first, from 'Die Verfassung Deutschlands' links peace and reconciliation with the comprehension of necessity:

> But if we recognize that what is is as it must be, i.e. that it is not arbitrariness and chance that make it so, then we recognize it as it ought to be. But it is hard for the ordinary run of men to rise to the habit of trying to recognize necessity and think it.[1]

The second passage taken from the Preface of his *Grundlinien der Philosophie des Rechts* makes much the same point as the 1802 essay:

> To recognize reason as the rose in the cross of the present and thereby to enjoy the present, this is the rational insight which reconciles us to the actual.[2]

Both Kaufmann and Bergman go wrong in attributing such a conception of necessity to Hegel because they do not bear in mind sufficiently clearly Hegel's philosophical purpose.[3]

It is of course possible to sympathize with their motives. The notion of historical necessity is one with which few people have sympathy at the present time and some such critics would hold that if Hegel's philosophical explanation of the development of the modes of experience in the contemporary world are held to be necessary then they say nothing. However, it is a mistake to attribute to Hegel a conception of necessity which he did not hold, and which he could not have held, in order to render his philosophical ideas more palatable to the taste of a less robust age.

It is one thing to assert that Hegel's explanations must be necessary, or at least must have been meant as necessary, quite another to show

---

[1] Lasson, *Schriften zur Politik und Rechtsphilosophie*, op. cit., p. 5.

[2] Glockner, op. cit., vol. VII, p. 35.

[3] It seems to me that Engels held the correct view here:

For Hegel the attribute of reality belongs only to that which is at the same time necessary—in the course of its development reality proves to be necessary.

In 'Ludwig Feuerbach and the End of Classical German Philosophy', in *Marx and Engels Selected Works*, vol. II, Moscow 1968, p. 361.

how he considered this necessity to be structured into both natural and social development. How is the development of consciousness and Spirit through its various stages so 'written into' both the natural and social worlds that it can be understood and comprehended by the philosopher as a rational and necessary process? Is the teleological development of consciousness a merely 'regulative ideal' for Hegel, that is to say something which we merely presuppose in our thinking about both nature and human society but cannot know whether it is a structuring principle of the world itself? Or is it some process totally immanent within both natural and social development? But, if so, how was this immanent development built in initially? Or is the development of consciousness the result of the creative activity of something approximating to the Christian God? It will be argued that there is no entirely unambiguous answer to these questions and it will be held further that this ambiguity while crucial, is also necessary, given a basic tension in Hegel's overall philosophical enterprise.

One point can be made without ambiguity, namely that the emergence, development and achievement of self-consciousness through natural and social developments cannot be merely a Kantian regulative idea. It is not something which we, as it were, work with on the assumption that it is true but which we cannot be sure applies to Nature and History considered 'in themselves'. First of all, Hegel would of course reject the notion of either Nature or History having the status of things-in-themselves, since he rejected the whole notion as we have already seen and he was certainly, even in his mature work, still sufficiently influenced by Schelling in that he still considered that Nature embodied consciousness in a petrified form and that this was something objective in Nature and not merely something presupposed in our approaches to it. The same would apply *mutatis mutandis* to the social and historical world. Professor Findlay has seen very clearly this and the consequence which follows from rejecting the view that the emergence of consciousness is a merely regulative idea:

> I do not think that it is enough to cherish Hegelian teleology as a sort of rational faith necessarily implied by our various higher order activities: one must be willing to give that faith some sort of metaphysical, ontological justification.[1]

If Hegel's teleology of consciousness is not a merely regulative idea then its structuring into the world requires some kind of metaphysical justification. Findlay, however, without good reason in my view, rejects

[1] 'Hegel's Use of Teleology', in *Ascent to the Absolute*, London 1970, p. 147.

the obvious interpretation of the metaphysical basis which Hegel does give to the teleological development of both the natural and social worlds, namely that his Spirit or Absolute Idea (the Categorical form of Spirit, considered prior in the natural and social worlds) is really a metaphysical counterpart of the Christian God. Certainly many philosophers who have both asserted the identity of thought and reality and have at the same time rejected the view that reality is a construction of thought have faced the problem confronting Hegel—Spinoza in his doctrine of substance in two modes; Leibnitz with his notion of the pre-established harmony; Schelling by the point of indifference; and, *mirabile dictu*, Wittgenstein in his concept of grammar.[1]

For Hegel this harmony is secured through the Idea, the categorical form of Spirit. So much may be agreed by most scholars, but what constitutes the Idea is a matter of sharp controversy. It would seem that the Idea stands in some kind of creative relationship to the world of Nature, creating an environment within which consciousness may emerge, and eventually a human world within which it can grow and eventually grasp philosophically in the minds of men the very structure of its own development. Considered in such a way, the Idea would stand in a creative relationship with the world, explaining how the necessary development of consciousness is built into reality and how the philosopher eventually is able to grasp it in its process of development. Such a view of the Idea is presupposed, for example, in the early paragraphs of his mature 'Naturphilosophie' in the *Enzyklopädie*:

> The divine Idea is just this: to disclose itself, to posit the Other outside itself and to take it back again into itself in order to be subjectivity and Spirit.[2]

In this passage the Idea is ascribed the attribute 'divine' and in the sentence preceding the first sentence quoted above the philosophical concept of the Idea is explicitly linked to the theological notion of God, although a notion which is to some extent theologically unconventional:

> If God is all-sufficient and lacks nothing, why does he disclose himself in a sheer Other of himself? (i.e. Nature).[3]

Similar passages to this may be found in Hegel's discussion of the

---

[1] For those surprised or shocked to see Wittgenstein in such company, see *Zettel*, Oxford 1967, p. 12:

Like everything else metaphysical the harmony between thought and reality is to be found in the grammar of the language.

[2] Glockner, op. cit., vol. 9, para. 247, additions.

[3] Ibid., para. 247, additions.

relationship between the Idea or Spirit and the social world. In his early essay on Natural Law Hegel, as we have seen, put forward the argument explicitly:

> The Absolute ever plays with itself a moral tragedy in which it ever gives birth to itself in the objective world, then in this form gives itself over to suffering and death and raises itself to glory from its ashes.[1]

The Absolute Idea structures the social environment so that consciousness develops out of fragmentation, overcoming bifurcation and eventually in the mind of the philosopher coming to a total self-awareness of the process of its own development. In *Die Vernunft in der Geschichte*, Hegel again explicitly links this process with the notion of God:

> The insight to which philosophy should help us is that the actual world is as it ought to be . . . God rules the world, the content of his plan is world history and its presupposition is that the ideal accomplishes itself, that only what accords with the ideal has actuality.[2]

Other factors too might lead the historian to take the view that Hegel considered the relationship between the Idea and the world to be comparable in some respects with the Christian notion of God and thus securing the reciprocity between man and his environment. Hegel took the view that philosophy and theology have the same content, deal with the same truths but whereas the theologian and the religious person apprehend their truths through images and *Vorstellungen*, the philosopher comprehends them through concepts, *Begriffe*, through detailed and specific judgements.[3] In addition, the very articulation of Hegel's own philosophical point of view is shot through with Christian images, to such an extent that his system would be difficult to describe without making reference to these symbols. For example, as early as his essay on Natural Law and 'Glauben und Wissen' he could see in the images of crucifixion and resurrection analogues to the development of the human mind through fragmentation and in overcoming fragmentation;[4] this image is revived in the very final lines of *Die Phänomenologie des Geistes*, a work in which he describes this process in detail:

---

[1] Glockner, vol. 1, p. 500.   [2] Ed. Hoffmeister, ed. cit., p. 77.
[3] This thesis is argued in *Die Phänomenologie des Geistes*, in the sections of the *Enzyklopädie* dealing with 'Absolute Spirit' and in more detail in *Vorlesungen über die Philosophie der Religion*, Glockner, op. cit., vols. XV and XVI.
[4] See above, pp. 80 ff.

History comprehended in thought forms at one and the same time the remembrance and the Golgotha of Absolute Spirit, the reality the truth, the certainty of its throne without which it was solitary and alone.[1]

Here again in a central work of Hegel's philosophy the relationship between Spirit realizing itself in the minds of men is described through Christian symbols. The image of the cross also appears in the Preface to *Grundlinien der Philosophie des Rechts*:

To recognize reason as the rose in the cross of the present and thereby to enjoy the present this is the rational insight which reconciles us to the actual.[2]

The reason for the pervasiveness of the imagery of the Passion, Crucifixion and Resurrection in Hegel's writings will be discussed shortly. In addition to this imagery one might note that the very word which Hegel uses to describe reconciliation, *Versöhnung*, has religious overtones in that it is the normal word used to denote the *atonement* wrought by Christ upon the Cross. Finally, and most extravagantly, Hegel sometimes draws an analogy between the three sections of his system, *Logik*, *Naturphilosophie* and *Geistesphilosophie* as analogous to the doctrine of the Trinity. The *Logik* on this view would be analogous to God existing as pure spirit, *Naturphilosophie* analogous to Jesus, uniting the pure spirit of the Father with the gross materiality of nature, and *Geistesphilosophie* corresponding to the Holy Spirit, relating the Father to the Son in the world and making explicit their relationship, whereas in art and religion and more particularly in philosophy man becomes aware of the structuring activity of Spirit in the world and is able to make its operations in human life explicit.[3]

Other, external evidence which might also lead one to consider Hegel's system as shot through with a counterpart to Christian theism is the attitude of the two most sophisticated of his contemporaries. Both Marx and Feuerbach regarded Hegel's philosophy as having an irreducible theological content, although that content was to some extent transposed into concepts such as *Idea*, *Spirit*, etc. Indeed, such an understanding of Hegel's work was a presupposition of Feuerbach's transformational method. Had he not considered Hegel's thought to have this irreducibly theological element, there would have been nothing for him to transform.

[1] Glockner, op. cit., vol. II, p. 620.
[2] Ibid., vol. VII, p. 35.
[3] Ibid., vol. IX, para. 247.

It is significant in this context to notice that both Findlay and Kaufmann deny the theological aspect of Hegel's work, or at least deny that it is to be taken seriously and are at the same time committed to the view that Hegel's philosophical explanations are not to be taken as necessary. This juxtaposition of views bears out in a negative fashion the point argued above, namely that the necessary development of consciousness in both the natural and the social worlds has to be given some kind of metaphysical grounding, and the obvious source of this in Hegel's work is his linking up of the notions of Idea and Spirit with something analogous to the Christian understanding of God. Obviously when the metaphysico-theological aspect of his thought is jettisoned as it is by both Kaufmann and Findlay, then the claim that his system was intended to elucidate necessary connections between modes of experience has to be abandoned too.

However, having argued that there is an analogy between the role of the notions of Absolute Idea and Spirit in the elucidation of human thought and experience and the Christian understanding of God and his relationship to the world, there arises a major problem. There is a profound tension in Hegel's thought at this point, which, once understood, must make his conception of the notions of Idea and Spirit appear highly ambiguous. The basic aim of Hegel's philosophical enterprise was to achieve harmony and coherence, to make man feel at home in the world, and a crucial factor in achieving this was the recognition of the necessity of certain types of experience and their particular character. To achieve the aim of coherence, all transcendence had to be exorcised from the world because Hegel recognized very early on that transcendence was a threat to community but, at the same time, in so far as he was committed to undermining the transcendent, necessity, in Hegel's sense, could not be structured into the world. Man can only be reconciled to the world through the recognition of necessity; but this necessity in turn has to receive some kind of metaphysical or transcendental accreditation in the Idea or Spirit. On the one hand transcendence is a threat to community; on the other hand the exorcising of the transcendent is a threat to the kinds of explanation of experience which Hegel thought could overcome alienation from social practices. If Idea and Spirit are to be considered in a way analogous to the Christian God, then it appears that there has to be a residue of transcendence beyond the grasp of human thought.

Certainly Hegel was aware of this problem and in his discussion of the relationship between the Idea or Spirit and the world he tries his best on the one hand to eliminate the transcendental aspects of the relationship and yet on the other to find in the relationship the source of the necessity which the philosopher is able to elucidate in his descriptions of the development of social life and institutions. He attempts to eliminate transcendence from the Idea and from Spirit by an analogical argument, playing upon the link which, as we have seen, he often draws up between the Idea and God. He argues that a correct understanding of God would be very different from that envisaged in traditional Christian theology and that this revised understanding of God in theological terms elucidates the notion of Idea/Spirit, the metaphysical counterpart to God. Traditionally in Christian theology divine transcendence has added up to the view that God is perfect, self-sufficient, complete in himself, distinct from the order which he has created, and is not modified, limited or affected by that order. God, fully perfect, fully self-conscious, creates a world from which he is essentially independent but within which he may intervene on occasion, these interventions being the source of man's knowledge of God and his nature. Hegel goes a long way towards revising such a conception of God and *mutatis mutandis* the argument applies also to the notions of Idea and Spirit.

The seeds of this argument are to be found in his early writings, particularly *Systemsfragment* (1800)[1] in which he argues that man can elevate himself to infinite life, that is to say in some rather vague way share in the infinite life of God through religious experience. In 'Glauben und Wissen' Hegel argues that finite and infinite are closely related and that this interrelation can be grasped by the philosopher[2] and in the essay on Natural Law he seems to argue that the activity of God in the world is central to God's *development*. In the *Enzyklopädie*, however, Hegel makes his point about the close interrelation between God and the world by asking a very pertinent question of the traditional conception of God:

If God is all-sufficient and lacks nothing, why does he disclose himself in the sheer other of Himself?[3]

This sheer other of himself is the natural and social world. If God is fully formed and fully perfect why did he need to create a world? The answer for Hegel is to be found in denying the presupposition of the question, namely that God is *not* fully developed, fully formed, self-sufficient when considered in himself and consequently his activity in the world is not a mere addendum to the infinite life of God, but the very means whereby God develops, and comes to full self-consciousness of himself:

[1] Nohl, op. cit., p. 347.   [2] Glockner, vol. i, pp. 292–3.
[3] Ibid., vol. IX, para. 247, additions.

The Spirit is declared in the element of pure thought and is simply this and essentially this, not only to be in this element but also actual. The *merely* eternal or abstract Spirit therefore becomes another to itself and enters existence. It therefore creates a world.[1]

The world is dependent upon God for its reality and for the specific character of its development, but at the same time God is not to be conceived as in the Judaic religion as the perfect, self-sufficient sovereign lord of the Universe, but rather in a deep sense dependent on his creation as the medium of his own development, a development which by taking place in the world can be comprehended by the philosopher. Comprehended in such terms all the mystical obfuscating elements of religious belief drop away and the notion of God with its traditional associations gives way to that of the Idea. We are now in a position to see why the crucifixion had a particular fascination over Hegel's mind. What from the religious point of view appeared as an infinite grief could be philosophically comprehended as part of the self-development of God, exhibiting in a concrete fashion his relation to and, indeed, dependence upon his creation becoming closely involved in the natural developments in human life.

It might be argued by the critic that there must still be a residual amount of transcendence left, the Idea as it was *before* creating a world or other and realizing itself in it through nature and the lives of men in society. Such is not the case, however, in Hegel's view because the philosopher can in fact fully comprehend both the process of the development in the world and the Idea as it existed before its self-realization in the world. This somewhat startling claim is made in *Die Wissenschaft der Logik*:

Accordingly, logic is to be understood as the system of pure reason, as the realm of pure thought. This realm is truth as it is without veil and in its own absolute nature. It can therefore be said that this content is the exposition of God as he is in his content is the exposition of God as he is in his eternal essence before the creation of nature and the finite mind.[2]

The *Logik* makes clear in abstract form, in a system of concepts, the structuring principles involved in both thought and being without considering how these principles are realized in concrete cases.[3] Given that these structuring principles are an expression of the Idea, the

---

[1] Glockner, vol. II, p. 587.   [2] Ibid., op. cit., vol. IV, p. 46.
[3] The system of logic is the realm of shadows, the world of simple essentialities freed from all sensuous concreteness. Ibid., vol. IV, p. 57.

metaphysical counterpart to God, then Hegel's position is perfectly legitimate on his own terms.

If Hegel's overall position is considered in relation to his philosophical aims, then it has a certain esoteric logic about it. Reconciliation can be achieved only through the intellectual apprehension of the necessity built into both the natural and social worlds; this necessity in turn can only be secured if it is in some way transcendentally accredited. This accreditation then constitutes a threat to the very reconciliation which the notion of necessity was introduced to secure. Consequently Hegel has to go on, driven by his own philosophical goals, to claim that, although in a sense outside of the world, the Idea is in a more profound way dependent on it for its own self-realization. Because the content of the Idea is fully realized in the world, it is within human comprehension and is in fact grasped in Hegel's own philosophy—a staggering and ambiguous claim, but one without which Hegel's goals could not be achieved and without which both the personal and social aspects of fragmentation and dissonance could not be overcome. To conceive of the infinite life of God or Idea was to press to its very extreme Hegel's claim that the philosopher could present the modern man with a home in the world.

A conceptual grasp of the world is necessary, therefore, to overcome its otherness, so that man the subject could come to feel at home in the substance of the world and this conceptual grasp is both metaphysical, revealing the structuring principles of the Idea/Spirit, and empirical, revealing in the detail of experience how these structuring principles are built into experience. Because of the complexity of a philosophical grasp of experience, a philosophical explanation cannot be given in a single proposition, but only in a complete grasp of the world in both its empirical and metaphysical dimensions and in a sense, therefore, the *whole* of Hegel's work can be seen as *the* conceptual grasp. Consequently philosophy has to be a systematic activity. The pursuit of coherence has to be conducted for every significant form of human experience[1] and it is only when these are seen in their interconnectedness, as embodying the structuring of the Idea, that man becomes reconciled to the totality of his experience in the modern world. Hegel probably made these points most explicitly in *Grundlinien der Philosophie des Rechts*:

> The series of concepts which this development yields is therefore at the same time a series of *shapes of experience* and philosophical science must treat them accordingly.[2]

[1] See Glockner, vol. I, pp. 60 and 71.   [2] Ibid., vol. VII, p. 82.

We have to be aware of the structuring principles of the Idea, laid bare in logic, basically the development of richness and depth through opposition and overcoming opposition, in all our basic modes of experience before we can grasp the essence of the world, because this essence consists only in the way in which the development has been achieved:

> The truth is the whole; but the whole is the essence perfecting itself through its development.[1]

It is because of this exacting need for philosophy to be systematic, tracing the Idea in all modes of experience, that Hegel talks in *Die Phänomenologie des Geistes* about the need to take on the 'exertion of the concept'. Conventional ways of thinking embody bifurcation and discord. They do not embody such a total grasp of experience, and consequently the task of philosophy is not seen as the analysis of the concepts of ordinary discourse, but the development of them so that they come to encapsulate the forms of experience which they present to the human mind in a bifurcated way. This process of development, which enables the philosophy to generate a conceptual framework adequate to the real interconnections in reality, is the process of dialectic.

The dialectic is intimately related to the way in which adequate concepts are reached, that is to say concepts which will enable a man to both grasp and become reconciled to his experience. He describes the requirement which leads to the development of the need for dialectic in the following passage from *Die Phänomenologie des Geistes*:

> In our times, the individual finds the abstract form ready-made: the exertion of grasping it and appropriating it is rather more the unmediated production of the inward and cut-off generation of the general rather than the emergence of the general out of the hetero-geneity of existence. The task facing us now therefore is less to purify the individual from the form of immediacy and the senses while making it into a thinking and thought substance, than to do the opposite: to overcome rigid thoughts and so actualize the general and infuse it with spirit.[2]

In the context it seems clear that Hegel is thinking in this passage about the highly abstract approach to experience to be found in the philosophy of his day. He stresses the disconnected character of the kind of structuring principles, which modern day philosophers adopt

---

[1] Glockner, vol. II, p. 24.   [2] Vol. II, p. 35.

in their approach to experience, when he talks of the 'unmediated production of the inward and cut off generation of the general' and no doubt once again Hegel has in mind here the kind of philosophical approach to particular modes of experience which he criticized Kant and Fichte for in his essay on Natural Law. Such approaches are one dimensional in that they do not encapsulate the detail of experience. The task of philosophy, properly conceived, is to see in detail how structuring principles can be discerned in experience; the philosopher should be concerned with the 'emergence of the general out of the multiplicity of existence'. Only when such an enriched grasp of experience has been achieved will man be reconciled. A set of concepts has to be developed to encompass this and in *Die Wissenschaft der Logik* Hegel describes in far more detail the way in which fixed, determinate and highly abstract ways of describing experience can be developed. In this process three notions hang together: 'Understanding', 'Dialectic' and 'Reason' and an account of the process of development has, therefore, to turn on an elucidation of these concepts. The fixed determinate thoughts which stand in need of philosophical development are at the level of the understanding; the Dialectic is the means of this development and Reason is the level which is reached when the development is far enough advanced for a coherent and rational grasp of experience.

'The Understanding' is the name of the attitude of mind in which notions are regarded as being fully determined, with a precise meaning and with a precise and restricted range of extension so that they can be applied rigidly and clearly to the differentiation of experience. This attitude is manifested in many spheres of activity, in conventional discourse, in mathematics and in certain types of philosophy, with those philosophers who, like Bishop Butler, insist that 'Everything is what it is and not another thing', the kind of philosophy which merely takes the concepts ready to hand in conventional discourse for its interpretation of experience without determining the adequacy of such concepts to reality. Hegel describes the role of the understanding in modern philosophy in *Die Wissenschaft der Logik*:

> Reflective understanding took possession of philosophy. We must know exactly what is meant by this expression which, moreover, is often used as a slogan; in general it stands for the understanding as abstracting, and hence as separating and remaining fixed in its separations.[1]

[1] Glockner, vol. IV, p. 39. One can see in Hegel's critique of the understanding both in common sense and in philosophy an echo of his early writings in which he argued that conventional discourse and literature had become abstract and divorced from the complex realities which it tried to describe, in

Clearly in Hegel's view the forms of description which were given to social experience both in conventional discourse and in philosophy in the late eighteenth and early nineteenth centuries in Western Europe were at the level of the understanding; they were abstract and involved bifurcation and discord. It is important to take note of the fact that Hegel does not consider the thought of the understanding to be devoid of value, but only that this level of thought has to be transcended if a coherent grasp of experience is to be attained. To analyse fully the notions of the level of the understanding might be useful as a prologomenon to their transcendence but certainly such activity only has this very restricted philosophical utility.

It is part of the abstract and formal function of the *Logik* to show that to stick to such fixed notions involves contradictions which can be overcome by the development of more adequate, less rigid notions. This generation of contradictions which shows up the inadequacy of the understanding is the process of dialectic. In his discussion of this process Hegel is at pains to point out that the generation of contradiction is not forced on to concepts by the philosopher but rather that the development of contradiction and its eventual resolution is part of the nature of the concepts themselves, and indeed of the material which the concepts describe. In describing the process of progress through the resolution of contradiction the philosopher is revealing the structuring role of the Idea in both the world of thought and reality:

'... the inner negativity of the determinations is the self-moving soul, the principle of all natural and spiritual life ...'[1]

A point which he makes in slightly less complicated form in *Grundlinien der Philosophie des Rechts*:

'... this dialectic is not an activity of subjective thinking applied to some matter externally, but is rather the matter's very soul putting forward its branches and fruit organically.'[2]

Obviously for Hegel the developing adequacy of conceptual grasp through the resolution of contradiction could not be merely 'wished on to reality' by the philosopher because there could be no guarantee that such a conceptual grasp really mirrored the nature of the world. Such an approach Hegel criticizes thus:

Dialectic is commonly regarded as an external, negative activity

contrast of course to the vivacity of Greek language. Hegel is after a conceptual scheme which will encapsulate reality much as Greek language did.

[1] Glockner, op. cit., vol. IV, p. 54.　　　　　　　　[2] Ibid., vol. VII, p. 81.

which does not pertain to the subject matter itself, having its ground in mere conceit, as a subjective itch for unsettling what is fixed and substantial or at least having for result nothing but the worthlessness of the object dialectically considered.[1]

Hegel's argument here is at one with his criticism of the Kantian regulative idea, an idea which is merely presupposed in our thinking and which we cannot be sure applies to reality considered as in some way standing outside of thought. Obviously Hegel's assertion that the Dialectic, the notion of progress through division and discord and overcoming such division and discord, applies both to thought and to being presupposes the argument discussed earlier in this chapter, namely that the harmony between thought and being is to be found in the Idea which structures the development of both in the same way. At the heart of Hegel's philosophy, therefore, there is not only the demand for the revision of concepts in accordance with the aim of philosophy, the pursuit of coherence, there is also the view that such a philosophical revision of concepts mirrors reality, and when used will grasp and appropriate the reality so mirrored.

The Dialectic implies progress through opposition and overcoming opposition and as such applies equally to both thought and reality. More adequate conceptions and more adequate modes of being are reached through this process but it must be borne in mind that those conceptions and those modes of being which are transcended in the dialectical progress are not in some sense lost either to thought or to reality. The more adequate forms of thought and the more adequate modes of being *include* within them what has been surpassed. It is precisely this which makes them more adequate, more rich. A Dialectical advance is one in which what has been surpassed is also preserved. In this sense it might be regarded as possessing increasing progressive import, a point which Hegel makes characteristically:

> Because the result, the negation is a specific negation, it has a content. It is a fresh notion, but higher and richer than its predecessor; for it is rich by the negation or the opposite of the latter, therefore contains it but also something more, and this is the unity of itself and its opposite. It is in this way that the system of notions as such has to be formed—and has to complete itself in a purely continuous course.[2]

The same applies *mutatis mutandis* to the progress of dialectic in reality. The implications of this thesis so far as a conceptual grasp of the social world is concerned are profound and provide the rationale for Hegel's

---

[1] Glockner, op. cit., vol. IV, p. 53.   [2] Ibid., vol. IV, p. 51.

practice in those explanations of social experience which we have discussed thus far. A grasp of a particular form of social experience cannot be had in a one dimensional way, disconnected from any consideration of its emergence from other less adequate forms, because the more adequate form emerges only as a consequence of some contradiction, some discrepancy, in the less adequate form. The point and the function of a particular mode of social experience can, therefore, only be understood in terms of what has preceded it, for what has preceded it gives it point at the present time and in some way is also carried over into it, for:

> What is sublated (overcome dialectically) is not thereby reduced to nothing. . . . To sublate (*aufheben*) has a two-fold meaning in the language: on the one hand, it means to preserve, to maintain, and equally it also means to cause to cease, to put an end to. . . . Thus what is sublated is at the same time preserved, it has lost its immediacy only but it is not on that account annihilated.[1]

A social institution cannot, therefore, be described in a one dimensional way, ignoring its development over time, a development which in turn is intelligible only in terms of the nexus of circumstances which occasioned it. Because of the close connection in Hegel's mind between thought and reality, the same applies to the concepts in terms of which we conceive reality. At the level of the understanding the concept of monarchy[2] for example may mean 'rule by one man'; at the level of reason this abstract disconnected kind of definition will not do. A definition would have to be given of monarchy which included within it some indication of the significant forms of monarchical institution the world has seen, the criterion of significance being, of course, the present understanding of monarchy, or the same point put more metaphysically, the present stage in this particular social institution as it has developed structured by the Idea for:

> The shapes which the concept assumes in the course of its actualization are indispensable for the knowledge of the concept itself.[3]

When such a conceptual grasp can be made on the whole of experience then the level of self-consciousness and Spirit is reached. The structuring of the Idea in all the modes of human experience and the natural worlds is able to be made explicit and because this structuring is at the same time necessary, reconciliation with the world is achieved.

---

[1] Glockner, op. cit., vol. IV, p. 120.
[2] I owe this example to Dr Pelcynski, see *Hegel's Political Writings*, p. 114.
[3] Glockner, op. cit., vol. VII, p. 38.

This reconciliation, however, is not merely to a brute and given reality for to see the world in the light of a philosophical grasp transfigures it. The world no longer appears as an alien place but as an environment which progresses and develops in the same way as the human mind and indeed is crucial to the development of mind:

> The conceptual grasp of an object consists in fact in nothing but that the self makes the object its own, penetrates it and brings it to its own form. Through the conceptual grasp of the mind, the being in and for itself of the object which it enjoys in direct envisagement and pictured thinking is transformed into a merely posited being.[1]

The world is not a construction of mind, as this passage makes clear. It is an independent environment, it has being in and for itself. Nonetheless, the human mind can appropriate it in thought and make it a structure which mirrors the human mind. This is achieved explicitly in Hegel's philosophy but this is in turn predicated upon the implicit harmony between thought and reality secured in the Idea.

Considered in this way, therefore, philosophy is the key to community, to overcoming alienation, to the reconciliation of man with his environment and thus curing the rootlessness of modern society. This of course could only be achieved if Hegel could give his work an educative function. The solution to the problem of alienation could not be merely *private* since the problem was a pervasive *social* one. Only if others could come to share in the philosophical perception of their environment, a perception which would transfigure their view of the world, could Hegel's problems be solved. Hegel does give his work such an educative function, insisting that a philosophical explanation because rational, is therefore open to all, unlike, for example, systems based upon intuition or faith, or the vagaries of personal feeling, with works such as Schelling's which dealt only with the 'dark invisible workmanship' which reconciles man with his world:

> Only what is completely determinate is at the same time exoteric, comprehensible and capable of being learned and thus becoming the property of all. The intelligible form of science is the way to science which is offered to all and made equal for all.[2]

Later on in the Preface to *Die Phänomenologie des Geistes* Hegel is scathingly contemptuous of those who base a philosophical grasp of the world on merely personal insight and in an interesting line he links up

[1] Glockner, vol. IV, p. 16.
[2] Glockner, vol. II, p. 19. I have used the translation of Walter Kaufmann in *Hegel*, op. cit., for this passage.

the rational dimension of philosophy with the achievement of human community:

> Those who invoke feeling as their internal oracle are finished with anyone who does not agree: they have to own that they have nothing further to say to anyone who does not feel the same in his heart—in other words they trample under foot the roots of humanity. For it is the nature of humanity to struggle for agreement with others, *and humanity exists only in the accomplished community of consciousness.*[1]

At the same time, however, the rational, reconciling grasp of experiences offered by philosophy is not easy to attain. Philosophy deals with the whole of experience in its metaphysical and its specific and individual dimensions and consequently the individual who seeks the reconciliation offered by philosophy has to take possession of it himself in both its detail and its necessity. Findlay has well characterized this educational process and linked it with the philosophical grasp of modes of experience which the individual must have for reconciliation:

> If systematic science (philosophy) is to arise in the individual he must recapitulate, relive and appropriate this procession of forms in his own experience.[2]

Only a complete understanding of these various modes can lead the individual to that understanding of the modern world, his relations to it and the modes of integration articulated in it which is the key to overcoming alienation from reality and the achievement of community in the modern world. There is however no quick or easy way to this. Hegel insists that the individual should take on the 'exertion of the concept':

> Impatience demands what is impossible, namely acquiring end without the means. First the length of the way must be suffered for every moment is necessary.[3]

---

[1] Glockner, op. cit., vol. II, p. 63. This was Hegel's criticism of Fries in the Preface to *Grundlinien der Philosophie des Rechts*. He describes Fries' political philosophy thus:

> This is the quintessence of shallow thinking, to base philosophic science not on the development of thought and the concept but on immediate sense perception and play of fancy; to take the rich inward articulation of ethical life, i.e. the state, the architectonic of that life's rationality . . . to take this structure and confound the completed fabric in the broth of 'heart, friendship and inspiration'.

Glockner, vol. VII, p. 27. His attack was based more on philosophical considerations and less on personal malice.

[2] Findlay, *Hegel, a Re-examination*, op. cit., p. 84.

[3] Glockner, op. cit., vol. II, p. 31.

In his *Lectures on Modern Idealism,*[1] Josiah Royce drew attention to the close analogy between the point and purpose of Hegel's system and the *Bildungsroman,* the educational novel, which had a certain vogue in Germany at the time and indeed in Europe generally after the publication of *Émile,* perhaps the first work in the genre. In that work Rousseau wanted to trace out an education whereby Émile might feel at home in an imperfect world and in his masterly *Genèse et structure de la phénomenologie de l'esprit,* Jean Hyppolite argues:

> Hegel found in this work a first history of the natural consciousness bringing itself to freedom by the way of personal and especially formative experiences.[2]

But whatever the influence of *Émile,* it is arguable that Goethe's *Wilhelm Meisters Lehrjahre* was a more profound influence on Hegel. In *Goethe und seine Zeit* Georgy Lukacs has drawn attention to the way in which the novel may have influenced Hegel. He contends:

> . . . the decisive point in the education of Wilhelm Meister consists precisely in his abandonment of a merely internal, merely subjective attitude towards reality and his working towards an understanding of objective reality and an active participation in reality just as it is. *Wilhelm Meister* is an educational novel, its content is the education of man for a practical understanding of reality.[3]

Such of course was precisely the function of Hegel's system.

[1] Op. cit., pp. 147–9.   [2] Paris 1946, vol. I, p. 16.
[3] Lukacs, op. cit., p. 62.

Chapter VII

Philosophy and Community

The ignorant man is unfree because he faces a world which is foreign to himself, a world within which he tosses to and fro aimlessly, to which he is related only externally, unable to unite the alien world to himself and to feel at home in it as much as in his home.

Hegel

It has so far been argued that any discussion of Hegel's political and social philosophy has to take into account the social and political concern of his philosophy as a whole. The pursuit of coherence and harmony was not for him a merely intellectual exercise, but a concern of utmost seriousness to life and community. The achievement of a grasp of reality as an environment within which self-consciousness could come to full development was the means whereby men would become reconciled to their society, with their social world, transfigured by philosophy. This conceptual grasp, deeply rooted in his metaphysics, is made most explicit so far as political experience is concerned in *Grundlinien der Philosophie des Rechts* and in the sections on *Geistesphilosophie* in the *Enzyklopädie*.

The task of the political dimension of philosophy, taken in the narrow sense, ignoring the social and political concern of his philosophy as a whole, as has already been seen in its tentative form in *Jenenser Realphilosophie I* and *II*, is to provide a rational and necessary explanation of the various modes of political experience, exhibiting in specific and individual detail the progressive development of the self-consciousness of the human mind in political contexts, a development exemplifying the structuring role of the Idea. The point of such explanation is of course fixed by Hegel's philosophy as a whole, that is to say to overcome the estrangement of man from political experience by showing the role of such experience in the development of human life and consciousness and to overcome the fragmentation of experience by bringing out the necessary connections *between* modes of experience, between, for example, politics and religion. There can, therefore, be no purely political philosophy, disconnected from an understanding of politics in a total pattern of human development, which in its turn has to be seen in connection with the emergence of the human mind and consciousness out of Nature. It is only with such a total grasp of experience as a whole that the problems of estrangement and fragmentation, the two crucial problems of the age can be overcome. In his *Grundlinien der Philosophie des Rechts*, Hegel implicitly makes precisely this point when he argues that the fundamental way in which political experience can be understood is in terms of the development of self-consciousness through the exercise, within the social world, of the human will. He argues that the general explanations offered in the work presuppose a knowledge of how the powers of the human mind have developed after the emergence of mind from Nature:

> The science of right is a section of philosophy. . . . As a section it has a definite starting point, i.e. the result and truth of what has preceded, and it is what has preceded which constitutes the so-called proof of the starting point. Here the concept of right, so far as its coming to be is concerned falls outside the science of right; it is to be taken up here as given and its deduction is presupposed.[1]

Hegel makes it very clear in this passage that in order to understand the nature of political experience it is necessary for it to be seen in connection with the emergence of consciousness from Nature and the distinctive powers of the human mind which are in turn developed and rendered concrete by participation in social and political experience:

> From our point of view Mind has for its presupposition Nature, of which it is the truth . . . (in this development, mind is preceded by external Nature).[2]

It is of course impossible to do justice to the sometimes breathtaking, sometimes scandalous, but always fascinating explanation which Hegel offers of the emergence of mind from the natural world. In this book, the deduction of mind from Nature will be taken as given and a brief

---

[1] Glockner, op. cit., vol. VII, p. 39, para. 2. Cf. para. 4, p. 50. See also Hegel's view in Dok. ed. Hoffmeister p. 219. Von der Natur komme ich aufs Menschenwerk.

[2] Glockner, op. cit., vol. X, p. 19.

discussion will be offered of the development of the specifically human characteristics of consciousness *before* they come require political and institutional embodiment.

Subjective Mind is the general title which Hegel gives to this discussion in the *Enzyklopädie* and it is divided into three sections, *Anthropology*, *Phenomenology* and *Psychology*. The first form which the human mind takes in its emergence from Nature is that of the *Natural Soul*, a quasi-mystical idea on Hegel's part of some kind of soul substance out of which individual souls are generated, and also specific souls, the souls of particular communities, their racial and national characteristics. At the level of the individual, the soul develops in certain clear cut stages from *Childhood*, 'the mind wrapped up in itself', *Youth* in which the soul tries to mould the world to its subjective fancies,[1] *Manhood* in which there is a correct, reconciled relation to the world, and finally old age. The particular ways in which these various stages develop depend of course upon general social and cultural conditions and their full specification requires the passage to *Objective Mind*, the social and political world. In the section on *Subjective Mind* Hegel is merely concerned to clarify the *formal* powers of the human mind which are then developed in a nexus of social and political circumstances in much the same way as in *Die Wissenschaft der Logik* he was concerned to elucidate the general structuring principles inherent in the Idea which in turn required their application and concrete realization in a natural and a social world. The first real advance in this formal structure is through sexual relationships in which people become related to one another through love which, in its turn, presupposes a richness of inner life on the part of the lover and a recognition of the beloved as another person. The same is true of the *Feeling Soul* (*die fühlende Seele*) in which

---

[1] It seems Hegel may be generalizing from his own passage from youth to maturity here:

> Youth is a struggle with a universality which is still subjective against his immediate individuality and that individuality marks the world which, as it exists, fails to meet his ideal requirements.

Manhood on the contrary is seen as the 'true relation of man to his environment, recognizing the objective necessity and the reasonableness of the world as he finds it—a world no longer incomplete'.

Glockner, vol. X, p. 104. Cf. also the additions to this paragraph: p. 105.

> At first the transition from his ideal life into civil society can appear as a painful transition into the life of the philistine . . . the impossibility of an immediate realization of his ideals can turn him into a hypochondriac. This hypochondria is not easily escaped by anyone. In this frame of mind the man is unable to overcome his repugnance to the actual world.

See above, p. 77.

the mind, the subject of sensation, patterns its sensations in certain ways and connects sensations one with another, into meaningful groups. This developing, but merely formal capacity of the mind is, however, an advance in self-consciousness because it involves:

> Waking up to the judgement in itself, in virtue of which it has particular feelings and stands as a subject in respect of these aspects of itself.[1]

There then follows, without much discernible justification in terms of immanent necessity, a discussion of *Habit*, which in its turn leads to a discussion of the *Actual Soul*, which is that level of consciousness formally reached when the mind is in control of its bodily functions and which, instead of regarding itself as dependent upon the body and, as such, sunk in the externality of Nature, can grasp itself as being, at least in conception, distinct from the body and having *Consciousness* as its essence. Again, the argument is purely formal. Hegel is attempting to elucidate the general pattern of human development in the void, fully realizing that such patterns of activity and development need to be realized in an external and detailed way in particular modes of life.

Phenomenology is the next section of the argument and is the study of the various general kinds of consciousness. At this level, the self-consciousness which the mind has made explicit in distinguishing between itself and Nature has to be developed, making the world its object through its grasp of reality:

> It is of the latter (i.e. the object), as external to it, that the Ego is first aware and as such it is consciousness. Ego is this absolute negativity . . . is itself that other and stretches over the object (as if the object were implicitly cancelled).[2]

There are various formal ways in which the mind can assert its power over objects: through *sense perception*, not really a very developed form in Hegel's view because it does not in any real sense subject the object to the demands of the Ego; through *intellect*, which is a more developed form of consciousness, although it, of course, dialectically presupposes perception, in that the chaotic manifold in sense perception is reduced to laws, issuing from the activity of the conscious Ego; through *desire* wherein the objectivity of the world is transformed to achieve the satisfaction of desire, rendering the objective world subjective, as Hegel puts it in his usual inimitable fashion. Desire and its satisfaction transform the objective world and as such contribute an

[1] Glockner, op. cit., vol. X, p. 204.
[2] Ibid., vol. X, p. 255.

advance in self-consciousness, but an even more significant advance is secured when the individual Ego can gain response not from merely inert reality, but from another free and developing consciousness. This demand for recognition, crucial to the achievement of self-consciousness is at the same time a battle:

> I cannot be aware of myself in another individual so long as I see in that other another and immediate existence, and I am consequently bent upon the suppression of this immediacy.[1]

Such a struggle for recognition, however, reaches an impasse. One side involved in the struggle has to give way; he becomes the slave, the other the master. But all this means is that the slave loses his conception of himself as a self-conscious being, whereas the master has achieved a merely *soi-disant* victory in that his recognition is now afforded by someone who is not a person in the full sense. Again these relations are merely formal. Hegel is elucidating the function of interpersonal conflict in the formal emergence of the human mind. Of course, this conflict has many forms in actual modes of social living. The patterns of domination and oppression are many, all that Hegel is doing is elucidating their general function for self-conscious growth.

The solution to the impasse of recognition can only be reached in a situation of reciprocal recognition, of individuals 'mutually throwing light on one another' as Hegel himself describes it. Of course such patterns of mutual recognition require some kind of detailed institutional embodiment, an embodiment which Hegel seems to believe has been afforded by the modern state, incorporating into its structure the rights of the free personality.[2]

Psychology is the third and final section of Subjective Mind and comprises a general discussion of the structure of the powers of the human mind reached at the level of *Universal Self-consciousness*, the level attained after the solution of the problem of recognition. Within this section Hegel distinguishes three types of human powers: *Theoretical Mind*, *Practical Mind* and *Free Mind*. Theoretical mind is the attempt of the self-conscious person to take possession of the world through the exercise of the intellect, but Hegel argues that without the supplement of practical activity such a grasp cannot be achieved. In practical activity man transforms objects and once they are thus transformed by human activity, the products can be appropriated by the human

[1] Glockner, op. cit., vol. X, p. 281.
[2] Obviously in this context the French Revolution and the reforms of Stein, abolishing serfdom in Prussia would probably have had an effect on Hegel's thought in this context.

intelligence. Full self-consciousness is achieved when the mind can fully elucidate its own relationship to the world in practical activity. This is a point of crucial importance. A conceptual grasp of an object can only be attained when that object has been formed and structured by human *praxis* which, of course, gives the logical justification to the *ex post facto* nature of philosophical explanation:

> As the thought of the world it appears only when actuality is there cut and dried *after its process of formation has been completed*.[1]

Accordingly, full self-consciousness is achieved when man can have a full grasp of the kinds of transformations which he has effected through his practical activity on a world which is not the mere product of his mind, but which can be shaped by his will, this process at the same time contributing to his own development as a person. The appropriation of the social world is one such activity of both the practical and the theoretical mind.

The realm of social and political experience is not, however, one which the mind happens, contingently, to realize itself in; on the contrary, the relationship between the powers of the mind considered formally and political experience considered in general is given a necessary explanation by Hegel. Man overcomes the brute otherness of the world largely through practical activity, which the mind then tries to grasp. This practical activity basically consists in an exercise of the will, which in turn is free. Consequently practical activity, transforming the world as the result of the will, is also an exercise in the achievement of human freedom:

> . . . the purposive action of the will is to realize its concept, Liberty, in these externally objective aspects, making the latter a world moulded by the former, which in it is thus at home with itself, locked together with it . . .[2]

The section of Hegel's *Geistesphilosophie* considered above is no doubt to the modern mind highly bizarre, at least in terms of detail. In conception perhaps not so. What Hegel is attempting to do is to elucidate the formal features of the concept of mind and how these formal features are related in terms of adequacy, in much the same way

[1] Glockner, op. cit., vol. VII, p. 36. This point, of course, bears out an earlier argument, namely that Hegel's philosophical development in Jena was intertwined with political developments, particularly the reformation in government achieved by Napoleon. This constituted the general praxis which he tried to grasp but, because it was developing and was not completed, the works of the Jena period have a somewhat prescriptive character.

[2] Ibid., vol. X, p. 382.

perhaps as a modern philosopher might try to elucidate a nexus of concepts such as intention, motive and will and attempt to make clear the interrelations of these concepts. Hegel then goes on to try to show how the development of these formal features of the mind is integrally connected to living in different kinds of social order, that different kinds of social and political practice help to develop one or other of the formal features of the mind while at the same time emphasizing that other features of the mind may well be ignored by the arrangements of a particular society. This kind of connection, of course, modern philosophers do not make. In Hegelian language they remain at the level of the Understanding, elucidating the concept of the mind in the void, without any specific and detailed reference to the kinds of situations within which minds are formed and developed. In his discussion of political experience in both his *Grundlinien der Philosophie des Rechts* and in the paragraphs on Objective Mind in the *Enzyklopädie* Hegel tries to achieve these connections, which, by showing the necessary relation between minds and societies, would help to overcome the alienation of man from his social world.

The political world, like other aspects and dimensions of the human milieu, is the realm within which man acts, which he transforms in his practical activity, in which he realizes his will. The will of man according to Hegel has two sides or moments: an element of individual caprice, the 'dissipation of every restriction and every content' and an element of universality. To be a fully rounded being, both of these aspects of the will have to be brought into harmony, otherwise a Kantian bifurcation would run through the individual's personality. This unification of the disparate dimensions of the will is initially to be found by the individual's participation in a nexus of social institutions and practices. Hegel argues that the truth behind the vague demand for the reunification of the aspects of the will is:

> that the impulses (i.e. the capricious element of the will) should become a rational system of the will's volitions. To grasp them like that, proceeding out of the concept of the will, is the content of the philosophical science of right.[1]

For a man to become fully self-conscious and to have a rounded, harmonious grasp of his experience, his own inner experience has to be brought into some kind of rationally discernible pattern of order and, in consequence, the indeterminate, particularizing element in the will has to be brought under some kind of rule-governed framework.

[1] Glockner, op. cit., vol. VII, p. 71, para. 19.

The demand is not that the arbitrary will should become insignificant, or should disappear, but that it should be structured by some rational pattern for only then could man be *bei sich selbst und also frei*. It is Hegel's argument that the social and political order can be seen in terms of this demand, that man cannot generate the principles of ordering for himself, but must find them within sets of norm-governed institutions. His philosophy of politics, therefore, is concerned to explain institutions in terms of this pattern, that is to say in the context of a developing pattern of personal control and self-consciousness. The three major types of institution which he discusses are Abstract Right, Individual Morality and Ethical Life, each of which is a progressively more adequate development of self-consciousness.

Abstract Right is the result of the basic relation between the will and the objective world. Only through the mastery and the transformation of the world can the will be actualized, the personality made concrete and alienation overcome. To be realized the will needs to possess and appropriate the external world and in so doing transform it for its own use, developing the mind in the process:

> personality is that which struggles to lift itself above this restriction and give itself reality ór, in other words, to claim the external world as its own.[1]

This relationship between the human personality and the external world immediately generates a social dimension—the object which is appropriated and transformed into mind dependence becomes property. Property is therefore for Hegel the institutional embodiment of the person's attempt to develop his own powers and come to self-consciousness by the appropriation of his environment. The philosopher's task is not to provide some *justification* for property, but rather to understand it, to comprehend it as a phase in the development of the human mind. Because the will as made concrete in property is a way in which *self*-consciousness is developed, it follows that the central characteristic of property is that it is *private*.[2] Any attempt to justify the common ownership of property on the grounds of some revisionary political and social theory will not do for Hegel because it ignores the role, brought out in his own work, which property has in the development of the self-awareness of individuals. Since property is the embodiment of the will, it is necessary to make clear the actual relationship involved between the willing subject and what he claims to be his

[1] Glockner, op. cit., vol. VII, p. 92, para. 39.
[2] Ibid., vol. VII, p. 99, para. 46.

property. Hegel distinguishes three types of such relationship. The first, *grasping an object*,[1] is perhaps the primordial form in which a man took possession of an object and Hegel argues that it still has its place in the signification of ownership but, at the same time, its use is greatly restricted and is appropriate only for certain types of object. *Moulding and transforming an object*,[2] particularly through labour, is perhaps the most personal and immediate way in which an object becomes closely identified with its owner because the personality of the owner is impressed upon it. The final general relationship which Hegel considers may obtain between a person and his property is the *use* of a thing.[3] Again this is an advance in the concrete articulation of consciousness because in use an object is brought within a long term trajectory of intention and purpose and is shown to have value in these terms. In labour and in the use of a thing, Hegel argues that Nature shows its truth—that it should be subordinate to mind. Again the harmony between the development and the human mind is asserted, its ground being in the structuring of the Idea.

Property may be alienated[4] because, although central to the development of personality, this or that particular form of property does not encapsulate the personality of the owner. The person requires property in order to develop the powers of his mind but the mind does not require *this* property as opposed to *that*, for if it did the development of self-consciousness would depend upon and be tied to the particularity of nature. The possibility of the alienation of property, thus inherent in the relationship between property and the human personality leads fairly naturally to the notion of contractual relationship.[5] We can see here in a particular case the pattern of explanation throughout Hegel's work, namely that a particular activity or an institution, in this case property, constitutes an advance in self-consciousness, in the conception of oneself as a particular person, and thus of differentiation of oneself from others with a consequent weakening of social bonds; at the same time, however, from another angle, from the *philosophical* point of view, such activities and institutions develop their own pattern of integration, appropriate to the more developed conception of the person produced by the activity—in the case of property contractual relationships between self-conscious property owners. This development through the resolution of fragmentation and opposition embodies the structuring of the Idea and the task of philosophy is both to grasp the contribution to human development made by fragmentation and

---

[1] Glockner, vol. VII, p. 108, para. 55.   [2] Ibid., p. 109, para. 56.
[3] Ibid., p. 113 ff., para. 59.   [4] Ibid., pp. 121 ff., para. 65.
[5] Ibid., pp. 130 ff., para. 72.

also how such diremption is overcome. In the case of property relationships, the philosopher has to show that:

> . . . contractual relationship therefore is the means whereby one *identical will* can persist within the *absolute difference between the property owners* . . . the wills are associated in an identity in the sense that one of them comes to its decision only in the presence of another.[1]

Contractual relationships in their turn become specified into a whole range of specific personal and social relationships: gift,[2] exchange[3] and letting[4] each of which in its turn is further specified.

A necessary consequence of the development of property and contractual relationships is that they may become violated by the unscrupulous and the criminal and the dialectical discussion therefore passes into a consideration of wrong doing, and into the various modifications of crime and punishment which in turn presuppose some notion of justice. Within the sphere of Abstract Right, Hegel distinguishes three types of offence: non-malicious wrong,[5] fraud[6] and crime.[7] Non-malicious wrong consists in an honest disagreement about property rights which on being resolved entails that one of the parties is in the wrong, albeit non-maliciously. Fraud on the other hand consists in a kind of equivocation on the part of the agent. He may well infringe property rights in general by his fraudulent activity and yet at the same time have respect for the particular property rights of certain individuals, without at the same time being aware of the self-contradictory nature of his attitude. Crime on the other hand consists in an explicit rejection of property rights on the part of the criminal through his criminal activity. In such a sense crime demands punishment and here again we see how Hegel shows how a social practice grows out of a development in self consciousness—through the ownership of property and through the structure of rights built upon such ownership.

Hegel's theory of crime and the method of its punishment marks the point at which the framework of Abstract Right has to be transcended. Hegel argues that in order to make sense of punishment, concepts have to be introduced into society, or rather develop *pari passu* with the development of punishment which are not intelligible within a general framework of social life which treats men merely as property owners,

---

[1] Glockner, op. cit., vol. VII, p. 131, para. 74.
[2] Ibid., p. 138, para. 80.　　　　　　　　　[3] Ibid., p. 138–9, para. 80.
[4] Ibid., p. 139, para. 80.　　　　　　　　　[5] Ibid., p. 144, para. 84.
[6] Ibid., p. 146, para. 87.　　　　　　　　　[7] Ibid., p. 147, para. 90.

as is the case with Abstract Right. The criminal who by his activity rejects the structure of property rights is in a state of contradiction. *Qua* human being his aim must be to secure the development of the powers of his mind, to come to self-consciousness and, as we have seen, this involves in Hegel's view that the individual has to own property in order to make concrete his personality; *qua* criminal, on the other hand, his activity involves a rejection of the very conditions which make the realization of himself as a human being possible.[1] Punishment is an attempt to resolve this contradiction, to restore to the criminal the correct perception of the role of property and property rights because in punishment he, as it were, pays off the debt, or annuls the wrong which he did against the structure of property and property relations. This restoration of the value of property rights, symbolized in punishment, in some sense embodies what the criminal *qua* rational human being must desire. It must be borne in mind that Hegel is not attempting to elucidate the justifications actually given in society for inflicting punishment on wrongdoers, rather he is attempting to give a philosophical and thus transfigured explanation of the role of punishment against the background of a similar treatment of the role of property in the development of the human mind.

Punishment is not to be regarded as some institutionalized form of revenge on the part of an aggrieved individual or of society. It has to be considered in the context of the development of the human mind and in particular the restoration of the correct course of such development in the mind of the criminal. Considered in this kind of way, the infliction of punishment must presuppose some conception of impartiality and justice, both of which are moral conceptions. Abstract Right cannot, however, secure the intelligibility of such conceptions because it is a system of particularity, of self directing individuals realizing themselves through the private ownership of property. Impartiality and justice cannot develop fully while the individual's experience remains at this level and yet their achievement is necessary to making the notions of crime and punishment intelligible:

The demand that this contradiction, which is present here in the manner in which wrong is annulled, be resolved like contradictions in the case of other types of wrong, is the demand for justice freed from subjective interests and a subjective form and no longer contingent upon might. . . . Fundamentally this implies the demand for a will which, though particular and subjective, yet wills the

---

[1] Glockner, op. cit., vol. VII, p. 155, para. 100.

universal as such. But this concept of Morality is not something demanded; it has emerged in the course of the movement itself.[1]

Property and Abstract Right make the will concrete and articulate, but at the same time the will actualized in the ownership of property is still capricious and sunk in particularity. At the same time the system of right still requires some notion of universality and impartiality to make sense of crime and punishment which are central to its self-maintenance. Hegel goes on to consider whether a set of universal rules of justice can be developed by the human mind without having to find them within social institutions. The argument does not imply that Hegel is considering man in the state of nature in his section on individual morality; all that the argument requires is that the possibilities of formulating rules of impartial morality come from the powers of the human mind alone, rather than finding such rules as they are embodied in social and political institutions.

Again the discussion of individual morality is a discussion of the mind in its development, not at this stage by its attempt to make itself concrete in the objective sphere by the ownership and manipulation of objects, but rather in turning back on itself in a reflective struggle to detach itself from its own self-interest and particularity so as to generate a set of impartial moral insights. The gain in self-consciousness at this level is in terms of autonomy and reflectedness. In the end, however, Hegel sees the whole enterprise as inadequate because the mind in its own particularity cannot, whatever the struggle, attain a set of intersubjectively valid moral principles. It cannot unite the particular will with the universal and thus harmonize its own two dimensions.

The attempt by the individual to generate his own moral insights must issue in action, which in its turn presupposes an ability on the part of the individual to formulate purposes and take responsibility. A man's environment is therefore structured and transformed not only by possession and labour, but also by his moral decisions which then result in different patterns of moral endeavour:

The finitude of the subjective will in the immediacy of acting consists precisely in this, that its action presupposes an external object with a complex environment. The deed sets up an alteration in the state of affairs confronting my will and my will has responsibility in general for its deed in so far as the predicate 'mine' belongs to the state of affairs so altered.[2]

[1] Glockner, op. cit., vol. VII, p. 161, para. 103.
[2] Ibid., pp. 172-3, para. 115.

An action is *mine* only in so far as it has formed part of my purpose. Since the human world within which moral activity takes place is so complex, a man is held responsible only for those actions which can be regarded as the *direct* result of his own purposes, and those purposes which he conceived on a given state of knowledge.[1]

The attempt by the individual to generate a set of universal moral rules has to be considered in its relation to its end and not merely to its form (that of the subjective trying to will the universal) and the basic moral end, Hegel argues, is that of welfare. All the possible objects of moral endeavour must be related to some question of the welfare of self-conscious beings:

> The welfare of many other unspecified particulars is thus also an essential end and right of subjectivity.[2]

The difficulty with the kind of subjective moral endeavour described in this section of *Grundlinien der Philosophie des Rechts* is that the content of welfare, the very object of moral concern, is not specified, except that of course the relationships in abstract right are presupposed. However, Hegel argues, the claims of welfare may conflict on occasion with those of right.[3] The subjective standpoint cannot, therefore, achieve a content for the notion of welfare by appealing to the articulation of merely legel relationships: on the one hand such relationships may well conflict with the requirements of welfare and in addition the legal relationships of abstract right merely protect the particularized articulation of the will in property and cannot therefore yield some notion of universal welfare. The conflict between right and welfare has in particular cases to be decided and for a decision recourse has to be made to *Conscience*. Conscience, Hegel says, wills what is good and the notion of goodness combines both those of right and welfare:

> Conscience is the expression of the absolute title of subjective self-consciousness to know in itself and from within itself what is right and obligatory, to give recognition only to what it thus knows to be good.[4]

The developing self-conscious mind therefore hopes to find some way from within itself of settling in an impartial manner any conflict between right and welfare. However, Hegel argues, that conscience is unable to bear the weight put upon it at this point in the development of morality. The subjective will, though striving to will the universal

---

[1] Glockner, vol. VII, p. 178, para. 120.   [2] Ibid., p. 184, para. 125.
[3] Ibid., p. 187, para. 128.   [4] Ibid., p. 196, para. 137.

and impartial, recognizing the need for so doing, must in conscience presuppose some kind of rule-governed procedure in order to secure the universality of its deliverances. However, such a rule in turn has to be developed by the conscience of each individual and the problem of impartiality arises again:

> Conscience is therefore subject to the judgement of its truth and falsity and when it appeals only to itself for a decision it is at variance with what it wishes to be, namely the rule for a mode of conduct which is rational, absolutely valid and universal.[1]

A man cannot develop or follow such a private rule. Its development presupposes the very notion of impartiality which the rule is designed itself to secure; following the rule can only be checked by some self-validating procedure of internal appeal.

Hegel's conclusion is that man cannot generate out of himself a moral world, but has to find his moral principles in the concrete on-going life of the community. Such a community is not as such a creation of his own powers, but nonetheless an environment within which his own powers can develop to the full.

In Hegel's discussion of *Ethical Life*, we can discern all the complex features of his philosophy noted thus far. There is metaphysical interpretation of experience, the understanding of political institutions in terms of the realization of consciousness, an interpretation which once grasped, transfigures such institutions so that instead of being seen as alien and external are regarded as necessary to the growth of the development of self-consciousness. In addition is the historical in the broad sense outlined earlier in the book, dealing in specific detail with such institutions as the family, corporation, public authority and the state. Philosophy provides a conceptual grasp of these institutions, a grasp which is no mere redescription but one which in Hegel's view brings out the actual nature of such institutions as opposed to their merely external characteristics recorded in conventional description.

In *Grundlinien der Philosophie des Rechts*, the transition from *Morality*, the world of subjective moral striving, is interpreted both phylogenetically, that is to say in terms of overall human development, in terms of the progress of the human race and ontogenetically, that is to say in the life of the individual. A brief consideration of this point

---

[1] Glockner, op. cit., vol. VII, p. 197, para. 137. It is interesting in this context to compare Wittgenstein on private rules in *Philosophical Investigations*, Oxford 1958, paras. 258 ff., particularly his assertion that to check a private rule privately is like someone buying several copies of the morning paper to assure himself that what it said was true (para. 265).

throws light not only upon the argument of the work but also on Hegel's mature view of his own development. The point is made most explicitly in the *Enzyklopädie* in which Hegel argues that the passage from subjective moral endeavour to the discernment of values and norms in the social order to hand is a passage from youth to maturity both within the individual and within the race. He describes youth in very much the same way as he describes the moral standpoint in *Grundlinien der Philosophie des Rechts*:

> In youth the ideal has a more or less subjective shape, whether it lives in him as an ideal of love and friendship or as an ideal of a universal state of the world . . . he therefore fancies that he is called and qualified to transform the world.[1]

In Hegel's view, the frustrations of the subjective standpoint, which as the earlier part of this book showed were part of his own experience, leads the youth to try to reconcile himself with the on-going life of the community which he had hitherto despised. He points out, however, that this accommodation to reality is often looked upon as mere submission, 'forced upon him by necessity'[2] but he goes on to argue in a passage of considerable importance for understanding the therapeutic role of philosophy that:

> . . . in truth, this unity with the world must be recognized not as a relation imposed by necessity but as the rational. The rational, the divine, possesses the absolute power to actualize itself and has, right from the beginning, fulfilled itself. . . . He can claim, therefore, with at least as much right, indeed with even greater right, than the adolescent to be esteemed as complete and self dependent . . . the insight into the rationality of the world, liberates him from mourning over the destruction of his ideals.[3]

In the life of the individual as well as of the race therefore an achievement of some kind of reconciliation of the moral world to hand in society is a development in self-consciousness. Man is compelled, as a result of the contradictions of the standpoint in *Morality*, to abandon the attempt to create a universal moral order from his own will, and he is driven on to find his values expressed in the morality of the community of which he is a member. *Ethical Life* therefore is the mature stage of consciousness in which man reconciles his particular and universal will by finding rational universal values within his own community:

[1] Glockner, op. cit., vol. X, p. 104. [2] Ibid., p. 106.
[3] Ibid., vol. X, p. 106.

They (i.e. the institutions of Ethical Life) are not something alien to the subject. On the contrary his spirit bears witness to them as its own essence, the essence in which he has a feeling of selfhood.[1]

This relationship with the world is not to be interpreted therefore as one of slavish submission, to see man's relationship to the moral world to hand in his community would be to ignore Hegel's claim that the patterns of morality within such a community are rational, that they can be grasped philosophically as embodying those values which will develop the self-consciousness of human minds. Of course this is a somewhat general claim as it stands and will have to be elucidated in detail with reference to Hegel's discussion of the various components of the modern community.

The *Family* constitutes the first specific form in which differentiated *Ethical Life* appears and within which self-consciousness is developed within a more universal objective framework.[2] It will be recalled that self-consciousness can only be attained when the particular interests and desires manifested in the will are structured by some universal or impartial principles. This proved to be impossible both in *Abstract Right*, in the ownership of property and in *Morality*, the world of abstract decision making. Although these forms of experience constitute significant advances in self-consciousness from one point of view, they still do not provide this structuring of the particular by the universal and thus the advance is not absolute. In the *Family*, however, the individual becomes weaned away from particularity because he has to become aware of and take into account the desires and needs of others. At the same time this developing universality in the will does not appear as imposed upon the individual, but as emerging both naturally and necessarily from the love which one member of a family feels for another, a situation in which one person finds his own life deeply reflected in that of another.

Although the family is an essential socially-oriented development of self-consciousness based upon the mutual recognition accorded in love, it is of necessity a somewhat transitory and restricted form of relationship. Transitory because of the growing maturity of children; restricted in that one family excludes another:

. . . a plurality of families, each of which conducts itself as in principle

---

[1] Glockner, vol. VII, p. 228, para. 147.

[2] Of course consciousness was made objective in *Abstract Right* in the ownership of property, but the will made concrete in property is only a particular will, a capricious will.

a self subsistent concrete person and therefore as *externally* related to its neighbours.[1]

Each family, although a unity in itself, pursues its own particular interests and tries to satisfy its own needs and considered in this way the family as a means of socialization, as a means whereby the universal dimension of the will is actualized, is definitely inadequate. However the fact that each family pursues its own needs leads such families into new and complex patterns of interdependence. As needs multiply and become more sophisticated with the result that the means of satisfying them become more complex and isolated, families and individuals come into very close, if somewhat arbitrary relationships through their mutual dependence in achieving satisfaction for their needs and desires. The system of needs is therefore the first form in which *Civil Society* appears, the kind of system within which men, by pursuing their own particular interests become related to others who can satisfy the needs made articulate in such interests. These relations of mutual inter-dependence in their turn come to require various sorts of control. Hegel characterizes the system of needs as a system within which:

. . . the particular person is essentially so related to other particular persons that each establishes himself and finds satisfaction through means of others.[2]

Man develops his capacities and powers, his self-consciousness by satisfying his needs and his desires. From one point of view this appears as a further development of social differentiation because it is a development in *self* consciousness; from another point of view, however, it appears as a way in which new profound types of social integration are established. In order to satisfy his desires and thus develop as an individual each man requires the activity of another. The self-realization of one person through the satisfaction of his desires is therefore to be achieved only through his relationship with others:

. . . there is formed a system of complete interdependence wherein the livelihood, happiness and legal status of one man is interwoven with the happiness of all.[3]

The system of commercial relationships, which, as we saw earlier, in this book both Hegel and many other social critics of his day and generation considered to be a cause of the fragmentation of society and the enervation of the individual, is now grasped philosophically not as

[1] Glockner, op. cit., vol. VII, p. 261, para. 181.
[2] Ibid., p. 262.   [3] Ibid., p. 263, para. 183.

merely an external system of relationships, but rather one in which the development of one man is linked with that of another. It is to be sure not the unmediated unity of the Greek city state, but at the same time men in contemporary society are very far indeed from being isolated atoms. The philosopher can grasp the interlocking relationships between the individuals in the system of needs beneath what appears as an anarchic veneer:

> The most remarkable thing here is the mutual interlocking of particulars which is what one would least expect because at first sight everything seems to be given over to the arbitrariness of the individual.[1]

At this stage in the argument Hegel's assertion that men are crucially related to one another in civil society is merely general; it is necessary to discern the laws which govern the operation of the system of mutual interdependence and at this juncture Hegel commends the work of the classical economists as constituting an attempt:

> ... to find reconciliation here, to discover in the sphere of needs this show of rationality lying in the thing and effective there.[2]

It will be Hegel's argument as the discussion progresses however that such interrelationships require some state regulation in order for the means of the integration achieved to be grasped as both calculable and rational and hence as a world within which man can find reconciliation.

One major form of mediated integration in modern society, Hegel argues, is the relationship between different classes:

> The infinitely complex, criss-cross movements of reciprocal production and exchange and the equally infinite multiplicity of means therein employed, becomes crystallized, owing to the universality inherent in their content, and distinguished into general groups. As a result, the entire complex is built up into a system of needs, means and types of work relative to those needs, modes of satisfaction and of theoretical and practical education, i.e. into systems to which one or other of which individuals are assigned.[3]

Hegel distinguished three social classes, the substantial, immediate or agricultural class; the reflective, acquisitive or business class and the universal class, or the class of civil servants. The substantial class, as its name implies, comprises those who stand in an immediate relation-

---

[1] Glockner, op. cit., vol. VII, p. 271.   [2] Ibid., pp. 271-2, para. 189.
[3] Ibid., p. 279, para. 201.

ship to the world, working on it, transforming it with the labour of their own hands, the character of their work being dependent on and closely tied up with the passing states of natural phenomena, the seasons and the weather. Because of this rather dependent relationship on the natural world, their work is concrete and substantial and yet at the same time members of the class show little independence of mind or self-consciousness.

The business class on the other hand[1] is the reflective class in that its whole existence depends upon its manipulating and transforming activity—by utilizing for its own advantage the complex system of interrelations established in the system of needs. Hegel argues that this class operates:

> essentially on the mediation of one man's needs and work with those of others.[2]

This class is further subdivided into *craftsmen*, those who make their products with their own hands and supply their products to a clear cut market;[3] those who labour in manufacturing industries, whose labour is abstract and distanced from the natural world, utilizing machines which impose some estrangement between man and what he produces and finally those who trade, exchanging products produced by others through the universal medium of money.[4]

The universal class is so called because it does not pursue particular or sectional interests, but rather the interests of the whole society by administering the legal machinery of the community. The complexity of modern society required some set of people to administer the society. The danger with such a class was, however, that it could represent sectional and particular interests. To prevent this Hegel argued that civil servants should either have a private income, or receive a salary from the state.[5]

The existence and the ethos attached to the particular social classes was not in Hegel's view a merely contingent matter. Classes rather arose as a result of the complexities of the system of needs and the progressive division of labour. People began to be grouped together not through accident of birth into particular estates but by their labour

---

[1] Glockner, op. cit., p. 280. Hegel calls this class *der Stand des Ewerbs*—the acquisitive class.

[2] Ibid., p. 282, para. 204.　　　　　　　　　[3] Ibid., p. 282, para. 204.

[4] Ibid., p. 282, para. 204.

[5] See Bruford, op. cit., p. 14: 'The growing complexity of society reflected in the rise of distinct classes and occupations based upon the division of labour and the increasing use of money had made a professional and non-hereditary civil service necessary from the thirteenth century onwards.'

into different social classes. The ethos of each particular class—substantial, acquisitive, universal—is explicable in Hegel's view in virtue of the kind of labour performed by men in each class. Again the division of labour, seemingly a form of fragmentation, can be seen to generate its own patterns of relationship in social classes and its own types of group ethos.

In addition, Hegel wishes to argue that belonging to a class is a development of self-consciousness on the part of individuals. Self-consciousness is achieved, at least in part, by the developing universality of the conceptions of the mind and social classes, though restricted in outlook from one point of view do provide a social dimension to a person's nature so that he becomes not merely *this* person with *these* particular needs and *this* private outlook, but a member of a social class with its own ethos and its own style of life. Membership of a class therefore lifts a man from the particularity and private pursuit of the system of needs.

The system of needs is the milieu within which individuals, motivated by particular needs and desires, attempt to satisfy these through labour, through trade and exchange and as such they come to have possessions and own property. It is necessary, therefore, for a system of justice to develop in order to protect these property rights. The administration of justice (*die Rechtspflege*), though essential to protect property rights and to safeguard the interests of consumers, is at the same time a further development of this integration through opposition which the structuring of the Idea makes discernible in social and political experience. Men isolated, although now in only a relative fashion, are able conjointly to recognize the *universal* authority of the system of justice:

> In Civil Society, the Idea is lost in particularity and has fallen asunder with the separation of inward and outward. In the Administration of Justice, however, Civil Society returns to its concept, to the unity of the implicit universal with the subjective particular.[1]

The system of justice, abstract in conception, becomes specific in the activity of the public authority. Hegel's notion of public authority draws very heavily upon the points made in *Jenenser Realphilosophie I* and *II* and upon Steuart's doctrine of the *Statesman*, although the discussion in *Grundlinien der Philosophie des Rechts* goes beyond his earlier views it some respects. In his Jena system, Hegel had argued that the system of needs was anarchic and blind and thus in need of control; in the present work, however, his position has modified

[1] Glockner, op. cit., vol. VII, p. 309, para. 229.

somewhat and his explanation of the role of the public authority in securing the integration of society has several dimensions.

The first aspect of the explanation is in terms of the natural generation, out of the system of needs of factors of common interest, such things as drainage, water supply, means of communication, etc. all of which Hegel argues:

Call for the care and oversight of the public authority.[1]

Such a justification would in the context have appeared unexceptional, this is particularly clear if Hegel's other name for the public authority, 'the Police' is utilized. Bruford makes the following point about the usage of the word during the period in Germany:

What was then called 'police' covered every kind of regulation considered necessary for the health, prosperity and moral welfare of the subject. Under this head were included the first sanitary regulations, concerning water supply, drainage, the removal of rubbish etc.[2]

The role of the public authority emerged too in terms of what might anachronistically be called consumer protection. Within the system of needs, the interests of producers and consumers could on occasion come into collision and at the level of mere self interest on both sides, there could be no rational way of securing an equitable outcome. Such possibly conflicting interests therefore require to be adjusted to one another which

. . . requires a control which stands above both and is consciously undertaken.[3]

A clear case of the necessity of this type of intervention on the part of the public authority would in Hegel's view, be the fixing of the prices of the commonest necessities of life, which he argues are offered by producers not so much to the individual consumer, but rather to the totality of consumers.[4] Again Hegel's discussion of this aspect of the role of public authority is not in the prescriptive mode. There was a tradition in Germany at the time that the police/public authority could regulate prices when and where necessary.[5]

Thirdly the intervention of the public authority into the commercial

---

[1] Glockner, p. 312, para. 235.
[2] Bruford, op. cit., p. 17. See also B. Chapman, *The Police State*, London 1970.
[3] Glockner, op. cit., vol. VII, p. 313, para. 236.
[4] Ibid., p. 313, para. 236.   [5] Bruford, op. cit., p. 17.

relationships of the system of needs is explained in terms of the need in the larger branches of industry to grasp the total situation within which the industry operates so that its activities could be based on a rational calculable footing. Hegel makes clear that he has in mind in this context the relation between an industry and the materials which it utilizes, but which are produced abroad.[1]

Hegel's position on the role of the public authority is therefore clearly much influenced by Steuart's view of the role of the statesman. At the same time, however, Hegel returns and extends a point which he made in 'Die Verfassung Deutschlands,' namely that such intervention should not be of a total and suffocating nature. He is reported as maintaining that in the modern world:

> ... two views predominate at the present time. One asserts that the superintendence of everything properly belongs to the public authority, the other that the public authority has nothing at all to regulate here because everyone will direct his endeavours according to the needs of others.[2]

The second doctrine, Hegel argues, cannot be maintained because of the arbitrary nature of the integration wrought in the system of needs; the first point he rejected in 'Die Verfassung Deutschlands' as being inimical to the development of individuality and self-consciousness. Both intervention *per se* and the particular character of the intervention of the public authority into the system of commercial relationships has to be understood in metaphysical terms. The anarchic nature of commercial relationships requires some sort of universal oversight in order to inject some kind of regulation into it and bring the particular pursuits of individuals into contact with more extensive and universal ends, and this is seen philosophically as being necessary to the achievement of self-conscious development. At the same time however, because such control has to be exercised over individuals who are conscious of their individuality and their freedom, it has to leave as large an area as possible to self-directing activities because these just as much as the development of universal patterns of order are necessary to self-consciousness.

Self-consciousness implies the union of the universal with the specific and the individual and in consequence the right of the individual to subjective freedom cannot be coherently denied in the modern world. In many passages Hegel insists therefore on both the need for public control of commercial relationships, but at the same time argues that

[1] Glockner, op. cit., vol. VII, p. 313, para. 236.
[2] Ibid., p. 314, additions to para. 236.

such control has to be consistent with freedom. In paragraph 236 of *Grundlinien der Philosophie des Rechts* Hegel asserts that strong public control could only be justified in a primitive community undertaking a gigantic economic task and in the context he mentions the building of the pyramids in Egypt. Such a society, however, had no real social differentiation and thus no very well developed notion of individuality and personal freedom. The situation of the modern world is, however, vastly different:

> The right of the subject particularity, his right to be satisfied, or in other words the right of subjective freedom, is the pivot and centre of the difference between antiquity and modern times.[1]

and he goes on to argue that this particularity is central to the development of the powers of the human mind and is fully articulated in the self-seeking of the system of needs.

Later in the argument Hegel goes on to give a further, highly ingenious explanation of the rise of the role of the public authority or of the 'external state', as he revealingly calls it. He points out that it is possible in certain circumstances for there to be an over-production of goods for the number of consumers in society and in conditions such as these the bottom may well drop out of the market in such goods and poverty for a great many people may result. This can be a social catastrophe in Hegel's view in that the poor may become a *rabble*, lacking any notion of respect and civic duty. Self-consciousness and self-respect are the products at least in part of labour and in these circumstances labour is denied to the poor with the consequent enervation of their personalities. Several solutions to this kind of social problem could be offered but none is acceptable given the present stage of the conscious development of individuals. It might be argued that the poor and out of work could receive income from the public authority which would in turn raise its revenue in various ways— Hegel mentions the rich, endowments to hospitals and monasteries, etc. Such a solution would not solve the problem according to Hegel given the stage of human development reached when problems like this arise.[2] Man comes to consciousness of himself and to a notion of self-respect through labour, transforming and moulding his environment and merely to dispense charity to the poor would not solve the personal dimension to the problem—the lack of self-respect which in its turn leads to the development of a rabble. An alternative could be to provide work but, as Hegel points out, the economic difficulties in

[1] Glockner, op. cit., vol. VII, p. 182, para. 124.
[2] Ibid., p. 319, para. 245.

the system of needs are a result of over-production[1] and consequently to subsidize the labour of the penurious rabble would merely intensify the problem.

This basic problem of over-production enables the philosopher to grasp a further dimension to modern economic activity, namely colonization and the need to seek and to capture new markets.[2] This activity, because it is so central to the survival of society, cannot be left to arbitrariness and chance and again has to be under the control of the public authority. Again we find central to Hegel's discussion of the various features of modern society a metaphysical dimension which cannot be merely thought away in any attempt to discern the identity or assess the significance of his thought.

As the system of needs predicated upon particularity and private self-seeking generates necessarily out of its own tensions various patterns of integration and universal control which, while not immediately and intuitively obvious, can be seen and grasped by the philosopher to be a significant development in man's consciousness of himself. The same point is implicit in Hegel's discussion of the corporation. As self-consciousness develops, so does the capacity for choice, for wishing and wanting with the consequence that the range of human needs develops as do the means whereby those needs are satisfied. This process leads to a progressive division of labour with further differentiations between individuals. At the same time, however, corporations emerge out of this progressive division and appear, once their role is philosophically grasped, as new and appropriate integrating forces in society. The corporations represent the interests of the various groups involved in the division of labour and Hegel, in an interesting passage, connects their integrating role with their development from a process of differentiation:

> Hence, a selfish purpose, directed towards its particular self-interest, apprehends and evinces itself at the same time as universal; and a member of civil society is in virtue of his own particular skill a member of a corporation, whose universal purpose is thus wholly concrete.[3]

The Corporation is a dialectical advance on public authority because the latter, irrespective of its philosophical explanation, may, at the level of practice appear to be somewhat external and imposed to those whose lives are affected by its operation. There is no conscious identity between controllers and controlled even though the need for such

[1] Glockner, p. 319, para. 245. [2] Ibid., p. 320, para. 246.
[3] Ibid., op. cit., vol. VII, p. 323, para. 251.

control may be grasped in philosophical terms. Within the corporation however, the identity between the universal aims of the corporation and the particular aims of the individual is secured reciprocally, by 'conscious effort for a common need'. At the same time, however, the interests of the corporation are only universal in a relative manner. Such interests certainly transcend the particular interests of the individuals within the corporation but at the same time such institutions merely express the interest of a sectional group in society, the interests of the acquisitive class and not the interests of society as a whole. The relationship between corporation and the public authority is thus complex. The corporation is not external, is not imposed, there is a close identity between it and its members; at the same time, however, its aims are universal in only a relative, *soi-disant* sense. The public authority on the other hand articulates the universal interest of society rather than the sectional interest of a group of individuals but at the same time appears as an external and imposed form of authority.

It is Hegel's contention that only the state can express the *universality* present in the public authority and the *specificity* and *individuality* of the corporation. The state provides the individual with universal ends so that his consciousness can rise above the particularity of his individual needs; it provides specific institutions within which these universal ends are made concrete and within these institutions some individual participation is allowed so that these universal ends become central to the minds of individuals acting within these institutions. The state is therefore a *concrete universal*, linking universality with specificity and individuality and as such:

> The state is the actuality of the ethical Idea. It is the ethical mind *qua* the substantial will manifest and revealed to itself.[1]

The state can be seen therefore as a supreme form of the structuring of the Idea in the human or the ethical realm; it emerges as a supreme and satisfying political form of integration out of the diremption and fragmentation of civil society and as such exhibits the growth and development through the resolution of contradiction and the reconciliation of fragmentation which is the exemplification of the Idea. The modern state,[2] correctly, that is philosophically understood, can therefore be seen in general terms to be the resolution of one of the major causes of the social fragmentation which, in Hegel's view, had been the heritage of the western world since the rise of aristocratic

---

[1] Glockner, op. cit., p. 328, para. 257.
[2] Hegel still has in mind the kind of state inspired by the reforms of Stein and his followers. See his letter to Hardenberg, one of Stein's circle, *Briefe*, vol. II, p. 242.

government in Rome—the divorce between man as an individual and man as a citizen, a divorce which had been taken much further in the economic life of the modern world. The modern state is able to reconcile this divorce when its institutions are understood and comprehended by the philosopher. These institutions do not attempt to remove particularity and sectional interest, for example as Rousseau had argued—the French Revolution had revealed the dangers of attempting to remove from society all intermediate sectional groupings—but rather by recognizing such particularity as being necessary for the development of self-consciousness and building into the state structure this element of particularity but at the same time fusing it with the universal ends of the state:[1]

> The principle of the modern state has prodigious depth and strength because it allows the principle of subjectivity to progress to its culmination and yet at the same time brings it back to the substantive unity and so maintains this unity as the principle of subjectivity itself.[2]

The state, because it arises by necessity out of the system of needs, has to allow for the consciousness of individuality realized there, but, at the same time it provided such self-realizing individuals with universal ends to which they are related through specific political institutions, particularly through the Assembly of Estates. Seen in this sense, the modern state is an essential development in the process whereby men become conscious of themselves and is not something imposed on them or external to them but rather constitutes an environment in and through which they may develop. Man no longer has the close, intuitive, *sinnliche Harmonie* which the Greek had to the political structure of his city state; man's contemporary relationship to the state has to be grasped through philosophy, through the exertion of the concept and as such is a mediated harmony.[3]

The actual way in which the state elevates the individual consciousness to universality through specific political institutions is by means of a framework whose main features are:

[1] Cf. Findlay in 'The Contemporary Relevance of Hegel' in *Language, Mind and Value*, London 1963, p. 229:

> We can see that the deep gulf of persons and classes of person is a necessary condition of their emergent rationality . . . only because they lived immured in selfish interests can morality and social obligation arise within them. The distinctness of persons is therefore a necessary condition of a rational life in common to them all and is therefore part of that life.

[2] Glockner, op. cit., vol. VII, p. 338, para. 260.
[3] Ibid., additions to paragraph 260, p. 338.

1. A Monarch who is hereditary and free from political faction.
2. A bureaucracy of civil servants able to pursue universal ends.
3. An Assembly of Estates through which the views of the various Estates on political policy are made known to the executive power.

Philosophically understood, the modern state, possessing these features constituted the solution to the political dimension of the fragmentation of society which had so preoccupied him.[1] As we have seen, Hegel had long since rejected the notion of a return to anything approximating to the political culture of the city state which he now describes as being based upon:

> . . . the notion of the substantial still undivided unity, a unity which has not yet come to inner differentiation.

This inner differentiation had developed as the result of a number of factors: the initial alienation of man from society originating in Rome; the development of Christianity with its emphasis on private ends and personal salvation, which took root in the declining Roman world; a subjectivity and a differentiation which was developed by the Reformation and which reached its zenith in political terms with the French Revolution and finally a differentiation which resulted from the growing and progressive division of labour. It is Hegel's claim that the institutions of the modern state are able to integrate men into a political community which could find a place for the values of freedom and individuality, the realization of which had been the correlation of the growth of differentiation.

At the head of the modern state stands the monarch, who, as it were, symbolizes in his own person the universality of the state's interest because he is raised above the particularity of class and group, a feature of the monarchy both crucial to the universality of the state and hence the development of the self-consciousness of the individuals within it. This, Hegel argues, can only be secured if the monarch is hereditary. At the same time, because the universality of the state's interest is made concrete in one man, it is also in a profound sense a universality made fully articulate in the dimension of individuality. The monarch, Hegel argues, has a share in the legislative power in that Hegel considers it to be the monarch's duty to take the final decision in any matter of policy but this final decision, although in a sense groundless, is not arbitrary. The monarch does not himself formulate the policy of the state. It rather comes to him in the form of

---

[1] Hegel argued in the letter to Hardenberg, cited on p. 171, that in his Rechtsphilosophie he was concerned to grasp 'conceptually in its principal features that which stands before us'.

counsel and countercounsel on the basis of which he has then to decide. This counsel basically is given to the monarch by the supreme council of the state, members of this council holding office by the fiat of the monarch. The dialectical role of the council is to act as the moment of specificity to the aspects of both universality and individuality realized in the monarch.

The legislative side of the state, the monarch in council, is therefore capable of being grasped as a philosophical universal, uniting the three necessary elements of universality, specificity and individuality. Such a view implies, however, that each moment is necessary and consequently the council in the state acts as a check on the power of the crown. The monarch in council as a concrete universal is, therefore, a philosophical transposition of the doctrine of constitutional monarchy. The constitutional side of Hegel's grasp of the role of the monarchy in the modern state also comes out in the universality of the monarch's concern which, Hegel argues, is made explicit in his respect for the constitution and the laws of the state.

The executive side of the state is concerned with carrying out the decisions of policy finally reached by the monarch acting on the advice of the state council. In a sense the public authority and the corporation already discussed are a part of the executive power of the crown, dealing particularly with the problems thrown up by the interplay of needs in civil society. This role within the executive power is emphasized by Hegel when he argues that positions of responsibility in the corporations are to be filled partly as a result of popular election with the final confirmation of appointment coming from 'higher authority', i.e. the crown.[1]

The other main branch of the executive is the civil service and this plays the role of the universal to the specific and ultimately individual dimensions of the corporations. Hegel again insists that the civil service must be impartial and freed from the particularity of interest, each civil servant finding his personal satisfaction in his pursuit of the universal interests of the state. Hegel makes two interesting points about the civil service over and above his major argument that it contributes to securing the rationality of the modern state.[2] One point is that within the universal function of the service there is room for specification of particular administrative duties because the division of labour has spread from society to government—the complexity of society leading to the development of different types of administrative expertise on the

[1] Glockner, vol. VII, p. 396, para. 288.
[2] Compare Weber's masterly essay on bureaucracy in *From Max Weber*, ed. H. Gerth and C. W. Mills, op. cit., pp. 196 ff.

part of civil servants;[1] the second point concerns recruitment to the service and here Hegel argues that it is rational for it to be recruited from the middle class because within this class intelligence is most fully developed and at the same time recruitment to the civil service would give to this class a sense of social duty which, along with the power of the crown and the role of the corporations, would neutralize its potentially upsetting and disruptive political strength.[2]

The monarch in council makes the decisions on policy, the civil service carries them out *sine ira et studio* and the Assembly of Estates communicates the views of the Estates in civil society on matters of policy. The three taken together, the Monarch, the Executive and the Estates, constitutes the legislature. The Assembly of Estates is a vital factor in Hegel's attempt to demonstrate that the modern state is an appropriate form of political community by mediating universal ends through the specific Estates to the individual lost in the particularity of self-interest in the system of needs. Through their relationship to the Assembly of Estates, the particular Estates bring into being:

... the existence of subjective, formal freedom, the public consciousness as an empirical universal of which the thoughts and opinions of the Many are particulars.[3]

The role of the Assembly of Estates is thus to relate the isolated self interested individuals in the system of needs to the political or universal realm. There can no longer be direct democracy, the progressive development of the powers and capacities of the individual had destroyed the relationship of the individual to the political realm which had been the presupposition of the direct participating democracy of the Greek city state. In the modern world the relationship between the private self-conscious individual engaged in the system of needs in the pursuit of his own self interest and his role as a citizen, concerned with the universal good of the community, has to be a mediated one. They are represented through organs within which their particular interests have grown more universal. Representation is through the Estates which in turn are elected from those who have held office in the relatively universal structures of corporations and occupational associations in civil society:

In making the appointment to the Estates, society is not dispersed

---

[1] Again compare Weber, especially pp. 240 ff., 'The Rationalization of Education and Training'.
[2] Glockner, op. cit., vol. VII, p. 403, para. 297.
[3] Ibid., p. 408, para. 301.

into atomic units, collected to perform only a single and temporary act and kept together for a moment and no longer. On the contrary it makes the appointment as a society, articulated into associations, communities and corporations, which, although constituted already for other purposes, acquire in this way a connection with politics.[1]

The Assembly of Estates is built up out of the representatives of the two non-universal classes in civil society, the substantial or agricultural class and the formal or business class, and each of these classes forms a chamber in the Estates Assembly, the agricultural class the upper chamber, the business class the lower chamber. The membership of the agricultural class in the upper chamber of the Assembly is comprised of the landed gentry whose position is thus neither based upon the favour of the mob nor of the monarch and as such they are in a better position to make articulate without fear or favour the true interests of the class. At the same time this class mediates between the crown on the one hand and the representatives of the business class on the other. On the one hand it obviously shares a certain amount of common ground with the monarchy in that membership of the Assembly is based upon entailed property and thus the hereditary principle, the basis of the monarchy; on the other hand, however, they know what it is to have specific interests and thus share in the ethos of the business class:

It is therefore fixed and has a substantive position between the subjective wilfulness of both extremes; and while it mirrors in itself the moment of monarchical power, it also shares in other respects the needs and rights of the other extreme and hence it becomes a support of both the throne and society.[2]

The representatives of the business class in the Assembly similarly are not elected in isolation direct from the pursuit of their particular and self interested concerns, but through the corporations, the institutions which within society helped to develop some universal standards in the activity of members of this class lost in the particularity of self-seeking. The deputies are elected to the Assembly from corporations and are thus in an analogous position to the landed gentry in the substantial class, and thus able to make a more universal assessment of the claims of their class and the claims of the community as a whole.

[1] Glockner, op. cit., vol. VII, p. 417. Cf. p. 411:
Regarded as a mediating organ the Estates stand between the government on the one hand and the nation broken up into particulars on the other.
[2] Ibid., p. 416.

The role of the Estates Assembly in political terms is manifold in Hegel's view. As a part of the legislature it of course performs the same function in relation to the business of legislation, which, Hegel argues, so far as it is concerned with individuals, comprises provision by the state for their well being and happiness, that is to say laws dealing with all sorts of private rights, the rights of communities, corporations and organizations affecting the entire Estate. As such the Estates would have a role in determining the policy of the public authority to commercial relationships, thus satisfying Hegel's demand made since the writing of 'Die Verfassung Deutschlands' that not only should public authority regulate commercial relationships but also that this regulation should not be merely external and imposed. In addition the Assembly of Estates is concerned with the extraction of services in terms of taxation from those who comprise the classes represented in the Estates.

Considered in their broader perspective, however, the role of the Estates is most important in linking the individual to the political world from which he has so long been estranged. To secure this role of involvement in politics which is at the same time a means of civic education Hegel argues in favour of the publicity of the debates in the Estates Assembly. Only with such publicity can a political consciousness be brought to the masses in such a way that they are able to discern the real possibilities in a situation:

... it then becomes clear that a man's castle building at his fire side with his wife and friends is one thing, while what happens in a great Assembly . . . is something quite different.[1]

When grasped philosophically, therefore, the modern state can be seen to provide a form of political community appropriate to the fundamental change in the human condition in the modern world compared with the Greek city state. In his discussion of modern political structures the main elements in Hegel's general philosophical position, discussed in the previous chapter, may be seen. He seeks to grasp the development of various social and political institutions in their universality, their specificity and their individuality as crucial for human self-realization in the modern world, a feature which Hegel regards as built immanently into such institutions by the structuring of the Idea, a structuring which reveals itself within the discernible progress through the emergence of new forms of integration out of differentiation and fragmentation both in society and in the human personality. At the same time this aim is therapeutic, to provide man

[1] Glockner, op. cit., vol. VII, p. 423, para. 315 additions.

with a home in the modern political community, to overcome that estrangement from political and social institutions which had so preoccupied him.

In the final section of *Grundlinien der Philosophie des Rechts*, Hegel gives a compressed version of his *Vorlesungen über die Philosophie der Geschichte* in which Hegel tries to trace the development of the notion of political community through world history, attempting to comprehend those realms of world history which he considers to be of crucial importance for understanding the development of the modern state. He distinguishes four such periods of history: the Oriental realm, the Greek realm, the Roman realm and the Germanic realm.

The Oriental world was on Hegel's view a substantial world, with no real division of consciousness between one man and another, within which there was no realization of the specific and unique qualities of each individual. In such a situation rule by one man was the appropriate form of political community and because there was no conception of *human* individuality, such a ruler was usually taken as being divine. Similarly such a rule was both naturally and appropriately despotic because there was no conception of personal freedom.[1]

Greek culture constituted a significant advance in human self-consciousness because it was in the Greek world that the principle of subjectivity first arose, although in a somewhat under-developed form—certainly not in such a form so as to enable a man to distinguish at all clearly between his own values and ideals and those of his community. There was, Hegel argues, in Greek society no deep fracture between the claims of personality and the demands of citizenship. This was largely the result of the institution of slavery. As we have seen, particularly in the works of the Jena period, Hegel argued that full self-consciousness and the development of private self-seeking develop as a result of progressive developments in the labouring process. The Athenian citizen, however, did not labour, the slave did:

. . . the due satisfaction of needs is not yet comprised in the sphere of freedom but is relegated exclusively to the class of slaves.[2]

The appropriate form of government at this level of human development is democracy. In such a society democracy could work because there was a coincidence between the individual's wants and the requirement of the community. The Greek stood, therefore, in a state of *sinnliche Harmonie* to his modes of social and political experience.

Hegel's discussion of the Roman world adds very little to the crucial

[1] See Glockner, op. cit., vol. VII, p. 452, para. 355.
[2] Ibid., p. 454, para. 356.

account given in 'Die Positivität der christlichen Religion' in which he described how aristocratic government had developed as a result of the accumulation of wealth by a few individuals as a result of the wars of conquest, and how this development had gone hand in hand with the alienation of the mass of the people from the political realm. Philosophically this development could be seen to be necessary as an advance in self-consciousness through the pursuit of private ends but, without the philosophically discernible rationality within it, it appears as a dark night of the soul, as a 'degenerate age', as Hegel had put the point in his earlier work, opening up a deep fracture between private and civic virtue and thus lying at the very basis of what he had earlier considered to be the unresolved crisis of the contemporary world:

> In this realm differentiation is carried to its conclusion, and the ethical is sundered without end into the extremes of private self-consciousness of persons on the one hand and abstract universality on the other.[1]

Philosophy could, however, discern in this 'infinite grief' that it was a necessary development in terms of self-consciousness because the mind progresses when new patterns of integration are produced out of deep diremptions. Philosophically understood the Roman world and its aftermath was part of the *Bildung* of consciousness.

The conclusion of this process is the Germanic realm, in which on the one hand the particularity of individual consciousness is taken to its extreme in commercial society but on the other hand is brought back to a form of universality and integration in the form of the state described above. The bifurcation between bourgeois man, maximizing his utilities in the market, and the impartial demands of citizenship are reconciled in the institutions of the modern state which can provide a form of *moralische Harmonie* in the modern world.

If Hegel's political philosophy is taken in the narrow sense, that is to say in terms of his concern to philosophically describe and explain both past and present forms of political community in terms of the discussion of political institutions, then the exposition of his thought would end at this point, but it has been a recurrent and central concern of this book to argue that Hegel's whole philosophy is socially and politically engaged and that any attempt to do justice to Hegel's general social and political concerns must take into account wider features of both his philosophical method and his substantive conclusions. Nowhere is this point more true than in the context of his religious

---

[1] Glockner, op. cit., vol. VII, p. 454, para. 357.

philosophy. In his early writings Hegel had been particularly concerned with the religious dimension of social life particularly from the point of view of the contribution which such experience could make to the achievement of an integrated community. Hegel had of course argued that the transcendental character of Christian religious experience had been a major element in the alienation of men from their social and political institutions, a situation which he summed up thus in *Der Geist des Christentums und sein Schicksal*:

> ... church and state, worship and life, piety and civic virtue, spiritual and wordly action never dissolve into one.[1]

Obviously Hegel could only consistently represent the modern political community as exemplifying appropriate patterns of integration into the modern world in so far as he was able to understand the role of Christianity within such a community and indeed the social dimension of his philosophy of religion is borne out by the inclusion within *Grundlinien der Philosophie des Rechts* of a long and sensitive discussion of the relationship between the political and the spiritual communities. In a passage which indicates that he had in mind his own earlier attitudes Hegel writes:

> ... religion may sometimes be looked upon as commanding downright indifference to earthly interests, the march of events and current affairs.[2]

However he goes on to make a very significant comment:

> ... but this suggestion seems to assert that politics is a matter of caprice and indifference.[3]

This assertion contains the germ of the solution to the relationship between politics and religion in the modern state. Hegel has demonstrated that the modern state and indeed other social and political institutions can be seen in terms of the development of self-consciousness, in terms of the development of the Idea as the structuring principle in this development, a development which once comprehended philosophically would realize Spirit in human life. But as was pointed out in the previous chapter, Hegel links up very closely this development understood philosophically in metaphysical terms and a correct understanding of the relation between God and the world. According to Hegel, correctly understood, the Christian religion is an attempt to

[1] Nohl, op. cit., p. 342.
[2] Glockner, op. cit., vol. VII, p. 348, para. 270.
[3] Ibid., p. 348, para. 270.

grasp in metaphors and in picture thinking the complete involvement of God in the world, the complete interrelation between the infinite and the finite. This dimension of religious experience of course, Hegel argues, comes out most clearly in the crucifixion, an event which symbolizes the unity of God and man. Religious experience is in this sense both inadequate to but at the same time the parallel of philosophical experience which can *comprehend* through the use of the notions of Idea and Spirit this unity of the infinite and the finite which religion merely *apprehends*. As political experience is along with other types of experience a way in which the Idea, the structuring element in the world is realized, it can also be seen in religious terms as a mode of God's realization in the world in such a way Hegel can claim:

Der Staat ist göttlicher Wille.[1]

In this sense there can be no fundamental discrepancy between religious experience and political life and instead of being considered as an enemy of good citizenship, philosophically grasped, becomes the very foundation of it. Thus he can argue:

. . . the church and state are essentially one in truth of principle and disposition.[2]

At the same time the philosophical grasp of the experience of the Christian religion is crucial for this reconciliation. Hegel is not implying that his earlier strictures on the anti-social elements in Christian belief were misplaced; on the contrary, he might well have continued to argue that when taken at the level of the understanding, that is to say in conventional terms, Christianity could still be anti-social. The crucial thing which Christians have to recognize, and it is in Hegel's view something which is brought home to them philosophically, is the symbolic importance of both the incarnation and crucifixion representing the union of the divine with the mortal and the infinite with the finite. Once understood in this way each man can see himself as part of God, or conversely see God not as some remote transcendent deity but as actualized both in modes of social experience and in the lives and self-consciousness of other men. Only in these circumstances will a spiritual community grow within the social world as opposed to being in deep discord with it. This point is made most clearly in Hegel's *Vorlesungen über die Philosophie der Religion*[3] in which he argues:

[1] Glockner, op. cit., vol. VII, p. 350, para. 270.
[2] Ibid., pp. 361–2, para. 290.
[3] Ibid., vols XV–XVI. The crucial argument is in vol. XVI.

God is but at the same time this Other (i.e. the natural and the social worlds), the Other in the sense that this Other is God himself.[1]

This comes out symbolically in the incarnation and the crucifixion of the God man and the task of the Christian community is to grasp that the whole world is in this sense the incarnation of God:

> It is with the consciousness of the Spiritual Community which thus makes the transition from man pure and simple to a God man, and to a perception, a consciousness, a certainty of the unity and the union of the Divine and human natures, that the Church or Spiritual Community begins and it is this consciousness which constitutes the truth upon which the Spiritual Community is founded.[2]

Obviously understood in this way there could be no deep cleavage between man as a citizen and man as a religious person.

The final sentence of the previous paragraph, however, brings out what has been insisted upon so far in this book, namely that philosophy in its rational educative role is the key to community. Modern man can live in an integrated political community so long as both his social and political and his religious experience is transfigured by philosophy. At the conventional level of thought man sees political institutions as imposed and arbitrary whereas the philosopher demonstrates that they are necessary in their development and expressive of the individual's will in character; in ordinary religious experience men take themselves to be engaged in the worship of a God who transcends the community, whereas the philosopher demonstrates that both the worshipper and his society is in fact a part of God's self-realization and that this self-realization is fully accomplished in the world. Only when such interpretations have been given can men live in community in the modern world. In such a sense, therefore, philosophy is at the service of the state, making men aware of their integration into modern modes of experience:

> With us in Prussia as distinct from Greece, philosophy has an existence in the open, an existence in touch with the public, an existence principally or only in the service of the state.[3]

The pattern of community in the modern world has therefore to be second order, mediated and philosophically based, an insight which Hegel put beautifully in *Die Phänomenologie des Geistes* when he argued that:

---

[1] Glockner, op. cit., vol. XVI, p. 635. [2] Ibid., p. 635.
[3] Op. cit., vol. VII, p. 29.

... humanity exists only in the accomplished unity of consciousness.[1]

It is Hegel's attempt to secure such a unity of consciousness and to solve the problems of fragmentation and dissonance which had beset him since his youth that constitutes the identity of his thought, an identity which makes *all* of his work pervaded by a deep humane concern for the life of men in his own society.

[1] Glockner, vol. II, p. 63.

Chapter VIII

Transfiguration or Mystification?

Hegel is to be honoured for having willed something great and having failed to accomplish it.

Søren Kierkegaard

So far in this book the argument has been historical in an attempt to determine, in so far as it is possible, the identity of Hegel's thought and we have seen that this identity is closely bound up with his general social and political preoccupations, preoccupations which had pervaded his thought from a very early age. At the same time his philosophical solution to these problems is inextricably bound up with his general metaphysical standpoint so that any assessment of Hegel's work ultimately comes back to an attempt to weigh the merits of his general philosophical orientation. In taking such a position on Hegel we have moved very far from Pelcynski's assertion that:

> Hegel's political thought can be read, understood and appreciated without having to come to terms with his metaphysics.[1]

On the contrary: reference to his general metaphysical position is crucial to making both his concern for politics and the particular character of that concern intelligible.

The activity of the critic therefore requires the formulation of some criteria for assessing a metaphysical system of the kind which Hegel produced and Hegel himself had views upon how his own work should be assessed. In *Die Phänomenologie des Geistes* he argues that:

> The subject matter of philosophy is not exhausted by any aim but only by the way things are worked out in detail. The aim taken by itself is a lifeless generality.[2]

[1] Pelcynski, op. cit., p. 136. [2] Glockner, vol. II, p. 13.

In suggesting how philosophy is to be appraised, Hegel appears to argue that attention should be directed less to the aims and presuppositions of a philosophical work and more to an assessment of the explanation given of the various modes of experience within the general philosophical framework. In the context of his own philosophy this would come down to the demand that the critic ought to look at his particular explanations of, for example, political and religious experience, and not concentrate his attention at the general level, merely discussing the aims of such explanations. Later in this chapter it will be argued that such an approach by the critic must be inadequate; that this is not the way in which a metaphysical system can be appraised. For the present, however, Hegel's recommendation will be followed and an attempt will be made to assess his thought in the terms which he urges upon the critic.

Hegel appears to argue that his system stands or falls by the explanation which it is capable of offering of all the modes of experience, but he does not give an explicit clue as to the criteria of adequacy which the critic could use to assess such explanations. Several criteria may, however, be extrapolated from Hegel's own practice which may provide crucial tests for his particular explanations.

In the first place it would seem that any criterion used must be rational. After Hegel's somewhat vituperative attacks upon philosophies which depend for their validity upon an appeal to feeling or intuition, it would be inconsistent if the appeal of his own system were to be determined by a similar verdict. This point seems to rule out as inappropriate for the assessment of Hegel's work the vague criterion of adequacy which W. H. Walsh puts forward in his *Metaphysics*:

. . . in the last resort it is a matter of inviting the reader to take the principles and see for himself.[1]

Such an account, however plausible in general, would not do for Hegel. In some sense the validity and truth of his position must depend upon some rational assessment of the explanatory power of his basic principles when they are applied to the complexities of various modes of experience. This being so, it would seem that Hegel's own practice generates three particular criteria which are conjointly necessary and sufficient conditions for a rational test of the adequacy of his explanations.[2]

The first of these criteria is to some extent controversial in that it

[1] London 1963, p. 182.
[2] My position here owes something to a paper by Prof. D. E. Christensen, ' "Authenticity" and "warranted belief" in Hegel's Dialectic of Religion', given to the Wooford Symposium in South Carolina, November 1968.

depends largely upon the general account of the purpose and role of Hegel's system offered in this book, namely his insistence that philosophical explanations must exhibit necessary connections between those things, practices or forms of experience which are explained. It has been constantly urged that the whole of Hegel's philosophy and indeed his earlier non-philosophical works may best be seen in terms of the pursuit of coherence, a pursuit articulated in philosophy as an attempt to overcome the estrangement of man from the world and the fragmentation of his experience by an attempt to understand the world in both its natural and social development as a rational and necessary process, this rationality and necessity being secured through the structuring of the Idea. Philosophy, it seems, must operate with some notion of necessity if its basic aim of reconciliation is to be achieved. Of course, the tough-minded critic might argue at this point that if such a notion of necessity is a central condition of the plausibility of Hegel's system, then the whole programme is vitiated from the outset. Hegel's attitude might be contrasted with that of the contemporary empiricist and the point of the analogy would be to argue that if Hegel wishes to operate with a concept of necessity in his explanations, then either he must be *stipulating* the meanings of the words, the descriptive terms which enter into his explanations, in which case his philosophical explanations become necessary because tautological and consequently with no claim on the facts; or alternatively he uses the descriptive expressions in his explanations in the normal fashion, in which case his explanations will become falsifiable through normal processes and hence not necessary. The argument for such a view would run like this;[1] any explanation of facts must include descriptive statements or phrases which stand in some relation to empirically detectable qualities or occurrences in the world; a detectable quality must be capable of being detected by empirical means because there must be some way of deciding whether a particular occurrence has the quality ascribed to it in the descriptive statement or by means of the descriptive phrase; in contrast to this would stand undetectable traits for which there could be no empirical means of deciding whether they are ascribed correctly to occurrences. An explanation of a body of facts is empirical in so far as it uses predicates which refer to detectable traits; metaphysical in so far as it does not. Because the ascription of empirical predicates to subjects must always stand open to revision, modification and falsification, it follows that there can be no necessary descriptions relating to detectable traits in the world. A metaphysical description

[1] See 'Are There Infallible Explanations?' by P. G. Morrison in *Studies in Hegel*, The Hague 1960.

may be necessary but it secures its necessity at too high a price, namely tautological insignificance.

It would seem on this view that Hegel's philosophy is caught on the horns of a dilemma. Either it has to give up the claim of necessary explanation, otherwise it could make no claim on the facts and could not therefore be in a position to secure its overall aim of reconciliation to reality; alternatively, the requirement of necessity could be built into the system but in such a case it would become, in Spinozistic manner, a long, rambling tautology.

This argument is strong and may well be irrefutable so far as the particular case of Hegel is concerned, but the principle on which it is predicated, namely a rigid distinction between analytic and synthetic statements has recently come under attack and the results of this attack have been used by some critics to extricate Hegel from the dilemma described above. The sharp bifurcation between analytic and synthetic statements has been brought into doubt by the writings of Wittgenstein and his followers. Indeed, the importance of Wittgenstein's work in helping to make Hegel's philosophy intelligible to the contemporary reader has been claimed by a recent reviewer:

> . . . in reacting against Logical Atomism, the later Wittgenstein came up with many of the old Idealist arguments in a new form. Hence the doubts cast upon the analytic-synthetic dichotomy, the corner stone of positivist thought.[1]

The example of Wittgenstein has led philosophers to realize that there is perhaps a middle way between the rather rigid distinction between relations of fact expressed in synthetic statements and relations of language and symbols expressed analytically. There has been a recognition in recent writings of what might be called contextual necessity or loose entailment.[2] Within a given community with shared traditions, customs and rules which go to make up the background of language and thought, some activities stand in close relationship, closer than a merely contingent relationship but not as close as a necessary relationship in the strict sense of the word. Some concepts are similarly regarded as being deeply connected with one another, again though, in the sense of loose entailment. Because of this 'tacit dimension' it is possible for those within the community to read off relations between activities and

---

[1] Anonymous article in *The Times Literary Supplement*, July 1969.

[2] See *Ethics* by P. Nowell Smith, London 1962. The basis of this development is to be found in Wittgenstein's discussion of the notion of *criterion* in the *Philosophical Investigations*. Cf. also Strawson's elucidation of a 'logically adequate criterion' in Chapter 3 of *Individuals*.

concepts, although such reading off is not to be construed as deduction in *sensu stricto* because, in a particular case, the relationship may not hold.[1]

It is arguable that it was some such conception of contextual necessity, mediating between the analytic and the synthetic, that Hegel had in mind. Indeed, Hegel characterized his philosophical position in 'Differenz des Fichte'schen und Schelling'schen Systems der Philosophie' as mediating between the polarities of the analytic and synthetic:

The method of philosophical science is neither analytic nor synthetic.[2]

Findlay perhaps among commentators has brought out this aspect of Hegel's thought when he argues that:

. . . at any point in the development of the dialectic only certain conditions would appear natural and fitting.[3]

'Natural' and 'fitting' indicate that Findlay has in mind a relationship closer than the externality of contingent, synthetic relationships, but not deducible in the strict sense of the word. Certainly there might be some plausibility attached to such a view because in his writings Hegel is always at pains to distinguish a dialectical explanation from a contingent historical one and yet at the same time he insists that the relations revealed in the dialectic are not analogous to the relations of deducibility in mathematics.[4] Such an elucidation of the notion of necessity in Hegel's system would go further than the arguments of Kaufmann and Bergman cited in Chapter VII. His work would consist in a great deal more than merely giving a reason for a particular development; it would consist rather in discerning retrospectively that a particular development was contextually implied. Other lines could have been open for development, but the one actually pursued can perhaps be seen in terms of loose entailment, as having been an intimation within the existing tradition.[5]

This argument is ingenious and may go some way towards providing an intelligible justification for *some* of the transitions which Hegel makes in the course of his explanations of particular modes of experience. Ultimately, however, the argument fails to rescue Hegel's position

[1] Of course the argument is implicit in Oakeshott's notion of the pursuit of intimations and the relationship between such intimations and tradition.
[2] Glockner, op. cit., vol. I, p. 72.
[3] *Hegel: a Re-examination*, op. cit., p. 74.
[4] See *Die Phänomenologie des Geistes*, Glockner, op. cit., vol. II, p. 40 ff.
[5] See Oakeshott's views on the flow of sympathy within a tradition.

from considerable logical difficulty. The kind of loose entailments discussed above presuppose a certain context, a certain tradition of rule and habit-governed behaviour. *Within* such a context certain relationships may well hold at the level of loose entailment, and indeed some of Hegel's arguments may fall into such a pattern. Most, however, decidedly do not. The vast majority of the developments in which Hegel is interested take place not within contexts with a shared pattern of behaviour, but *between* contexts when the shared tradition of rule-governed behaviour has broken down or has become inconsistent. It would, for example, be difficult to argue that the transition in both *Grundlinien der Philosophie des Rechts* and in *Vorlesungen über die Philosophie des Geschichte* between the Oriental world and the Greek world could be interpreted on the model of contextual implication because there was no shared context, no shared tradition of behaviour.

This objection could be mitigated in Hegel's favour but at what must be too high a price. It might be possible to argue that Hegel was concerned with transitions against a shared background, within a shared context, this background and context being supplied by the Idea. The Idea could on this basis provide a kind of a transcendental context to act as a backcloth to the kind of contextual implications in which Hegel is interested. The intimations in a given situation would in this sense be intimations within the Idea. Again this argument is ingenious, and there are passages in Hegel in which he talks of the Idea as if it had a transcendental content, but such passages are inconsistent with other demands in his philosophy. The exorcism of the transcendent, the comprehension of the infinite, was a key to the achievement of harmony and this exorcism was to be completed on the basis of Hegel's claim, discussed in Chapter VII, that the Idea has no content other than its realization in the world, a realization which can be fully comprehended by the philosopher. The Idea could not, therefore, constitute the concrete and articulate background to make intelligible the transitions between one mode of life and another in terms of the notion of contextual entailment, or the pursuit of intimations. There is therefore a tension between the two demands in Hegel's work. Reconciliation can be achieved by the comprehension of the necessary form which experience takes at any particular time and by exorcizing all transcendental elements in human experience. The need for the latter rules out the possibility of making the former intelligible. At the most Hegel could restrict the task of philosophical explanation to the comprehension of how developments within a particular tradition could be seen as contextually implied but at the same time taking that tradition as a datum and not seeing it as implied by something external to itself because that would presuppose a transcendental, between-traditions context.[1]

The other two general criteria of adequacy which may be used in the assessment of Hegel's particular explanations of various modes of experience are derived from a consideration of certain formal features involved in the notion of dialectic and from a consideration of Hegel's view of the relationship between a philosophical treatment of a mode of experience and what is known on other, empirical grounds about such experience.

The first of these criteria might appear as deeply unhegelian in that it consists in extrapolating a crucial *formal* feature of dialectical explanation *per se* and using this as a test of adequacy in the case of particular dialectical explanations. The notion of a 'formal feature of dialectic' has an unhegelian ring about it in that Hegel would always deny that a meaningful distinction could be drawn between form and content in philosophy. On the other hand Hegel himself wrote *Die Wissenschaft der Logik* in which he adumbrated in considerable detail the general character of the dialectical process and this discussion is notoriously carried on at a very abstract level. No doubt the full meaning of the dialectic may be gathered only in a concrete case but at the same time for the concrete case to be recognized as an example of dialectical development it would have to possess the formal features of dialectic. As was argued in Chapter VI[2] the dialectical process is concerned with the unification of contradiction and opposition, transcending the isolated notions of the understanding and connecting them up at a higher and more adequate level, a process which is in turn mirrored in the development of being which also develops through the resolution of opposition and fragmentation. However, Hegel makes it clear that both in thought and being this development through overcoming diremption and fragmentation does not entail that what is overcome is lost either to thought or to reality:

 . . . because the result, the negation, is a specific negation it has a

---

[1] Perhaps this is too strong. Perhaps such a view need not imply necessarily that this between-traditions context has to be transcendental. In his 'Political Education', in *Rationalism in Politics*, op. cit., p. 126, Oakeshott refers to 'a tradition of a vaguer sort which is shared by a number of societies'—such a view, if made more concrete, could provide the kind of context which is necessary to make sense of some of Hegel's transitions, but again I doubt it. Hegel connects up societies separated by deep gulfs in political, artistic and religious practices and it is difficult to see how they could be said to share a context unless such a context is the metaphysical operation of the Idea, with all that such a view would imply for the coherence of Hegel's philosophical position.

[2] See above, pp. 142 ff.

content. It is a fresh notion but higher and richer than its pre-
decessor; for it is rich by the negation of the latter and therefore
contains it.[1]

The same would apply of course *mutatis mutandis* to the dialectical
development of reality.

Dialectic has therefore increasing import, what is superseded is
preserved at the higher level. This point therefore provides a criterion
of adequacy for assessing particular dialectical explanations. Adequate
dialectical explanations have to fulfil this necessary condition of preserving at the more developed level patterns of experience or notions
developed further back. In so far as Hegel's explanation of social and
political experience is concerned, this feature of the dialectic is more
than a purely formal consideration because it is Hegel's contention that
the modern state can preserve within itself the consciousness of subjectivity and freedom developed in morality and in the system of needs.
In order to secure this end, this formal feature of dialectic has to be
fulfilled and its non-fulfilment would not merely be a 'logic chopping'
objection to Hegel's thesis but would also at the very same time
constitute a failure on his part to demonstrate that the modern state
can be considered as a form of political community adequate for the
conception of the free personality worked out in the course of European
history. Certainly at a very general level, Hegel argues that the modern
state, the culmination of the dialectical development within the social
world, does include within its universality the conscious recognition of
the right to subjectivity and self direction:

> The principle of the modern state has prodigious depth and strength
> because it allows the principle of subjectivity to progress to its
> culmination and yet at the same time brings it back to the substantive
> unity and so maintains this unity as the principle of subjectivity
> itself.[2]

At the general level, this formal feature of dialectic, in this case so
crucial to the comprehension of the integration of modern man into
the political community, appears to be satisfied, but of course Hegel
would himself be the first to admit[3] that this general point has to be
shown in its working out in specific detail. It is at the level of detail,
and in particular the discussion of the individual's rights against the

---

[1] Glockner, op. cit., vol. IV, p. 51.
[2] op. cit., vol. VII, p. 338.
[3] In view of his criticism of the generality of the claims of Fichte and Kant
in 'Über die wissenschaftlichen Behandlungsarten des Naturrechts', Glockner,
vol. I.

state, that doubts about the extent to which the standpoint of individuality is preserved at the higher dialectical level of the state begin to creep in. The following passage for example seems to 'mediate' the subjectivity of the private individual in such a way that it becomes transposed and unrecognizable:

> The state is absolutely rational in so far as it is the actuality of the substantial will which it possesses in the particular self-consciousness once that consciousness has been raised to consciousness of its universality. The substantial unity is an absolute, unmoved end in itself, in which freedom comes into its supreme right. *On the other hand this final end has supreme right against the individual whose supreme duty it is to be a member of the state.*[1]

Certainly the point is not unambiguous. Hegel certainly considers that the state in general gives full scope to the subjective, merely bringing it into contact with the universal, but at the same time at the level of detail it is not so clear how the right to subjectivity is given political expression in any really meaningful form. What is clear is that this is a point in his argument which is so crucial that Hegel cannot really afford to be ambiguous or equivocal. Only through a detailed and rational comprehension of the reconciling features of the modern state can man become united with it—hence any ambiguity in the comprehension must render it inadequate.

The final internal criterion of adequate explanation which can be extrapolated from some of Hegel's *obiter dicta* and also from his practice is that a philosophical explanation of a mode of experience, a form of life or of an institution, must cohere with what is known on empirical grounds about such modes, forms and institutions. This point may first of all be illustrated from Hegel's practice in the following way. The dialectician or the philosopher does not conduct 'first order' empirical enquiries into the nature of those things which he then explains philosophically. Indeed, the task confronting the philosopher, that of providing a grasp of the totality of experience, interpreting it in some rational and interconnected manner, would be daunting enough without having to conduct first order empirical enquiries into such forms of experience. Findlay makes this point with reference to history and then goes on to generalize it:

> . . . in his theodicistic philosophy of history he bases himself on ordinary sources and documents, on actual works and products, on the researches of scholars and on the work of reflective but non-

---

[1] Glockner, op. cit., vol. VII, p. 258.

philosophical historians and critics. The Owl of Minerva only wings its interpretative flight, to modify one of Hegel's most famous statements, when all this common or garden spade work is completed.[1]

It would seem therefore that, so far as Hegel's practice was concerned, for a philosophical explanation to be adequate, it would have to be consistent with what could be known on other non-philosophical grounds about the things to be explained.

The point is made explicitly, however, by Hegel and in such a way that coherence with empirical material becomes a standard of philosophical adequacy:

> Philosophy has to correspond to reality and experience. This correspondence can be regarded as at least an external standard for the truth of philosophy.[2]

Hegel emphatically declares here not only that philosophy has to presuppose empirical research relating to those things with which the philosopher wishes to deal but further that such research cannot be used as a detachable taking-off point for speculation, but rather that the coherence of philosophical thought with empirical research is a criterion of the truth of philosophical explanation. This abstract-seeing demand perhaps has a social dimension coming from deep in Hegel's early work. He was preoccupied by the fact that so much contemporary thought and language appeared to be disconnected from the world which it attempted to describe, a factor which cuts off the philosopher from the life activity of the people. Similarly in the case of Jesus in 'Der Geist des Christentums und sein Schicksal', his message was cut off from the mundane life of the Jews and was a failure. In Hegel's view the philosophical description of an experience, while transfiguring the experience must still be deeply rooted in the conventional character of it.

In principle this formal requirement means that Hegel's theories can in a sense be tested on a contextual basis by asking the question of whether his descriptions of a particular mode of experience or whatever in fact cohered with what was known about such a mode on non-philosophical grounds. In the case of the philosophical transfiguration of the social world, this demand is ambiguous but at the same time crucial. It is fairly clear how the critic might assess the extent of the coherence between, for example, Hegel's discussion of electricity in his *Naturphilosophie* and what was known about electricity by scientists at

---

[1] *Hegel: A Re-examination*, op. cit., p. 75.
[2] Glockner, op. cit., vol. VIII, p. 47.

the time,[1] but the situation is far more complicated in the case of Hegel's claim that the state in the modern world is a universal force, not the representative of any particular narrow sectional interest. What could count as the analogue of the scientist's view of electricity in this context where the notion of empirical as opposed to philosophical knowledge is far from clear. Again the point, although logical, has a social dimension in that the transfigured character of the state, that is to say the modern state, comprehended as the universal element in society was a crucial factor in Hegel's attempt to reconcile modern man to his political experience and thus lay the foundation for a regenerated political community. Yet Hegel seems to imply that this philosophical view of the state must also cohere with what is known empirically about the actual character of such states. It is here, for example, that Marx's evidence becomes important. As is well known, Marx initially adopted something akin to the Hegelian view of the state as the universal element in the social world, but soon became disabused after his close contact with the state's activity during the period that he was a reporter on the *Rheinische Zeitung*. In his first contribution to the newspaper dealing with the proceedings of the sixth Rhenish Parliament, he wrote in a very Hegelian manner of the law:

> Laws are as little repressive measures directed against freedom as the law of gravity is a repressive measure against movement. . . . Laws are rather bright, positive, general norms in which freedom has attained to an existence that is impersonal, theoretical and independent of the arbitrariness of the individual.[2]

Indeed, it is clear that Marx considered the modern state *in toto* to be an embodiment of freedom, the guardian of the general or universal interest of society:

> Modern philosophy considers the state as the great organism in which must be realized the juridical, moral and political freedom and in which the individual citizen, in obeying the laws of the state only obeys the natural laws of his own reason, that is to say of human reason.[3]

At the very same time, however, Marx already realized at the level of theory that there was considerable tension between this philosophical analysis of the nature and function of the modern state and political

[1] This kind of thing is done by M. J. Petry in *Hegel's Philosophy of Nature*, op. cit., vol. I.

[2] Marx and Engels *Historische Kritische Gesamtausgabe*, Frankfurt, Berlin and Moscow 1927, vol. I, 1 (1), p. 247.

[3] Ibid., p. 249.

actuality, but at the same time used the Hegelian theory of the state as a yardstick for measuring the adequacy of particular states:

A state which is not the realization of rational freedom is a bad state.[1]

Marx therefore stressed the need to consider, when examining the actual constitution of the modern state, the concrete nature of the circumstances (*die sächliche Natur der Verhältnisse*).[2]

Such consideration led Marx to cast doubt upon Hegel's philo-sophical interpretation of what Marx took to be political reality. His report for *Rheinische Zeitung* on the law concerning the stealing of wood from forests led him to see in the law not an expression of universal rationality, but the undue influence of one sectional group in civil society;[3] the plight of the wine growers in the Moselle region also constituted a concrete circumstance which led Marx away from his earlier Hegelian position; and the final breach occurred with the censorship introduced by the government which involved the banning of *Rheinische Zeitung* and Ruge's *Deutsche Jahrbücher*, together with the great liberal paper of the age *Leipziger Allgemeine Zeitung*. The state appeared in reality very differently from its transfigured philosophical form, being seen as the instrument of one sectional group and not the guardian of the universal interest of society.

Obviously, given Hegel's view of the relationship between philosophy and the character of everyday experience, the example of Marx poses at least a problem for his interpretation of the state. One does not have to be a Marxist to realize that the emphasis which Hegel places on the universality of the state's interest is much over-stressed and in point of fact is inconsistent with Hegel's own more concrete analyses of political events and processes. In 'Über die englische Reformbill'[4] he stressed the extent to which the government in a modern state can be biased in favour of those sections of the population which are strongest within civil society, a point which was in fact the very basis of Marx's opposed analysis. In so far as such arguments have a limited amount of validity, then it would seem that the philosophical interpretation of the role of the modern state which Hegel gives must stand in need of some revision if the correspondence between philosophy and experience

. . . can be regarded as at least an external standard for the truth of philosophy.[5]

---

[1] Marx and Engels, op. cit., p. 248.   [2] op. cit., p. 360.   [3] Ibid.
[4] Lasson, *Schriften zur Politik und Rechtsphilosophie*, op. cit., p. 286. I owe this point to Dr Zbigniew Pelcynski.
[5] Glockner, op. cit., vol. VIII, p. 47.

Once revised, however, such a situation would have very profound effects upon Hegel's overall philosophy of the political community. Membership of the modern state was a form of integration and a development of self-consciousness, but if the state is not the universal element which it appears to be, then self-consciousness cannot realize its universal element in the political world.

It seems, therefore, that Hegel's system cannot survive the tests of adequacy which can be extrapolated from his own theory and practice and this fact is no minor structural matter. It fails the test of adequacy at substantive points, points at which Hegel had hoped to secure the reconciliation between man and the social and the political world around him.

If Hegel's philosophy is to be rejected on the grounds of its failure to survive his own implied tests of adequacy, what might be said about it in more general terms, particularly as the key to community in the modern world? Hegel seems to have envisaged that the modern form of community must crucially depend upon a philosophical interpretation of its modes of life, particularly its politics and its religion. We have already seen the disruptive ambiguities which surround Hegel's philosophy of politics and a similar ambiguity runs through his teaching on the correct interpretation of religion, an ambiguity which, however, appears to be no particular fault of Hegel's own work, but is an ambiguity in the role of religion in modern society.

As we saw early in this book Hegel was taught his theology in Tübingen by two dogmatists, Flatt and Storr, who utilized the Kantian distinction between phenomenon and noumenon to argue that *qua* noumenon, God must be beyond human grasp and community and must reveal himself to us in revelation. Such a view of God Hegel regarded, following Rousseau and Schiller, as socially disruptive. The solution to the problem as he was eventually to see it was in the philosophical reinterpretation of religion so that religion became not concerned with the worship of a distant and transcendent God, but with the apprehension of how the Other of the world was structured by God and was in fact the self-realization of God. Understood in this way, religion would become a force for cohesion in the community. Taken in the non-philosophical and conventional sense religion was divisive. Given that a philosophical reinterpretation of religion is required by the demand for the achievement of community it is difficult to see why when the philosophical perspective is reached, religion, shot through as it is with concepts and images implying transcendence and infinity, should be necessary at all. If religion has to be translated into metaphysical terms, into concepts such as Idea, Spirit, Other, etc., it seems difficult to see why it is still needed within the community which must have achieved the philosophical perspective on its own activity in order to exist as a community.

This ambiguity is, however, something deep in the present structure of religious belief and its role in society. In some ways our own situation *vis-à-vis* religion is analogous to the position facing Hegel as a young man. It is interesting that the last thorough-going treatment of Hegel's religious thought, Mactaggart's *Studies in Hegelian Cosmology*, published within ten years of Karl Barth's *Römerbrief*, heralded a return to the perspective of Flatt and Storr. Barth's views of God, based upon what he took to be the infinite distance between God and man revealed in the Bible, are socially disruptive in a wider sense than the political; they produce a profound cultural dichotomy within a society with developing patterns of secularization. They disconnect man's experience of God from other forms of experience available in society, and cut off the description of religious experience from other kinds of description through the use of concepts such as revelation and infinity. Such an understanding of the Christian religion cuts it off from the on-going culture within modern society and there is a correlative demand that religious discourse should be made relevant to the totality of human social and cultural concern by being translated into some terms taken from that wider culture. Such a demand is in a sense Hegelian. Hegel saw the need to translate Christian discourse into a community-based metaphysic and thus reconnect it with the life of society; the modern non-Barthian theologian sees the answer not as translation into metaphysical terms, because any kind of relevant metaphysic would be as disconnected as the theology which it was to translate, but into some other terms, usually of a vaguely existentialist sort or in terms of various modish political views. Here again, though, the ambiguity noted in Hegel's treatment re-appears. If such translations succeed, then what is the point of the religious dimension to the discourse?[1] On the one hand we appear to be faced with a Barthian dogmatism which in terms of both experience and description separates religion from the on-going life of the secular community; on the other with a demand that Christian discourse should be translated into secular terms in which case it is difficult to see the point of retaining it.

This ambiguity in his treatment of Christianity seems to have been implicit in Hegel's mind in a confusing way. It has been the central argument of this book that philosophy is the key to community, that

[1] See A. C. MacIntyre, 'God and the Theologians', in *Against the Self-Images of the Age*, London 1971.

it is only when political and religious experience are reinterpreted philosophically that a harmonious community can be generated and this point was linked up in Chapter VII, with the rational educative role of philosophy. However, at one or two points Hegel seems to assert that the common man must find his source of integration into the community through religion, because philosophy is too abstract and difficult to provide the core of common culture, that overall interpretation of experience necessary to provide that community of consciousness central to humanity.[1] In a letter to Duboc, Hegel writes of the role of religion in a way in which it would indicate that he saw in it a common man's metaphysic:

> I can exempt myself from saying that for mankind in general, truth is primarily revealed in the form of religion, enlivened and enriched by one's experience of himself and life, for seizing it in the form of thought and knowing it through thought is a different need.[2]

In his Berlin inaugural lecture he again makes the point in an oblique manner saying that:

> Religion is the way in which men generally achieve the consciousness of their being.

This kind of view, albeit put in a somewhat oblique fashion, brings out the ambiguity of Hegel's view of religion. It is only when it is philosophically comprehended that religion becomes a way in which mankind comes to achieve the consciousness of his being, that is a being involved with other beings in the self-realization of God; understood conventionally religion is concerned with the being of man only in so far as it is related to a *transcendent* God, if it were not so it would be difficult to see the need for a philosophy of religion. On the one hand Hegel has to acknowledge the hold which religion has over people, so much so that it is a common man's metaphysic, but without the philosophical comprehension such religious views were socially divisive. Religion can only be socially benign when grasped philosophically but once grasped in this way it is difficult to see the point of religion within the community.

Hegel's philosophy had an inextricable social concern and this applies equally to its presuppositions as to its working out in detailed explanation of the various modes of social experience. Hegel certainly regarded the absolute presuppositions of his own work as lifeless generalities taken without this detailed connection with specific

[1] Glockner, op. cit., vol. II, p. 63.   [2] *Briefe*, op. cit., vol. II, p. 326.

attempts at explanation, but we are not forced to follow his assessment. What can be made of the basic presuppositions of his work—the need for some kind of rational coherent grasp of the structure of experience and its connection with the developing powers of the human mind?

It might of course be objected at this point that, if pursued, the discussion must lapse into nonsense because all that can be said significantly about absolute presuppositions is that they are pre-supposed, the implication being that *qua* absolute presuppositions, they cannot be assessed. These views are familiar as being those of Collingwood, argued most fully in his neglected work *An Essay on Metaphysics*. Concerning absolute presuppositions, Collingwood argues:

> An absolute presupposition cannot be undermined by the verdict of experience because it is a yardstick by which experience is judged.[1]

Experience cannot in any conceivable way be used to assess the value of the notion of the pursuit of coherence as a fundamental presupposition because what counts as a real experience may well depend upon the notion of coherence. This is certainly true, for example, of Hegel's distinction between the actual and the merely real. An actual experience, institution or practice is one which develops a pattern of coherence; a merely real experience, institution or practice exists but not in a significant manner from the point of view of the development of coherence. Collingwood's views may not, however, be the end of the matter and a closer examination of them may well throw light on the basic orientation of Hegel's own thought.

According to Collingwood, the philosopher merely makes articulate the absolute presuppositions of his age, the basic orientation towards experience upon which his society is predicated. In this context he argues, for example, that Kant made explicit the presuppositions of Newtonian physics. Considered in this way philosophy is an historical enterprise, concerned with describing the basic structuring principles brought to the interpretation of experience by his own or another society. As these principles may well vary from society to society, from epoch to epoch, philosophical systems too will vary according to the nature of the presuppositions which they make articulate. The case of Hegel, however, fits very badly into Collingwood's pattern. The impetus to his own philosophizing was that the presuppositions of his age, articulated in politics, in morality, in philosophy and religion were based upon bifurcation and discord and this was not acceptable to Hegel. He sought, as we have shown, to change and revise the description

---

[1] London 1940, p. 193.

of experience in his society so that patterns of integration and community could be discerned. Philosophy for Hegel was at least in part revisionary; merely to draw out the implications of a set of bifurcating presuppositions would seem to him to be both pointless and inhumane in that, *pace* Collingwood, it seems to be central to Hegel's thought and perhaps most particularly to *Die Phänomenologie des Geistes* that behind the different patterns of thought and rationality in any age lies a demand for reunification, for harmony and coherence and the duty of the philosopher is to the understanding of the thought and activity of a society in terms of this metaphysical demand and not to the way, sometimes involving misunderstanding, diremption and discord in which this metaphysical demand is made articulate in the presuppositions of conventional thought.

Because Hegel links the achievement of coherence and harmony with the need to develop self-consciousness on the part of individuals, it might be argued that the appeal of the principle is less likely to be found by philosophical analysis and more in psychology and psychiatry. On such a view the pursuit of coherence would be understood in terms of the satisfaction of a deep human need, the correct understanding of which being the province of the psychologist or psychiatrist. An explicit argument on these lines is to be found in Richard Wollheim's book *F. H. Bradley*, a philosopher much influenced by Hegel. He comments on Bradley's attempt to establish a systematic grasp of experience as follows:

> The ideal of harmony and comprehensiveness, of system, the monistic ideal enjoys a certain authority in the most characteristic activities of mankind. . . . What then is the appeal of monism? . . . the true answer must lie deep in the recesses of the human mind.[1]

He goes on to argue that its appeal may well be psychological:

> . . . there is an analogy between the metaphysical attachment to the idea of an undivided reality and the desire to establish whole objects which is of such crucial importance in infantile development.[2]

And in this context he mentions particularly the work of Melanie Klein. In the case of Hegel this account has a good deal of *prima facie* plausibility. We know from both his letters in his earlier years and in his mature discussions of sanity, madness and rationality that Hegel did regard the total grasp of experience as a very deep human necessity and that before he had developed such a grasp through his philosophical work, he was in a state of considerable psychological difficulty and after

[1] London 1959, p. 283.　　　　[2] Wollheim, op. cit., p. 283.

developing such a grasp of experience regarded the failure to do so as a pathological state. However a psychological or psychoanalytical explanation will not do to explain the appeal of the pursuit of coherence. Psychoanalytical explanation, for example, far from explaining the role of coherence in fact presupposes it. It assumes that some kind of coherent self-understanding may in most cases be crucial both for thought about oneself and having a correct bearing towards both the world and towards other people. Psychoanalytic explanations, because they establish a pattern of coherence between apparently disconnected human activities, exemplify coherence but do not explain it.

Wollheim's argument, however unwittingly, points the way in which we should look at the role of the pursuit of harmony and coherence when he argues that such ideals:

. . . enjoy a certain authority in the most characteristic activities of mankind.[1]

His argument goes wrong in not seeing psychoanalysis as one similar activity, equally in need of explanation. Surely in some way these ideals are presupposed in all our higher order mental activities and since religion, art, politics and morality seem to presuppose that a pattern of experience is being sought which is universal, unifying and intersubjective, it might also be argued that such activities presuppose that coherence is in some sense there to be found. It certainly does not seem to be the case that all such activities involve continual frustration; on the contrary, we can clearly recognize developments within them. If we adopt some such position there seems to be no reason why the philosopher should not look for coherent connections between patterns of experience. Obviously our approach has to be more sceptical than that of Hegel, we can no longer regard any such connections as being necessarily written into the nature of reality, and if connections are not to be found, they should not be forced. The correct approach might seem to consist in an attempt to look first of all at different types of human experience on their own terms, attempting to bring out the rules, standards of intelligibility, and patterns of rationality within them, describing them in their own terms and then, this having been done, to look for analogies and connections between them. At the same time the powers and capacities of the human mind required by participation in such types of experience could also be elucidated and again when this process has been completed connections and analogies looked for. Only then will we be able to develop that perspicuous

[1] Wollheim, op. cit., p. 283.

representation, that overall view which Wittgenstein argues consists in seeing connections not merely *within* different types of experience or different language games, but *between* them.[1]

Hegel certainly failed to provide a unified grasp of experience but his struggle and failure to do so are instructive. He claimed too much when he saw in philosophy a way out of the social and political problems which beset him, and his claims led him to postulate connections between experiences which palpably could not be made. But a more sceptical approach, more concerned to elucidate types of experience from within, might well succeed where Hegel failed.

Such an approach to experience, transposed into our own present day idioms of thought has a great deal in common with the intimations in Wittgenstein's later work, intimations which have perhaps been followed furthest by Peter Winch who argues in more concrete terms for a philosophical orientation described abstractly in the previous paragraph:

> On my view then, the philosophy of science will be concerned with the kind of understanding sought and conveyed by the scientist; the philosophy of religion will be concerned with the way in which religion attempts to present an intelligible picture of the world; and so on. And of course these activities and their aims will be mutually compared and contrasted.[2]

The rationale of this kind of approach is the attainment of that 'perspicuous representation' of our experience, noting and not attempting to reinterpret discrepancies and divisions, making articulate connections if and when they can be discerned. The achievement of this comprehensive view of experience is connected by Winch, as it was by Hegel, with a deep human need. On this point Winch quotes Burnet who wrote in his *Greek Philosophy*:

> We have to ask whether the mind of man can have any contact with reality and if it can, what difference it will make to his life.[3]

As we have seen, for Hegel the inability to secure a comprehensive grasp of experience within which man's relationship to reality is secured exercises a baneful, but philosophically eradicable influence on the life of man.

At the same time the modern philosopher may well learn from Hegel

---

[1] *Philosophical Investigations*, op. cit., para. 122. Wittgenstein also saw the failure to achieve this as something pathological.

[2] *The Idea of a Social Science*, op. cit., pp. 19–20.

[3] London 1930, pp. 11–12.

about the way in which he should approach such modes of experience in his attempt to understand the mode of discourse and pattern of understanding within them. Hegel continually stressed the way in which conceptions of man, of art, of politics, and morality are not disembodied but are embedded in forms of social life and modes of practice within social life generally and that, given this internal relationship between a practice and its conceptual self-understanding, the philosopher's approach must in some sense be detailed and historical. As societies develop over time along with the modes of experience within them, so do the forms of self-understanding. This example is not in fact lost on those philosophers who have learned something from Hegel: Alasdair MacIntyre argues, for example, in *A Short History of Ethics*:

> Moral philosophy is often written as though the history of the subject were only of secondary and incidental importance. . . . that moral concepts can be examined and understood apart from their history. . . . In fact of course moral concepts change as social life changes. . . . Moral concepts are embodied in and partly constitutive of social life.[1]

Concepts and modes of experience cannot be discussed in a one dimensional manner but have to be identified in their persistence over time and their forms of self-understanding discussed in the same way.

At a more abstract and metaphysical level it seems that the modern philosopher adopting the orientation argued above may also learn, and perhaps already is in the process of learning, from Hegel about the relationship between the powers of the human mind and the modes of human experience and practice. Most contemporary philosophers are content to analyse in an abstract way the concept of mind as it is differentiated into certain particular forms—intelligence, behaviour, action, will, motive and intention, etc. At the same time, however, within most analyses conducted in this kind of way is the possibility of their self-transcendence. Most contemporary philosophers under the influence of Wittgenstein and Strawson now have a tendency to look at the ability to *identify* and describe the powers of one's own mind as parasitic upon a public language with public rules set in a background of social convention, habits and traditions. For example, the identification of the emotions has now been linked to context and convention so that what makes a feeling a particular emotion is not the character of the feeling as pure state, but the context within which the feeling occurs.[2]

[1] London 1966, p. 1.
[2] See E. Bedford, 'Emotions' in *Essays in Philosophical Psychology*, ed. D. F. Gustafson, New York 1964.

Similarly it might be argued of this thesis that the ability to form and to identify intentions is parasitic upon the forms of description, the *Gedankenwelt* of a particular society, which, as was pointed out in the previous paragraph, does not exist 'in the air' but is related to and constitutive of the modes of experience to hand in society. One does not approach the social world with a richly differentiated inner life of intentions, motives, emotions which one then proceeds to actualize in some objective external realm. Rather, the possibility of *having* inner experience in the sense of differentiated, structured, coherent forms of inner experience is necessarily linked to public language, public rules and forms of description. In this sense self-consciousness, the awareness of the character of one's inner experience, is closely linked with the modes of experience and the capacities of description embodied in such modes of experience available in one's social milieu.

There is a growing awareness among philosophers of the implications of this social dimension to the individuation of the contents of one's own mind. It emerges particularly clearly in very general terms in *Thought and Action*[1] and *Feeling and Expression*[2] by Stuart Hampshire. In the former work he summarizes his position linking it explicitly with Hegel:

> . . . a transcendental argument of the kind that Kant and Hegel attempted is always needed to show the necessary connexion of art with morality and with positive knowledge and thereby show its necessary place in the development of individuals and human societies.[3]

It emerges in more concrete form in some recent moral philosophy in arguments which perhaps have their implications for political philosophy. In her essay 'Modern Moral Philosophy'[4] Professor Anscombe made the point very strongly that moral philosophy, in the sense of understanding moral discourse, depends in a crucial way upon the philosophy of mind because the crucial notions involved in morality are those of wanting and needing, the fulfilment of which would give content to the notion of human flourishing which she takes as crucial to morality.

Thus far the argument might be seen in terms analogous to Hegel's assertion in the beginning of *Grundlinien der Philosophie des Rechts* that the notion of human willing is crucial to politics and the philosophical comprehension of political experience. Closer inspection reveals that Anscombe has not gone far enough in that she tends to

[1] London 1959.   [2] London 1960.   [3] Op. cit., p. 245.
[4] *Philosophy*, vol. XXXIII, 1958.

take the view that moral principles and moral beliefs are in some sense derived from wants, whereas as D. Z. Phillips and H. O. Mounce point out in 'On Morality's Having a Point',[1] the notion of a human want and the way in which it is individuated may well depend upon the morality within which one moves and has one's being. Wants presuppose a social background which contains objects which may be wanted. They do not exist in the void, but within particular forms of life. The case is similar with desires. They are not simple, indubitable entities but have to be individuated within a particular context. What we desire depends entirely on what objects of desire have been presented to us and consequently the pattern of a person's desires has a history of intelligible response to that to which he has been exposed. The same is true of the other powers of the human mind. We have to follow through Wittgenstein's insight that the identification of an inner experience presupposes a background of linguistic rules and habits and see in detail how this dependence operates.

The modern philosopher has to learn from Hegel that:

. . . the Ego is by itself only a formal identity. . . . Consciousness appears differently modified according to the difference of the given object and the gradual specification of consciousness appears as a variation in the characteristics of its objects.[2]

In a sense, such an approach is implicit in the work of Wittgenstein and those who follow him. Using an argument analogous to that used by Hegel to show that a man cannot follow a private moral rule, cannot give the word 'good' a private definition through the operation of his conscience, Wittgenstein argues that man has to be seen in a socio-linguistic context in order for him to make sense of his experience. In such a way Wittgenstein gives as much a metaphysical deduction of human society as does Hegel. At the same time Hegel went beyond Wittgenstein, and was surely correct in doing so, in connecting up the realization of specific human powers and capacities with living in and participating in particular modes of experience. In the idiom of contemporary philosophy this demand would come down to an attempt to show how different language games presuppose and develop different kinds of human powers.

It seems, therefore, that an understanding of Hegel's thought in its total context in an attempt to determine its identity leads to unconventional conclusions about its significance. The significance of his thought perhaps lies less in the detail of his philosophy of the state

---

[1] *Philosophy*, vol. XI, 1965.   [2] Glockner, op. cit., vol. X, p. 259.

or of civil society and more in the salutary nature of his views of the role of the philosopher *vis à vis* experience in general, and political experience in particular. A clear understanding of his significance in seeing the philosopher as interested in the detail of social and political experience and what such experience contributes to the achievement of self-consciousness may lead philosophy from the analytical scholasticism which has disconnected it from any serious attempt to understand social and political experience and its role in human life for over half a century.

Bibliography

A. Hegel's Works

H. Glockner (ed.), *Sämtliche Werke*, Frommann, Stuttgart 1927–30.
J. Hoffmeister (ed.), *Dokumente zu Hegels Entwicklung*, Frommann, Stuttgart 1936.
Briefe von und an Hegel, Felix Meiner, Hamburg 1952–4.
Jenenser Realphilosophie I, Felix Meiner, Leipzig 1932.
Jenenser Realphilosophie II, Felix Meiner, Leipzig 1932.
Die Vernunft in der Geschichte, Felix Meiner, Hamburg 1955.
G. Lasson (ed.), *Schriften zur Politik und Rechtsphilosophie*, Felix Meiner, Leipzig 1923.
Jenenser Logik, Metaphysik und Naturphilosophie, Felix Meiner, Leipzig 1923.
H. Nohl (ed.), *Hegels Theologische Jugendschriften*, Mohr, Tübingen, 1907.

B. Works of Hegel's Contemporaries

A. Ferguson, *An Essay on the History of Civil Society*, Creech and Bell, Edinburgh 1767.
J. G. Fichte, *Sämtliche Werke*, Veit, Berlin 1845–6.
J. W. Goethe, *Sämtliche Werke*, Cotta, Berlin 1902.
J. G. Herder, *Sämtliche Werke*, ed. B. Suphan, Weidmann, Berlin, 1877–1913.
F. Hölderlin, *Stuttgarter Ausgabe*, Cotta, Stuttgart 1946.
I. Kant, *Gesammelte Schriften*, Drusck, Berlin 1955.
J. J. Rousseau, *Oeuvres Complètes*, Gallimard, Paris 1964.
F. W. J. Schelling, *Sämtliche Werke*, Cotta, Stuttgart and Augsburg 1856–61.
J. C. F. Schiller, *Werke* (Nationalausgabe), ed. L. Blumenthal and B. von Weise, Bohlau, Weimar 1943.
J. Steuart, *An Inquiry into the Principles of Political Economy*, ed. A. Skinner, Oliver and Boyd, London 1966.

C. Books on Hegel

P. Asveld, *La Pensée religieuse du jeune Hegel*, Publications Universitaires de Louvain, Louvain 1953.
P. Chamley, *Économie politique chez Steuart et Hegel*, Dalloz, Paris 1963.
L. Dupré, *The Philosophical Foundations of Marxism*, Harcourt Brace, New York 1966.
J. N. Findlay, *Hegel: A Re-examination*, George Allen and Unwin, London 1959.
Introduction to *Hegel's Philosophy of Nature*, translated by A. V. Miller, Oxford University Press, Oxford 1970.
R. Garaudy, *Dieu est mort*, Presses Universitaires de France, Paris 1960.

F. Gregoire, *Études Hégéliennes*, Bibliotheque philosophique de Louvain, Louvain 1958.

J. Hyppolite, *Genèse et structure de la phénomenologie de l'esprit*, Aubier, Paris 1946.
Studies on Marx and Hegel, translated by J. O'Neil, Heinemann, London 1969.

W. Kaufmann, *Hegel: Reinterpretation, Texts and Commentary*, Weidenfeld and Nicolson, London 1966.

G. A. Kelly, *Idealism, Politics and History*, Cambridge University Press, Cambridge 1969.

T. M. Knox, Preface to *Early Theological Writings*, Chicago University Press, Chicago 1948.

A. Kojève, *Introduction a la lecture de Hegel: leçons sur la phenomenologie de l'esprit*, Gallimard, Paris 1947.

G. Lukács, *Der junge Hegel: über die Beziehung von Dialektik und Oekonomie*, Europa, Vienna, 1948.

H. Marcuse, *Reason and Revolution*, Routledge and Kegan Paul, London 1941.

Z. Pelcynski, *Hegel's Political Writings*, Oxford University Press, Oxford 1964.

A. T. B. Peperzak, *Le Jeune Hegel et la vision morale du monde*, Nijhoff, The Hague 1960.

M. J. Petry, *Hegel's Philosophy of Nature*, George Allen and Unwin, London 1970.

K. R. Popper, *The Open Society and Its Enemies*, Routledge and Kegan Paul, London 1945.

K. Rosenkranz, *Georg Wilhelm Friedrich Hegels Leben*, Berlin 1844, reprinted by Wiss. Buchges, Berlin 1969.

J. Royce, *Lectures on Modern Idealism*, Yale University Press, Yale 1915.

J. H. Stirling, *The Secret of Hegel*, Longman, London 1865.

D. Books on Hegel's Contemporaries

R. Buchwald, *Schiller*, Insel, Wiesbaden 1953.

D. Ewen, *The Prestige of Schiller in England, 1788–1859*, Columbia University Press, New York 1932.

X. Leon, *Fichte et son temps*, Colin, Paris 1922.

G. Pons, *G. E. Lessing et la christianisme*, Didier, Paris 1964.

R. G. Smith, *J. G. Hamann*, Collins, London 1960.

E. Wilkinson and W. H. Willoughby, Introduction to *Schiller's Letters on the Aesthetic Education of Man*, Oxford University Press, Oxford 1967.

E. Other Books Cited in the Text

W. H. Bruford, *Germany in the Eighteenth Century*, 2nd ed., Cambridge University Press, Cambridge 1965.

BIBLIOGRAPHY

R. G. Collingwood, *An Essay on Metaphysics*, Oxford University Press, Oxford 1940.
J. N. Findlay, *Language, Mind and Value*, George Allen and Unwin, London 1963.
Ascent to the Absolute, George Allen and Unwin, London 1970.
E. Fromm, *The Sane Society*, Routledge and Kegan Paul, London 1963.
H. Gerth and C. W. Mills, *From Max Weber*, Routledge and Kegan Paul, London 1948.
T. Gilby, *Between Community and Society*, Longman, London 1953.
D. Gustafson, *Essays in Philosophical Psychology*, Doubleday, New York 1964.
J. Habermas, *Technik und Wissenschaft als Ideologie*, Suhrkaup, Frankfurt 1968.
S. N. Hampshire, *Thought and Action*, Chatto and Windus, London 1959.
T. M. Knox, *A Layman's Quest*, George Allen and Unwin, London 1969.
A. C. MacIntyre, *Against the Self Images of the Age*, Duckworth, London 1971.
A Short History of Ethics, Routledge and Kegan Paul, London 1966.
M. Oakeshott, *Experience and Its Modes*, Cambridge University Press, Cambridge 1933.
Rationalism in Politics, Methuen, London 1962.
Introduction to *Leviathan*, Blackwell, Oxford 1955.
W. Pannenberg, *Basic Questions in Theology*, S.C.M. Publishing House, London 1970.
R. Plant, *Social and Moral Theory in Casework*, Routledge and Kegan Paul, London 1970.
W. Simon, *The Failure of the Prussian Reform Movement 1807–19*, Cornell University Press, Cornell 1955.
W. H. Walsh, *Metaphysics*, Hutchinson, London 1963.
P. G. Winch, *The Idea of a Social Science*, Routledge and Kegan Paul, London 1958.
L. Wittgenstein, *Philosophical Investigations*, Blackwell, Oxford 1953.
Zettel, Blackwell, Oxford 1967.

F. Articles on Hegel

F. Bergman, 'The Purpose of Hegel's System' in *Journal of the History of Philosophy*, 1964.
P. Chamley, 'La Doctrine économique de Hegel et la conception hégélienne du travail' in *Hegel Studien*, Bonn 1965.
'Les Origines de la pensée économique de Hegel' in *Hegel Studien*, Bonn 1965.
W. Kaufmann, 'Hegel's Early Anti-theological Phase' in *Philosophical Review*, 1954.

209

G. Articles on Hegel's Contemporaries

E. Cassirer, 'Schiller and Shaftesbury', in *Publications of the English Goethe Society*, 1935.

G. B. Parry, 'Enlightened Government and Its Critics in Eighteenth-Century Germany' in *Historical Journal*, 1963.

R. Pascal, *'Bildung* and the Division of Labour' in *German Studies, Essays in Honour of W. H. Bruford*, Harrap, London 1962.

'Herder and the Scottish Historical School' in *Publications of the English Goethe Society*, 1938.

H. Other Articles

G. E. M. Anscombe, 'Modern Moral Philosophy' in *Philosophy*, 1958.

D. Z. Phillips and H. O. Mounce, 'On Morality's Having a Point' in *Philosophy*, 1965.

There are two important books on Hegel of interest to the reader of the present work, but which appeared only recently:

H. Küng, *Menschwerdung Gottes: eine Einführung in Hegels theologisches Denken als Prologomena zu einer kunftigen Christologie*, Herder, Freiburg 1970.

Z. Pelcynski (ed.), *Hegel's Political Philosophy*, Cambridge University Press, Cambridge 1971.

INDEX

Estates, 103, 116–7, 119, 165, 172–3, 175–7
Estrangement, 49, 70–1, 79–80, 97–8, 106, 125, 130, 147, 165, 177–8, 186 (*see also* Alienation)

Family, 109, 162–3
Fate, 70–1, 94, 96
Ferguson, A., 17, 21, 22, 24
Feuerbach, L., 15, 130, 134
Fichte, J. G., 78, 82–87, 90, 92, 103, 105, 115, 125–6, 188, 191
Findlay, J. N., 15, 98, 131, 145, 172, 188, 192
Flatt, J. F., 34, 196–7
Formalism, 89–90, 92, 103–4
Fragmentation
  of culture, 18, 31, 50
  of person, 23, 63–4, 75–6, 88, 95, 101–2, 107, 117, 125, 148, 155–6, 163, 166, 173, 177, 178, 183, 186 (*see also* Bifurcation and Divisiveness)
France, 25, 96, 112, 121
  French Revolution, 51, 54–5, 72–3, 82, 151, 172–3
Frankfurt, 22, 56, 72, 77, 130
Freedom, 84, 154, 168, 169, 175, 178, 191, 194 (*see also* Liberty)
Fries, J. F., 145
Fromm, E., 34

Garaudy, R., 73
Garve, C., 17, 113
Gedankenwelt, 17, 27, 79, 204
Germany, 16–17, 24–6, 32, 51, 60–1, 96, 112, 117, 119, 120, 167, 178–9
Geschichte, 128
God, 34, 36, 43, 53, 59–62, 80, 86, 122–3, 131–3, 135–38, 180–2, 196–8
Goethe, J. W., 16, 22–3, 27, 29, 36, 73, 113, 146
Golgotha, 134
Good Friday, 80
Greece
  art, 17
  language, 30–1, 141,
  poetry, 28
  religion, 26, 27, 32, 34, 36, 42–3, 48, 59, 63

Greece—*continued*.
  social and political order, 25, 46, 51, 71, 73–4, 125, 178, 182
Gregoire, F., 125
Guilds, 119

Habermas, J., 109
Habit, 150
Hampshire, S. N., 204
Harmony, 26, 38, 87–8, 105, 125–6, 132, 135, 142, 144, 153, 155, 172, 178, 189, 198, 200, 201 (*see also* Coherence)
Hamann, J. G., 16, 23, 77
Hardenburg, 171, 173
Hartshorne, C., 80
Haym, R., 54
Heidegger, M., 128
Herder, J. G., 17–19, 21, 23, 26–7, 29–30, 36, 42
Historie, 128
History, 28, 57, 64, 127–8, 130–1, 133 (*see also Historie* and *Geschichte*)
Hoffmeister, J., 19
Hölderlin, F., 16, 19, 32, 39, 40, 51, 56, 76–8
Holy Roman Empire, 25
Humanität, 17
Humbolt, A. von, 18, 49
Hume, D., 33, 100
Hypochondria, 77, 149
Hyppolite, J., 31, 146

Idea, the, 132–3, 135–9, 141–4, 147, 149, 155, 166, 171, 177, 180–1, 186, 189–90, 196
Ideas, regulative, 85, 99, 131, 142
Idealism, 82, 187
Idealist, 187
Indifference, the point of, 86
Infinite, 100
  the good infinite, 101
  the bad infinite, 101
Intention, 153
Intuition, 86–8, 144, 185
Italy, 112, 119

Jacob, 70
Jacobi, 85, 126
Jena, 26, 76, 98–100, 112, 119–20, 122–3, 152, 166, 178